Tra

P & O Handbook issued to travellers to the Far East, *c.*1928.

Travellers' Singapore

An Anthology

Compiled and Introduced by
JOHN BASTIN

KUALA LUMPUR
OXFORD UNIVERSITY PRESS
OXFORD SINGAPORE NEW YORK
1994

Oxford University Press

Oxford New York
Athens Auckland Bangkok Bombay
Calcutta Cape Town Dar es Salaam Delhi
Florence Hong Kong Istanbul Karachi
Kuala Lumpur Madras Madrid Melbourne
Mexico City Nairobi Paris Singapore
Taipei Tokyo Toronto

and associated companies in

Berlin Ibadan

Oxford is a trade mark of Oxford University Press

Published in the United States
by Oxford University Press, New York

First published 1994

British Library Cataloguing in Publication Data
Data available

Library of Congress Cataloging in Publication Data
Data available

ISBN 967-65-3078-6

Typeset by Indah Photosetting Centre Sdn. Bhd., Malaysia
Printed by Kim Hup Lee Printing Co. Pte. Ltd., Singapore
Published by Oxford University Press,
19–25, Jalan Kuchai Lama, 58200 Kuala Lumpur, Malaysia

For
MARIANNE

Acknowledgements

THE Author and Publishers gratefully acknowledge the permission of the copyright holder to reproduce Passage 60: Masanobu Tsuji, *Singapore: The Japanese Version*, Trans. Margaret E. Lake, ed. H. V. Howe (Ure Smith, Sydney, 1960).

They also wish to record their gratitude for copyright advice relating to other passages given by The Publishers Association, 19 Bedford Square, London, WCIB 3HJ; Reed Book Services, Sanders Lodge Industrial Estate, Rushden, Northants, NN10 9RZ; Random House UK Limited, 20 Vauxhall Bridge Road, London, SW1V 2SA; Conway Maritime Press Limited, 101 Fleet Street, London, EC4Y 1DE; and A & C Black (Publishers) Limited, Howard Road, Eaton Socon, Huntingdon, Cambs., PE19 3EZ. They are particularly grateful to Victor Gollancz Limited, Villiers House, 41/47 Strand, London, WC2N 5JE, with respect to the book, *From Golden Gate to Golden Sun: A Record of Travel, Sport and Observation in Siam and Malaya* (H. F. & G. Witherby, London, 1923) by H. Norden. All attempts at tracing the copyright holder of this book were unsuccessful.

The Author has made every effort to trace copyright holders of passages in this anthology. The Author and Publishers offer their apologies to any holder of copyright of any passage published, trusting that they will understand that every endeavour has been made to trace them.

Contents

Introduction

JOHN BASTIN

TRAVELLERS to Singapore this year (1994) will number nearly 6.5 million. On average they will stay three and a half days, most of them in the 25,500 rooms in Singapore's 71 gazetted hotels. About 13 per cent of them will be business travellers and the rest mainly tourists. One-third of them will come from ASEAN countries, one-fifth from Japan and Taiwan, nearly 7 per cent from Australia, and nearly 5 per cent from the United Kingdom. Eighty per cent of them will come by air, which makes them different from the travellers in this anthology, who all arrived by ship. This was the case with all travellers to Singapore before the Second World War, except for a few who arrived by train or, during the 1930s, on international flights from Europe and Australia. They were all travellers in the traditional sense, and are to be distinguished from the thousands of Asian immigrants from China, Hong Kong, India, and South-East Asia, and the large number of Muslim pilgrims from Indonesia, the Philippines, and Malaysia, who came to Singapore to board ships on the Haj to Mecca. Most travellers to Singapore were European and American, but there were also Asians, generally silent travellers, who left little evidence of their visit, and few accounts of their impressions of Singapore.

Travellers in the early decades of the nineteenth century arrived at Singapore in sailing ships as merchants or seafarers, but there were occasional adventurers who met the cost of their own passage on East Indiamen sailing from Europe round the Cape of Good Hope to Singapore and China. A number arrived direct from India and, as the century progressed, went on to Java. Some also arrived on ships from Australia. Residents of the Indian subcontinent often travelled for reasons of health, but from the middle of the century many of those arriving at Singapore by way of India had sailed from Europe through the Mediterranean to Alexandria, then journeyed overland to Cairo, and either on to Suez or along the Nile to Luxor and across the desert to Quseir, 250 miles south of Suez. From there, or from Suez, they took passage by ship along the Red Sea to India. This overland route dramatically cut the distance between Europe and Asia, and when the British occupied Aden in 1839, travellers were provided with an intermediate port of call on the way.

The introduction of steam vessels into the Mediterranean by the Peninsular and Oriental Steam Navigation Company (P&O), and the dispatch of the wooden steam paddler *Hindostan* into the Red Sea in 1843 to convey passengers to India, led to the overland route becoming the most popular way of travelling from Europe to Asia. Passengers were taken to Calcutta or, after 1854, to Bombay, from where they travelled further east. When the Suez Canal was opened in 1869, passengers on P&O ships more commonly sailed directly to Galle and on to Singapore and Hong Kong. The popularity of the route is shown by the remarkable increase in the number of P&O ships, which grew from 7 when the company began operating the Alexandria overland route in 1840, to 42 in 1855, and 51 on the eve of the opening of the Suez Canal. At this time a large part of the freight between Europe and Asia was still carried on sailing ships round the Cape of Good Hope, but the Suez Canal soon established the supremacy of steam in carrying freight and passengers to Asia, and, in so doing, 'changed the face of the Eastern seas'.

The economic viability of P&O was assured by securing the mail contract between England and Alexandria, and then between Suez and Calcutta. In 1844 the contract was extended to Singapore and Hong Kong, and the first P&O mail steamer, the *Lady Mary Wood*, reached Singapore on 4 August 1845, only 41 days out of London. On her return voyage she carried 4,757 letters from Singapore, the bulk of them for Great Britain and Europe. The arrival of the P&O monthly mail packet had an enormous influence on the economic and social life of Singapore, which was now more immediately affected by commercial and political events in the outside world. These contacts were further accelerated in 1853 when the P&O mail packets were increased to two a month. The first left London on the 8th of each month for Galle, Penang, Singapore, and Hong Kong, and the second left on the 24th of each month for Galle, Calcutta, Penang, Singapore, and Hong Kong. The P&O mail packets reached Singapore on the 15th and the 10th day of each month respectively. They sailed from Singapore on the 17th and 28th day of each month, the first via Bombay, and the second via Calcutta, both reaching Marseilles in 44 days, before sailing on to Southampton. The cost of a passage from Singapore to Southampton in 1855 was $528, but this was raised shortly afterwards, due to the increased cost of coal, to $600. Fares from England to Singapore were about the same.

Travellers to Singapore now enjoyed a direct and reliable service from Europe, and their number increased accordingly. One must assume from later figures, and from the testimony of travellers in this anthology, that Singapore was regarded only as a port of call on the way to other places in Asia, as well as to Australia, after a P&O branch line was opened. Rival European steamship companies soon began to challenge P&O's virtual monopoly of steam navigation east of Suez, notably the Compagnie des Services Maritimes des Messageries Impériales, later renamed Messageries Maritimes, which extended its services to the Far East as a result of French colonial expansion in Cochin China. The first Messageries Impériales steamer to arrive at Singapore from Suez was the *L'Impératrice Eugénie* on 21 November 1862, inaugurating a monthly service which gave way at the end of the century to a fortnightly one between Marseilles and Yokohama, the outward and homeward bound ships generally arriving at Singapore on the same day.

The Hamburg–America Line also began to operate a monthly service from Hamburg and other European ports to China and Japan by way of Singapore, and the North German Lloyd Company, founded at Bremen in 1856, commenced a monthly service from Europe to Singapore and the Far East in 1886, both services increasing at the end of the century to fortnightly sailings. The Nederland Steamship Company, founded in 1870, operated a fortnightly service from Southampton to Surabaya, via Singapore, and it co-operated with the Rotterdam Lloyd Line in providing an alternate weekly service after 1892. At the same time, the Japanese Mail Steamship Company, Nippon Yusen Kaisha, began a fortnightly service between Yokohama and London by way of Singapore and Marseilles. The Italian Compania Transatlantica Line operated monthly passenger sailings between Liverpool and Manila, calling at Singapore, and the Austrian Lloyd Line also provided a monthly service to Singapore on ships sailing between Trieste and Kobe. The Glen, Ben, and Shire Lines all offered the more venturesome traveller first-class accommodation to Singapore on some of their cargo steamers. The British India Steamship Company, with its large fleet of ships, operated a fortnightly service between London and Calcutta, with transhipment facilities from there and Madras for Singapore, and by the end of the century it operated an alternate weekly mail service to Singapore with P&O, whose steamers sailed via Colombo. When the British India Steamship Company merged with P&O in 1914, it became the largest British shipping line, providing most of the passenger accommodation between Europe and Asia.

All of these transocean shipping companies, as well as companies operating in Asian waters like the Royal Dutch Packet Company, Koninklijke Paketvaart Maatschappij, and the Straits Steamship Company, brought thousands of travellers to Singapore every year, and to these were added American travellers sailing from San Francisco across the Pacific to the Far East once the Union Pacific and Central Pacific railroad companies linked the eastern and western seaboards of the United States in 1869. By the end of the century, North American travellers could also take the Canadian Pacific Railway to Vancouver and from there sail on one of the CPR's *Empress* steamers on the fortnightly Japan and China service to Yokohama, Kobe, Nagasaki, Shanghai, and Hong Kong. This was a shorter route than was offered by ships of the Pacific Mail Steamship Company on the 18-day service from San Francisco, by way of Honolulu, to Japan and Hong Kong. The Nippon Yusen Kaisha Line also operated a fortnightly service for travellers between Seattle and Hong Kong. North American passengers wanting to travel on to Singapore boarded one of the P&O or Messageries Maritimes steamers at Hong Kong.

The extension of steam navigation to Singapore had a considerable impact on its economic and physical development. In the early days, sailing ships anchored in the open roadstead and the cargo was carried in lighters to the mouth of the Singapore River and unloaded into godowns along Boat Quay. With the increase in trade, and the growing number of ships, watering and coaling facilities for steamships proved inadequate, even after the building of Collyer Quay in the 1860s. Before the opening of the Suez Canal, P&O held reserve stocks of 8,000 tons of coal at Singapore, which was mainly supplied from Great Britain, with smaller quantities coming from Labuan and Australia. Five years after the opening of the Canal, imports of coal into Singapore rose to 230,000 tons, dropping back to 142,000 tons in 1879. The need to store coal and service its steamers obliged P&O to build a wharf at Tebing Tinggi, on the north side of New (Keppel) Harbour, and its example was followed in the late 1850s by Jardine, Matheson & Co., John Purvis & Son, the Borneo Company, and, in 1864, the Tanjong Pagar Dock Company, which built wharves capable of accommodating 4 ships in 1866, 12 ships in 1868, and 20 ships in 1884.

The number of vessels using these wharves rose from 99 steamers and 65 sailing ships in the half-year ending August 1869, to 185 steamers and 63 sailing ships in the same period three years later, the increase in steam vessels being a consequence of the opening of the Suez Canal. In 1879 no less than 541 steamers and 91 sailing ships tied up at the Tanjong Pagar wharves, where passengers now disembarked, except for those on P&O ships, who landed at the P&O wharf, and those on Messageries Maritimes and North German Lloyd mail steamers, who came ashore at the Borneo Company's wharf, a distance of less than 2 miles from town. The construction of Anson Road in 1880, and Cecil Street five years later, provided a direct connection between Tanjong Pagar and the area of Raffles Place, and at the same time Keppel Road was built between Tanjong Pagar and Telok Belanga, past the P&O wharves at Tebing Tinggi. In 1885–7 lines were laid for the running of steam trams along Pasir Panjang Road and Keppel Road to the Tanjong Pagar docks, and from there along Anson Road and Cecil Street to Collyer Quay. A branch line ran from the junction of Tanjong Pagar Road and Anson Road to South Bridge Road, and then across the Singapore River by Elgin Bridge to Rochore. This tramway service lasted only until the end of 1892 due to competition from rickshaws, which had been introduced in numbers into Singapore as public transport in 1881. Electric trams followed, but the rickshaws matched the competition, rising to an average of more than 20,000 between 1900 and

1924. They provided travellers to Singapore with endless adventures, generally involving arrival at wrong destinations.

At the beginning of the twentieth century, a traveller's first impression of Singapore after disembarking from the steamer would be gained by proceeding along Keppel Road and Anson Road, where the electric tramway ran, to Cecil Street, past the Netherlands Trading Society building to Collyer Quay, and left into Battery Road and Raffles Place, formerly Commercial Square. Here the large European business houses were situated, as well as the departmental stores of Robinson & Co., and John Little & Co., the latter occupying the spectacular new building designed by Swan & MacLaren in 1907. Returning to the waterside, the traveller would pass the buildings of the Singapore Club and Chamber of Commerce, the Post Office and the Harbour Department, with the Hong Kong and Shanghai Bank opposite. After crossing the Singapore River by Cavenagh Bridge, he would come upon the government offices, and the Victoria Memorial Hall, incorporating the old Victoria Theatre, built to designs of Swan & MacLaren between 1902 and 1905. He would catch a glimpse behind of the old Supreme Court building before approaching the Esplanade and its tree-lined carriage path, still the social focus of Singapore residents taking their early evening drives. The new enclosure and pavilions of the Singapore Cricket Club and the Singapore Recreation Club would now come into view, as well as Thomas Woolner's large bronze statue of Singapore's founder, Sir Stamford Raffles, which had been erected on 27 June 1887 to mark Queen Victoria's Jubilee. He would pass on the landward side of the Esplanade the Hotel de l'Europe and see St Andrew's Cathedral, built by Lieutenant-Colonel Ronald Macpherson of the Madras Artillery between 1856 and 1862. Further along he would pass Raffles Girls' School and, at the corner of Beach and Bras Basah Roads, he would finally arrive at the favourite resort of so many travellers to Singapore, Raffles Hotel.

The Armenian Sarkies brothers had established the hotel in 1887, and when the main building was constructed in 1899 by Swan & MacLaren after designs by R. A. J. Bidwell, and the Bras Basah wing, comprising 20 suites on two floors, was added in 1904, the hotel offered a standard of accommodation and quality of service hitherto unknown in Singapore. It was challenged by the Hotel de l'Europe, the oldest and only establishment facing the Esplanade, after it was rebuilt in 1907 with 120 bedrooms and a large dining-room, claimed to be the finest in the East. It was said that Americans invariably stayed at Raffles Hotel while many British travellers preferred its rival. The Hotel de l'Europe eventually lost its prime site facing the Esplanade when the new Supreme Court, designed by F. Dorrington Ward, was built in 1937–9. There was also the Adelphi Hotel overlooking the grounds of St Andrew's Cathedral, where 'sea-breezes sweep the premises night and day making life in Singapore healthy and invigorating'. It had opened in 1863 in a building in Coleman Street and was rebuilt on its then existing site in 1904, again by Swan & MacLaren. Together with the Sea View Hotel at Tanjong Katong—'the hotel on the Palm fringe of Singapore'—it became extremely popular with travellers in the 1930s, after weathering, like most of the hotels in Singapore, the harsh economic effects of the Depression. Both offered the latest comforts, including hot and cold water, electric fans, and modern sanitary installations. Another first-class hotel was the Goodwood Park, which occupied the former premises of the Teutonia Club in Scott's Road, and advertised itself in the 1930s as being 'the most charmingly situated hotel in Singapore'.

The hotels all had runners to meet the ships as they berthed at a wharf of the Singapore Harbour Board (the successor to the Tanjong Pagar Dock Company) and arrange for passengers and their luggage to be taken to their respective establishments. The runners were joined on board ship by the local Thomas Cook agent, who offered transit passengers various tours of the island, including, invariably, the Botanic Gardens. Travellers to Singapore were now arriving in some of the most luxurious ships in the world, such as the modern express ocean liners of the North German Lloyd Line, *Scharnhorst*, *Potsdam*, and *Gneisenau*, which took only 22 days to reach Singapore from Southampton, and 14 days from Genoa; those belonging to the Nederland and Rotterdam Lloyd Lines, particularly the crack liners, *Baloeran* and *Dempo*; the luxurious one-class motor ships operated on a three-weekly service by the Danish East Asiatic Company between London, Rotterdam, Marseilles, and Singapore; the modern liners of the Lloyd

The Hotel de l'Europe after the arrival of a European mail boat at Singapore, from Hugo V. Pedersen, *Door den Oost-Indischen Archipel: Eene Kunstreis*, H. D. Tjeenk Willink & Zoon, Haarlem, 1902.

Triestino Line sailing from either Venice and Trieste or Naples and Genoa; and those of the Nippon Yusen Kaisha Line, including the *Nitta Maru*, which offered travellers the latest degree of comfort, including air-conditioning throughout, when it was introduced on the Japan–Europe service immediately before the outbreak of the Second World War.

As well as travellers by ship, a small number arrived at Singapore from 1933 on weekly flights from London operated by British Imperial Airways, using, from Karachi, Armstrong Whitworth AW15 Atalanta monoplanes, especially designed for the Tropics, carrying 9 passengers at 130 mph. Royal Dutch Airlines (KLM) operated a twice-weekly service, later increased to three times a week, to Indonesia, via Singapore, with Douglas DC3 airliners on five and a half day-long flights from Amsterdam, connecting with London. During these flights travellers enjoyed a full night's sleep at first-class hotels along the way, the cost being included in the return fare of £234, which was about twice that by ship. Commercial aircraft arriving at Singapore first used the RAF Seletar airfield, but the opening of the $9 million Kallang Airport in June 1937, providing combined facilities for land and marine aircraft, allowed the introduction in the following year of the legendary Short S23 Empire flying-boats operated by British Imperial Airways, the most successful of all pre-war civil aircraft, carrying 24 day, or 16 night berth passengers at 165 mph. Travellers to and from Australia on the Qantas leg of the journey flew via Jakarta, Surabaya, Bima, and Kupang. Although hardly recognized at the time, these overseas commercial airflights constituted a dividing line in the history of travel to Singapore, between the so-called 'golden' age from 1880 to 1939 and the new post-war period of Lockheed Constellations, Boeing jumbo jets, cheap package tours, and skyscraper hotels, offering a service and a degree of comfort unimagined by the travellers recorded in this anthology.

* * *

The passages in this anthology have been selected from books written by the travellers themselves. In a few instances, passages have been taken from accounts by residents of Singapore, where it was found necessary to provide information on such important subjects as the Singapore Mutiny of

1915. The passages have been chosen to provide a chronological sequence, reflecting the changing perceptions of Singapore by succeeding generations of travellers. In order to record the contemporary scene, the old spelling of names and places has been preserved. Some brief explanation of local terms is given in footnote references. The source of each passage is indicated at the end, together with the relevant page numbers. The compiler has been particularly concerned to give adequate coverage to women travellers to Singapore, and to include many passages written by Americans. Although the anthology contains one passage by a Malay, and two passages by Japanese authors, it has proved impossible to include any passage written by a Chinese. There is only one known nineteenth-century Chinese traveller who left an account of his visit to Singapore. This was Li Chung Chu, who spent a month in Singapore in 1887 before returning to China. His account is not particularly informative, though he noted the relatively small number of Chinese and European restaurants in Singapore, and the difficulty which Asian passengers encountered in hiring small boats to carry their luggage ashore from ships anchored in the harbour. In remembering him, we also recall the thousands of other Asian travellers to Singapore whose impressions of their visit, if they had been recorded, would have given another dimension to this anthology.

1
The First Survey of Singapore

CAPTAIN DANIEL ROSS
1819

Captain Daniel Ross commanding HEICS Discovery *and Lieutenant John G. F. Crawford commanding HEICS* Investigator, *both of the Bombay Marine, arrived from Macau in mid-December 1819 to make a hydrographic survey of the Straits of Malacca. They were immediately engaged by Sir Stamford Raffles to assist him in his search for a suitable trading post, and after surveying Pulau Kerimun they accompanied him and his entourage to Singapore, where, on 30 January 1819, a preliminary treaty was signed with the local Malay ruler, Temenggong Abdul Rahman of Johore, allowing the East India Company to establish a factory on the island for an annual payment of 3,000 Spanish dollars. Ross, who had earlier pointed out to Raffles that Singapore might be approached by ships nearer than shown on the existing charts, immediately commenced a survey of the surrounding waters. He completed his report on 7 February 1819, concluding that 'the Singapore Straits, will afford a safe anchorage in all seasons, and being clear of hidden danger, the approach to it is rendered easy by day or night'.*

THE town of Singapore, on the Island of the same name, stands on a point of land near the western part of a bay, and is easily distinguished by there being just behind it, a pleasant looking hill, that is partly cleared of trees. Between the point on which the town is situated, and the western one of the bay, there is a creek, in which the native vessels anchor close to the town, and it may be found useful to European vessels of easy draught to repair in. On the eastern side of the bay, opposite to the tower, there is a deep inlet lined by mangroves, which would also be a good anchorage for native boats; and about north from the low sandy point of the bay, there is a village inhabited by fishermen, a short way to the eastward of which, is a passage through the mangroves, leading to a fresh water river....

The coast to the eastward of the town, is one continued sandy beach; and half a mile to the eastern point of the bay, or two miles and half from the town, there is a point where the depth of water is six or seven fathoms, at three or four hundred yards from the shore; and at six hundred yards a small bank with about three fathoms at low water; the point offers a favourable position for batteries to defend ships that may in time of war anchor near to it.

Fresh water is to be had at several places in the vicinity of the town, and there are some small rivers along the coast to the eastward, where the water appears red.

D. Ross, 'Report of a Survey of Singapoora Harbour, 7 February 1819', *Calcutta Journal, or, Political, Commercial, and Literary Gazette*, 6 April 1819, pp. 59–60.

2
Discovery of the Singapore Stone

MUNSYI ABDULLAH BIN ABDUL KADIR
1819–1822

Abdullah bin Abdul Kadir had worked as a young scribe for Raffles at Malacca in 1810–11, prior to the British invasion of Java, and he was one of the many Malays who travelled to Singapore from Malacca when news arrived of the new British settlement. His account is contained in his Hikayat Abdullah *(The Story of Abdullah), which was published in Singapore in 1849. Although written later in his life, the details he gives of the new settlement are vivid, though not always accurate. He refers here to Sultan Husain, with whom Raffles had concluded a second treaty on 6 February 1819, granting the East India Company the right to establish trading factories on the island in return for annual payments of 5,000 Spanish dollars to the Sultan, and 3,000 Spanish dollars to Temenggong Abdul Rahman. He also refers to the disagreement between Raffles and the first Resident of Singapore, Lieutenant-Colonel William Farquhar, about the layout of the town. More interesting is his account of a visit he made with Raffles and the Protestant missionary, the Revd Claudius Henry Thomsen, to the mouth of the Singapore River to see the recently discovered stone, inscribed with characters which are now thought to be Javanese* kawi *of the tenth to the thirteenth centuries. Abdullah wrongly blames the destruction of the stone on George Dromgold Coleman, who was responsible for designing many of Singapore's early buildings, when, in fact, it was demolished in January 1843 by the Acting Settlement Engineer, Captain D. H. Stevenson, during work to widen the Singapore River.*

WHEN the Settlement of Singapore was about four months old I arrived . . . from Malacca. I found that there were no houses yet on the far side of the river. It was covered with jungle, mangrove trees and mud. People lived only on the near side. Sultan Husain Shah was just starting to build his palace at Kampong Gelam. But the area was covered with mangrove and there was no means of approach over the land. People going to Kampong Gelam, used only the route along the shore. They feared the journey through the swamp, though they had some fear also of the shore route.

The Sultan's entire family in Riau, his attendants, his household and entourage, moved to Singapore together in hundreds of boats. Some lodged with the Sultan, some with the Temenggong, and others opened up new ground inland, everyone choosing according to his own wishes.

Every day without ceasing murders took place along the road to Kampong Gelam. There were policemen on duty here and there but they themselves were often murdered. Colonel Farquhar employed no small labour force cutting down the bushes and clearing away the scrub bordering the road, making up the surface, and repairing the [East India] Company's houses, each section having its particular task. All the workmen were Malacca Malays who lived in crowded quarters up against a *nibong** fence near the Temenggong's

*A tall, thorny palm.

premises. They built themselves an oratory, that is a house for prayer, round which were grouped the huts in which they lived....

Since Singapore has become a settlement chintzes from Europe have been used as bathing clouts, broadcloths as trousers, Bugis satins and the *batek** silks of Java as hats. People carry silk umbrellas in their hands and wear leather sandals, and talk fluently in English, Benggali and Tamil. If an Englishman addresses them in Malay they reply in English....

As time went on the numbers of foreigners and white merchants greatly increased and the fame of the Singapore settlement spread far and wide, confirming the fact that it was a permanent settlement. Many people from other countries moved to Singapore, and some gave agencies to traders in Singapore, sending in goods from various places. All these factors increased the population of the settlement, which became filled with various races plying their different trades and crafts, all of them living in Singapore. Among them there were poor men who became rich and some who brought capital of tens of thousands of dollars from their own countries only to lose it all and become beggars. Everyone traded on his luck for, as we say, 'If you have the luck of coconut fibre you float, if of a stone you sink.'...

There is a story about how Mr Raffles and Colonel Farquhar together debated the best way to enlarge the Settlement. Colonel Farquhar considered that Kampong Gelam should become the business quarter, that is to say a trading centre with markets and so forth. But Mr Raffles thought that the business quarter should be on the near side of the river. Colonel Farquhar said 'This side is very unsuitable as the ground is all muddy and the water is not good. It will be very costly to reclaim the land. Besides, where can we obtain sufficient earth for banking?' Mr Raffles replied 'If Kampong Gelam were to become a business area this side of the river would remain unimproved for as long as a hundred years.' Each of the two men held firmly to his own opinion, the one saying this the other that, each trying to find support for his view. They thought the matter over for three days. Then it occurred to Mr Raffles that the small hill near Tanjong Singapura might be broken up and the earth used for

*A patterned cloth, printed, or drawn in wax and painted.

banking on the near side of the river. The next day the two of them considered this idea and agreed to it. The people must have been amazed to see the work being carried out. The next day men under the orders of Mr Raffles and Mr Farquhar came round calling for Chinese, Malay and Indian labourers, and some two or three hundred labourers were paid one rupee per head per day to dig and carry the earth. There were men breaking up rocks, for many very large rocks lay about. Every man had his task. There were scores of overseers, looking like men going to war. Labour became more and more expensive from day to day. Every afternoon sacks of money were brought to pay the workmen. Twice a day Mr Raffles used to appear on the ground directing the workmen and besides this there were many people supervising them at work. Colonel Farquhar too was there early every morning without fail to divide up outlying sections of the land. Part was sold by auction and part was given away free as long as it could be cleared quickly, for the whole place was covered with scrub....

After three or four months the hill was flattened out and all the muddy pools, narrow water-channels and swampy ground were levelled off. There remained a few huge rocks, some as tall as elephants, and others even larger. These rocks were very useful, for the Chinese came in scores and broke them up for house building. There was no payment for the work, for everyone rushed to ask for the stone which was just given away.

It was then that they found at the point of the headland a rock lying in the bushes. The rock was smooth, about six feet wide, square in shape, and its face was covered with a chiselled inscription. But although it had writing this was illegible because of extensive scouring by water. Allah alone knows how many thousands of years old it may have been. After its discovery crowds of all races came to see it. The Indians declared that the writing was Hindu but they were unable to read it. The Chinese claimed that is was in Chinese characters. I went with a party of people, and also Mr Raffles and Mr [C. H.] Thomsen, and we all looked at the rock. I noticed that in shape the lettering was rather like Arabic, but I could not read it because owing to its great age the relief was partly effaced.

Many learned men came and tried to read it. Some brought

flour paste which they pressed on the inscription and took a cast, others rubbed lamp-black on it to make the lettering visible. But for all that they exhausted their ingenuity in trying to find out what language the letters represented they reached no decision. There the stone rested until recently with its inscription in relief. It was Mr Raffles's opinion that the writing must be Hindu because the Hindus were the oldest of all immigrant races in the East, reaching Java and Bali and Siam, the inhabitants of which are all descended from them. However, not a single person in all Singapore was able to interpret the words chiselled on the rock. Allah alone knows. It remained where it was until the time when Mr [S. G.] Bonham was Governor of the three Settlements of Singapore, Penang and Malacca. Mr [G. D.] Coleman was then engineer in Singapore and it was he who broke up the stone; a great pity, and in my opinion a most improper thing to do, prompted perhaps by his own thoughtlessness and folly. He destroyed the rock because he did not realize its importance. Perhaps he did not stop to consider that a man cleverer than he might extract its secrets from it, for I have heard it said that in England there are scholars with special knowledge who can easily understand such writing, whatever the language or race. As the Malays say 'If you cannot improve a thing at least do not destroy it.'

When all the swampy low-lying ground and pools of muddy water had been banked up, the land was marked out and sold by auction. If anyone wishes to know the site of the hill which Mr Raffles broke up to make banks for the watery morass on the near side of the river, it is at the end of Tanjong Singapura in Lorong Tambangan. They laid out a garden there, planting all kinds of flowers and trees. I heard it said that they meant to have a house built there containing a statue of Mr Raffles, as a reminder to all people that it was he who had done such great work. I do not know why the project was dropped. . . .

Munsyi Abdullah bin Abdul Kadir, 'The Hikayat Abdullah', an annotated translation by A. H. Hill, *JMBRAS*, XXVIII, 3 (1955): 142, 144, 146–8.

3
Old and New Singapore

JOHN CRAWFURD
1822–1823

John Crawfurd, a Scotsman, was the second Resident of Singapore, succeeding Lieutenant-Colonel William Farquhar in that post in June 1823. He first visited the island between January and February 1822 on a political mission to Thailand and Cochin China as Agent to the Governor-General, the Marquis of Hastings, and his long and informative account of early Singapore comes from his account of the mission, which was published in London in 1828. Crawfurd was an extremely able man, and served under Raffles as Resident at Yogyakarta during the British occupation of Java. He remained Resident of Singapore until December 1825, but he was not popular during his term of office, finding it difficult to compete with his predecessor, Farquhar, who was held in great affection by the inhabitants of the island.

LAST night my old friend Colonel Farquhar, resident of Singapore, sent his staff, Captain [C. E.] Davies, on board to invite us on shore. We landed this morning; and Mr [C.] Scott, a merchant of this new settlement, and the son of my respected friend, Mr Robert Scott, an experienced and most intelligent merchant of Penang, hospitably and obligingly gave his house up for our accommodation. In the evening we dined with Colonel Farquhar, and went through the greater part of the new settlement. Notwithstanding the state of abeyance in which the political question regarding the settlement was involved, there was universally an air of animation and activity. Several miles of new road were already formed, and the habitations were so numerous, and the population so great, that we could hardly imagine that the whole was the creation of three short years....

I walked this morning round the walls and limits of the ancient town of Singapore, for such in reality had been the site of our modern settlement. It was bounded to the east by the sea, to the north by a wall, and to the west by a salt creek or inlet of the sea. The inclosed space is a plain, ending in a hill of considerable extent, and a hundred and fifty feet in

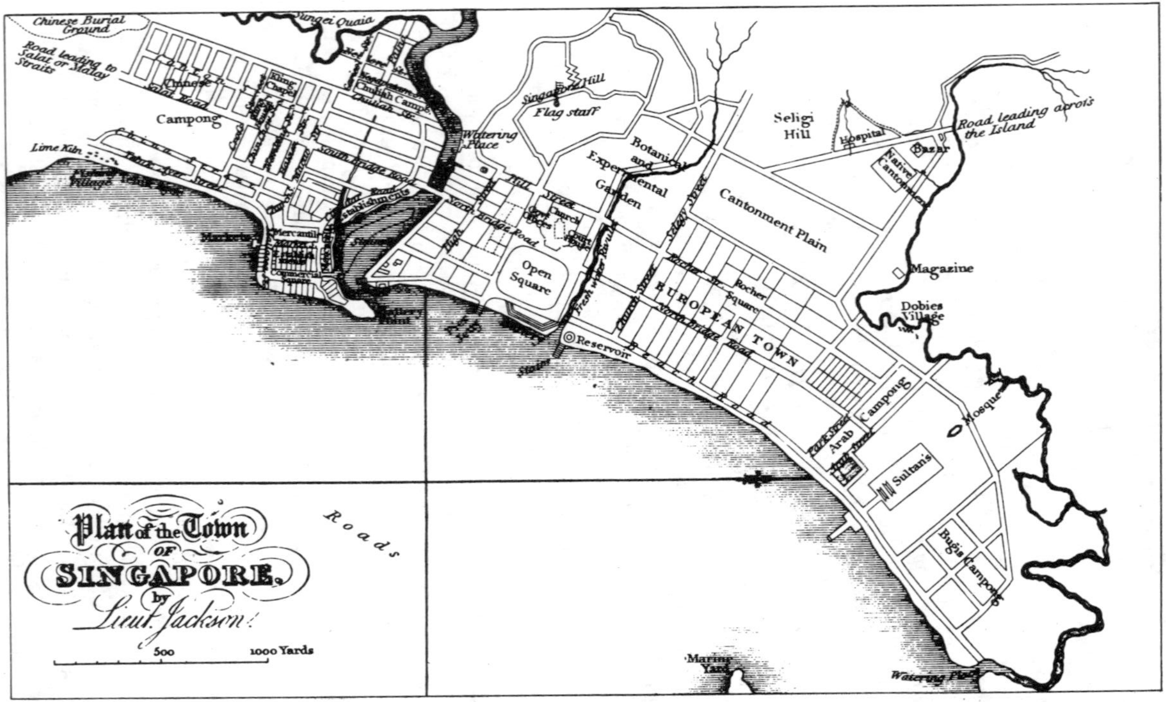

Plan of the Town of Singapore by Lieutenant Phillip Jackson, *c.*1823–4, from John Crawfurd, *Journal of an Embassy from the Governor-General of India to the Courts of Siam and Cochin China*, Henry Colburn, London, 1828.

height. The whole is a kind of triangle, of which the base is the sea-side, about a mile in length. The wall, which is about sixteen feet in breadth at its base, and at present about eight or nine in height, runs very near a mile from the sea-coast to the base of the hill, until it meets a salt marsh. As long as it continues in the plain, it is skirted by a little rivulet running at the foot of it, and forming a kind of moat; and where it attains the elevated side of the hill, there are apparent the remains of a dry ditch. On the western side, which extends from the termination of the wall to the sea, the distance, like that of the northern side, is very near a mile. This last has the natural and strong defence of a salt marsh, overflown at high-water, and of a deep and broad creek. In the wall there are no traces of embrasures or loop-holes; and neither on the sea-side, nor on that skirted by the creek and marsh, is there any appearance whatever of artificial defences. We may conclude from these circumstances, that the works of Singapore were not intended against fire-arms, or an attack by sea; or that if the latter, the inhabitants considered themselves strong in their naval force, and therefore thought any other defences in that quarter superfluous.

On the stony point which forms the western side of the entrance of the salt creek, on which the modern town of Singapore is building, there was discovered, two years ago, a tolerably hard block of sand-stone, with an inscription upon it.... The only remains of antiquity at Singapore, besides this stone, and the wall and moat before mentioned, are contained on the hill before alluded to. After being cleared by us of the extensive forest which covered it, it is now clothed with a fine grassy sward, and forms the principal beauty of the new settlement. The greater part of the west and northern side of the mountain is covered with the remains of the foundations of buildings, some composed of baked brick of good quality. Among these ruins, the most distinguished are those seated on a square terrace, of about forty feet to a side, near the summit of the hill. On the edge of this terrace, we find fourteen large blocks of sandstone; which, from the hole in each, had probably been the pedestals of as many wooden-posts which supported the building. This shows us, at once, that the upper part of the structure was of perishable materials; an observation which, no doubt, applies to the rest of the buildings as well as to this. Within the square terrace is a circular inclosure, formed of rough sand-stones, in the centre of which is a well, or hollow, which very possibly contained an image; for I look upon the building to have been a place of worship, and, from its appearance, in all likelihood, a temple of Buddha. I venture farther to conjecture, that the other relics of antiquity on the hill, are the remains of monasteries of the priests of this religion. Another terrace, on the north declivity of the hill, nearly of the same size, is said to have been the burying-place of Iskandar Shah, King of Singapore. This is the prince whom tradition describes as having been driven from his throne by the Javanese, in the year 1252 of the Christian era, and who died at Malacca, not converted to the Mohammedan religion, in 1274; so that the story is probably apocryphal. Over the supposed tomb of Iskandar, a rude structure has been raised, since the formation of the new settlement, to which Mohammedans, Hindus, and Chinese, equally resort to do homage. It is remarkable, that many of the fruit-trees cultivated by the ancient inhabitants of Singapore are still existing, on the eastern side of the hill, after a supposed lapse of near six hundred years. Here we find the durian, the rambutan, the duku, the shaddock, and other fruit-trees of great size; and all so degenerated, except the two first, that the fruit is scarcely to be recognized.

Among the ruins are found various descriptions of pottery, some of which is Chinese, and some native. Fragments of this are in great abundance. In the same situation have been found Chinese brass coins of the tenth and eleventh centuries....

The site of the town is remarkable for its salubrity, and the fevers and dysenteries of ordinary tropical countries are of very rare occurrence. I have no recollection, indeed, of any European having fallen a victim to the climate in the long period of nine years, since the formation of the settlement. This may appear at first view the more remarkable, since a considerable portion of the site of the town, and much of the neighbourhood, is a low and even noisome marsh. The healthiness of the situation is, I conceive, chiefly ascribable to the free ventilation which prevails, and which precludes the formation of those poisonous miasmata, which are the true source of most endemical diseases in warm countries. Sea-breezes prevail with considerable regularity, but chilling land-winds are scarcely known—probably another reason for the salubrity of the place. In the north-east monsoon, from October to March, the settlement is refreshed by stiff breezes blowing in from the China Seas. The westerly monsoon, interrupted by the Straits of Malacca and the neighbouring lands, is not felt. That the free ventilation of the town now mentioned is the chief cause of its salubrity, may be inferred from this, that the climate is not equally good in the only other part of the island where a considerable population is collected. This is the beautiful and romantic spot called 'the new harbour', which is landlocked, and where fevers and dysenteries of a fatal character are sufficiently frequent among the Malay settlers who occupy it....

The agricultural capabilities of Singapore, distinct from soil, are not inconsiderable. The alterations of season are so trifling, that there is a perpetual succession of flowers and fruits; and every period of the year, therefore, seems almost equally suited for conducting the labours of agriculture.... Before quitting this subject, I ought to observe, that the agriculture of Singapore, of whatever description, is almost exclusively carried on by the Chinese.

The manufactures carried on in Singapore, however trifling, deserve some notice. The most considerable is that of pearl or white sago. The raw sago is imported, as mentioned in another place, from the north coast of Sumatra. The process of converting it into pearl sago is sufficiently simple, and consists in nothing more than frequent edulcorations, drying the farina, granulating it in sieves, and finally drying, or rather baking it by a slow fire, in iron pots. The sago thus treated is at first of a pure white colour, and has all the look of new-fallen sleet, but in time it becomes more or less discoloured according to the degree of skill with which the process has been performed. The manufacturers are all Chinese, and a manufactory employing about a dozen labourers will produce at the rate of five piculs per diem. The cost of production is reckoned at about five Spanish dollars per picul, equal to about a farthing per pound. The art of manufacturing pearl sago is a recent one, and invented by the Chinese. It was first practised at Malacca about fourteen years ago, and introduced into Singapore only in 1824. This last place is now the principal seat of manufactory.

Ship-building has not hitherto been carried to any extent, but two establishments exist, capable of giving ordinary repairs to vessels of any size, and at which a few small craft, constructed of the timber of the island, have been built. This timber however, as already mentioned, is not fit for building durable ships. Should at any period the abundant supply of teak timber produced in Siam become available, it may be expected, as there are many situations convenient for the formation of docks and slips, that the business of ship-building will be established at Singapore upon an extensive scale. The only other manufactory which may be worth noticing is the fabrication of native arms, and of domestic and agricultural implements for exportation throughout the Archipelago. In 1825, there were upward of sixty forges employed by the Chinese chiefly in this business.

The chief importance of Singapore is as a commercial emporium, and in this view it has certainly answered the most sanguine expectations. When it was founded, in 1819, it was inhabited by a few hundred piratical Malay fishermen. Down to the year 1819, both the island and the harbour may be said to have been almost unknown. It was indeed not only not frequented by European shipping, but carefully avoided. In 1820, the very year following its occupation, not less than 13,000 tons of native vessels cleared out from the port, all employed in one description of trade or another; and no less than 55,000 tons of European shipping touched at it, either for trade or refreshment. For the first three years of its occupation, no attempt was made at an estimate of the amount of the trade carried on. I made an effort to remedy this defect in 1823, when the exports were found to amount to 5,568,560 Spanish dollars....

There is no Asiatic and few European ports of which the trade is so diversified as that of Singapore....

The town of Singapore is naturally divided into three portions, namely, the Malay part; that which contains the dwellings of the European merchants, the public offices, and the military cantonments; and the Chinese, or commercial portion. The two first are situated upon a plain fronting the harbour, running to the length of about a mile and a half along the shore, and having its breadth confined to about one thousand yards by a range of hills of from one hundred to one hundred and fifty feet high. The commercial portion of the town is divided from the other two by the salt creek already named, and is situated upon a narrow peninsula, lying between this last and the sea to the westward. The Malayan portion of the town lies at the eastern portion of the plain, and is chiefly occupied by the Sultan of Jehore [Johore] and his followers, from whom we purchased the island, and who is our pensionary. The dwellings of the merchants and the military cantonments occupy the central and western portion of the same plain, and the highest portion of the range of hills which I have named is occupied by the Government-house, other portions by the dwellings of public officers or merchants. Almost all the best warehouses and the whole dwellings of the Chinese are on the peninsula, to the western side of the creek, which is connected with the plain by a very good wooden bridge. The whole of the warehouses, and all the dwelling-houses in the principal streets in their vicinity, are built of brick and lime, and roofed with red tile. The more distant dwelling-houses and shops are built of wood, but roofed with tile also; and it is only in the distant outskirts that any huts with thatched roofs are to be found, although, five years ago, nearly the whole of this portion of the town was composed of dwellings of this last description. The streets are formed upon a regular plan, intersecting each other at right angles; and the roads, both in the town and the immediate vicinity of the settlement, are constructed of a mixture of sand with a clay-iron-ore, which, constituting the crust of all the hills in the island, is of course abundant.

J. Crawfurd, *Journal of an Embassy from the Governor-General of India to the Courts of Siam and Cochin China; Exhibiting a View of the Actual State of Those Kingdoms*, Henry Colburn, London, 1828, pp. 42–7, 533–7, 555–6.

4
A Dutch Account of Singapore

BARON H. G. NAHUIJS VAN BURGST
1823

The Dutch colonial official and military officer, Baron H. G. Nahuijs van Burgst, arrived at Singapore in May 1824 after travelling along the west coast of Sumatra, where he visited Raffles at Bencoolen (Bengkulu). He had been expelled from Java after the British conquest of Java, but he returned in 1816 and was afterwards appointed Resident at Yogyakarta. He established a direct personal friendship with Raffles by sending Lady Raffles at Bencoolen a pretty Java pony, and Raffles reciprocated the favour by writing flatteringly about him to his future parents-in-law when he was courting their daughter. During his travels in Sumatra and Malaysia he addressed letters to his friend at Jakarta, Lieutenant-General H. M. de Kock, and these were later published as a book at Breda in 1826. His report on Singapore is one of the best informed accounts of the early settlement.

I believe that no person with any feeling can help being impressed when setting foot in Singapore, because he can now see as a seat of European trade and industry a place which only five years before was a cavern and hiding place for murderers and pirates.... Before the occupation of Singapore by the English, some Chinese living a few miles inland earned a livelihood by planting and preparing the gambier.*

Ground standing vacant is obtainable by any person without payment whatsoever. Anyone desiring it simply applied to the Resident, who thereupon issued a grant free of charge, unless the ground was owned or occupied by natives, in which case it was necessary to make an agreement regarding the transfer with the natives beforehand.

The land is mostly hilly and is thickly covered with trees. Many of the hills in the neighbourhood of the beach are already adorned with houses of various Europeans....

The house of the Resident also stands on such a hill. From it one has the best view of the Roads, the Straits of Singapore and the Straits of Malacca, as well as the neighbouring islands. The house itself, however, did not attract me very much and seemed very cramped.

The roads to all these hills although very useful for carriages are not first class, whilst the lower roads leading to the houses of the Europeans are in very good order. Amongst

***Uncaria gambir*, producing an astringent extract for use with betel or for tanning.

all these one road stands out, which is almost three miles long, on the right bank of the river. This is 42 feet wide and raised at least 8 or 10 feet above the morass, leading to a very pleasant country house standing on a nice hill. This belongs to Mr [J.] Pearl, ships's captain and owner of a pepper and gambier plantation.

Very few Europeans devote themselves to agriculture. The cost of laying out and upkeeping the plantations are also not very encouraging. Those who have acquired land must first clear it of extensive timber, which is usually done by contract with Malays who are particularly skilled and like that work. The further cleaning up and bringing into good order of the ground as well as the planting and upkeep must be arranged with Chinese day labourers, whose daily wage amounts to from one-half to one rupee.

The houses of the settlers or traders are close to the shore and are well built. Most of them are raised high above the ground and roofed with stone tiles, which are partly brought from Malacca and partly from China.

Most of the houses are on the left bank of the river, which divides the town into two parts. A few are on the right bank, where the Chinese and Arab settlement containing more than one hundred good houses is situated. There is a good bridge over the river 200 feet long and 32 feet broad.

Singapore can already boast of about thirty tastefully built European houses. These are placed a short distance from one another and in front of them runs a carriage-way, which they all make use of in the afternoons. This riding and driving appears to me to be very similar to riding around in a riding-school, because one has to go round the same circular road four or five times in an afternoon in order to make a tour worth the name....

The cost of living in Singapore is very high, because the island produces little or nothing. Workmens' and servants' wages are excessive....

Many servants and coolies are Chinese, whose number totals about 5,000; most of them are occupied in agriculture. The Malays seldom work for the Europeans; they are too lazy and indolent by nature to devote themselves to a definite daily task. The Malays settled in Singapore for the most part submit to the so-called Malayan Tommagung [Temenggong], the former head of the pirates, whom the British Government support with a monthly payment of Sp. Piaster 700*.... In addition to this income of Sp. Piaster 700 per month he also enjoys certain revenue arising out of the ferrying across the river and some small charges which he levies on native vehicles and on the cutting of timber. This Tommagung is generally said still to have a very good understanding with his elder brothers the pirates and to maintain an active correspondence with them, giving them regular news of the comings and goings in Singapore harbour and the destination, cargo and strength of the different ships. The Tommagung lives with his dependents a short distance away from the European town on a site allotted to him by the British Government of Singapore, on account of the frequent quarrels and murders for which his dependents have been responsible.

Over all these people as well as over the Bouginese [Bugis] settled in Singapore, the British Resident has not the least authority, even when they attack the Europeans....

Interference on the part of the British administration with native affairs was to cost them dear. When a Malay ran amok and in his mania killed some people and even went so far as to dangerously wound the British Resident, Colonel Farquhar, Lieutenant-Governor Raffles desired that the body of the evil doer should be hung up on a gallows for some days as a warning to others; against which the native authorities objected on the ground that as the evil doer had given his life against other lives, all further punishment terminated. The Lieutenant-Governor, who was in possession of the body of the murderer, had that, notwithstanding all the objections of the natives, hung on a gallows guarded by soldiers, which had the effect that all the natives adopted a threatening attitude and awakened considerable fear amongst the citizens. All of them, garrison, civilians, settlers and traders, as well as the Chinese who took the side of the Europeans, were night and day under arms, and this unsettled state of affairs lasted just so long as the body was hanging up, terminating on the third day, when Mr Raffles considered it wiser to hand over the body of the misdoer to his friends and compatriots for burial. Since this upset there has been no very great sense of security amongst the merchants of Singapore,

*A Spanish dollar was roughly equivalent to 5*s* sterling.

and if one touches them on this tender spot one will most likely hear complaints about the small garrison and the limited power which the British Government in Singapore possesses.

Two Companies of Bengalese and a detachment of 25 European Artillery must hardly suffice to ensure the safety of their people and the large values which are lying in Singapore warehouses in the way of goods, especially opium and piece goods, two valuable articles which the natives particularly prize. Many of the residents are not without anxiety that a man like the Malayan Tommagung, tempted by the large treasure, could easily be induced with the underlings and a great many of his friends the pirates, to attack the weak garrison and citizens unexpectedly and then clear off with his booty to places where he could not easily be traced. People were hoping therefore that a good fort would be built, that the garrison would be strengthened and the port guarded by a couple of the Company's cruisers from Bombay.

As a measure of precaution the British Government after the minor dispute with the natives have ordained that nobody other than of high rank, whose names must be registered at the police station, shall have the right to go about within the European establishment carrying a kris or other weapon....

In the fundamental laws which were laid down by Sir Stamford Raffles on the foundation of Singapore all gambling, without exception, was forbidden and it was assumed that this would never be permitted, even though farmed out. The leasing of the dice gambling by the Resident has put up the backs of most of the good settlers, especially the magistrates, of whom many have tendered their resignation. It appears to me that one cannot deny that such gambling in a place where there are so many bad people must give encouragement to robbery and murder, and at the very least must always have the natural effect of bringing the lower-class working people to poverty and distress.

Another circumstance which makes the settlers in a sense dissatisfied with the present Resident is that he is very economical and saving with the country's funds and undertakes few public works in contrast with Lieutenant-Governor Raffles, who was not very sparing with Government money and laid it out for the public benefit and for the improvement of Singapore. So long as the fate of Singapore is undecided and it is still uncertain whether that establishment is to remain in the hands of the English it seems to me cautious and sensible not to lay out too much money on this insecure possession....

Judging by everything I saw myself of Singapore I believe that its situation has been very well chosen for trading purposes by Sir Stamford Raffles; but that this place could not be raised to such a state of general trading activity as on the one hand was feared and on the other hand was hoped. Do not attach too much value to appearances. The twelve English merchant houses already settled there, which for the most part are working not with their own capital but with that of merchants in Bengal, Madras, Batavia, Bombay, Poeloe [Pulau] Penang and England, appear to me more than sufficient, together with the Armenian, Chinese and native traders who are settled there, for the trade of Singapore; and if a greater number, which is not improbable, turn in that direction then I consider it certain that many of them will suffer disappointment, in case that has not already happened and is happening to many. Therefore it seems to me that the authorities in Singapore make too much fuss about the trade there, going so far as if this place, to the exception of all others, was the only one in the Straits of Malacca enjoying this distinction....

Baron H. G. Nahuijs van Burgst, 'Extracts from the Letters of Col. Nahuijs', trans. H. E. Miller, *JMBRAS*, XIX, 2 (1941): 192–9.

5
A Resort for Invalids

THOMAS PRINSEP
1829

Thomas Prinsep, a Captain in the Bengal Corps of Engineers, was one of six brothers who served in India during the early years of the nineteenth century. Having been advised to leave India for the recovery of his health, he travelled in 1829–30 to Penang, Singapore, Jakarta, and Australia, recording his impressions of the places he visited in a series of letters, which were edited by his sister-in-law, Mrs Augustus Prinsep, and published in London in 1833. The book was accompanied by a separate folio of topographical engravings, after drawings made by Prinsep during his travels, but unfortunately there is no view of Singapore. He later died in India after falling from his horse.

AT length I have reached this infant Hercules of commerce, which has already strangled the two snakes, Penang and Malacca, that thought to eat him up in his cradle. The island of Sincapore lies at the extremity of the scraggy peninsula of Malacca, divided from it by a very narrow channel, only navigable for small boats, and forms a kind of centre to the countless islands around.... The first appearance of this place from the sea pleased me even more than Penang, with its cheerful row of detached houses along the beach, each within its neat little enclosure, and the small hills rising behind, topped with bungalows, all open to the sea and sea-breeze; but when you see the whole settlement, you heave a sigh at its insignificant extent, and feel what a prison it is!...

Sincapore has become quite the fashionable resort of Calcutta invalids, and seeing the effects so marked upon all their countenances, I will give it the chance of beautifying my own. Prison as it is in extent, if it succeeds in this, I shall think it sufficiently agreeable to reside in, even for six whole months....

At a distance there is a beautifully variegated frame of green islands, which seems to hug the ocean into a lake. Have I not well chosen my point of sight? But come, now, let us to the Esplanade, for here we may walk out and brave the sun with impunity, protected solely by an umbrella. Many even make pic-nic parties upon the water, and indulge in the freedoms and rural amusements of England. The beach, with its cottages and lawns, may remind you of an English watering place; but unhappily you are soon undeceived by following the road a mile either to the right or left. That to the right, after passing this pretty Esplanade and Lilliputian fort, leads to the town. A little muddy river runs into the bay, and is covered with an infinite number of Chinese and Malay boats, busily employed in the traffic to and from the junks and merchant-vessels in the harbour. Cross this river on a

View of the Singapore River and Government Hill, by Edmond-François Pâris, 1830, from C. Laplace, *Voyage autour du monde par les mers de l'Inde et de la Chine exécuté sur la Corvette de sa Majesté la Favourite*. . . , Arthus Bertrand, Editeur, Paris, 1835. (National Museum, Singapore)

crazy, tottering wooden bridge, and you will find on each side of you a salt marsh, out of which rise hundreds of buildings, standing, as it were, upon stilts, ten or twelve feet above the mud, which is covered by the tide only at high water; a raised causeway through this leads to the rest of the town, which is built substantially on *terra firma*, but more than half is on these piles. This artificial elevation, and the streets or canals being of a tolerable width, give the town a more important appearance than it otherwise would have. Great numbers of Chinese live in these wretched looking boxes (houses I cannot call them); their only entrance is by a narrow plank from the causeway, over which dangerous pathway the inmates and even the little children are continually running. Most of them are shops in which the owners may constantly be seen, indifferent to the inconveniences of their situation, pursuing merrily their various occupations. They are excellent carpenters, and the island furnishes some very beautiful specimens of wood, particularly well adapted for ornamental household furniture. The Chinese inhabitants far exceed the Malays in number; they come down from the coasts of China and Siam in swarms, insomuch that they and their descendants have become too numerous to find subsistence here in an honest way, and have recource to theft, in which they are great adepts. This they practise almost without restraint, such is the indolence and carelessness of the police, who, in some rather violent tussels, having allowed the offenders to gain the advantage, they have acquired so much boldness, that scarcely a night passes without some depredation being committed....

The whole extent of the road being no more than three miles, our walk will not be far to the English quarter. Behind the row of detached Bungalows on the beach, the ground is still unredeemed from swamps, and is inundated at every tide. From this rise three or four little hills, like islands on a lake, upon which are built some very pretty villas, commanding a delightful prospect of the harbour. Great pains have been taken in forming and ornamenting the gardens attached to them, but to little or no purpose; for the hills are mere rocks with scarcely sufficient soil for the raising of a few vegetables. The low grounds are equally unfit for cultivation, though from a very different cause. They are thickly covered with an unwholesome vegetation, producing at night such noxious vapours, that the inhabitants are obliged to close their doors and windows as securely as if they were in danger of an attack from wild beasts. But who can calculate upon the effects of malaria? Here, in the very focus of its production, it is an extraordinary fact, that not a death from local sickness has taken place among the residents for years. In the day-time all the rooms are opened as much as possible to the sea breezes, which at this, the coolest season of the year, occasionally recalls to my memory the luxurious feeling of a warm day by the sea-side in Devonshire. But if there be little variety of amusement on shore; the sea and harbour, with its multitudes of vessels of all descriptions, is a never-failing source of interest and entertainment. During the fortnight I have been here, two or three ships have either sailed out or in every day....

This place is so directly in the course between Bengal, Madras, Bombay, and China, that the harbour is constantly full of Indiamen, large and small. Most of the Bengal captains bring down sheep with them, which sell at an enormous price. I forgot to say, that there is not an acre of pasturage here for cattle of any description. No quadrupeds are to be seen but horses, dogs, pigs, and goats. With the utmost care a sheep can scarcely be kept alive here longer than a month. Provisions of every description are extremely dear; fish, pork, and fowl, are the principal articles of consumption, with rice. Fish, in great variety, is found in these straits. Pork is reared with success by the Chinese; and poultry and rice are brought from Java and the surrounding islands. Vegetables, as I mentioned before, are not to be grown, even upon the hills, in sufficient quantity to supply the market. I have omitted, however, one great delicacy, at least it is so considered by the Chinese, who rear them in great abundance for their own tables, viz. puppies! Malacca, though at a distance of a hundred miles, supplies Sincapore in profusion with fruits of delicious flavour, and of so many different kinds, that I have not as yet learned all their names. Oranges, pumalos, mangoes, plaintains, pine-apples, custard-apples, leechees, loquots, are brought in perfection; and at length I have tasted the mangosteen, which alone would supply the place of all. I need say no more than that, high as my expectations had been raised, its great fame was noways exaggerated. It is about as large as a moderate-sized apple, having a very thick rind, which, when cut, yields a red juice, and is employed, I believe, as a dye. The fruit within is disposed in compartments, like an orange, and has a pulp of a snow-white appearance, of the most refreshing, uncloying sweet you can imagine.

In point of society, I am better off than I should be at almost any interior station of India. There is an amazing number of merchants, and no less than nine lady-families....

[T. Prinsep], *The Journal of a Voyage from Calcutta to Van Diemen's Land: Comprising a Description of that colony during a Six Months' Residence*, from Original Letters, Selected by Mrs Augustus Prinsep, Smith, Elder and Co., London, 1833, pp. 17–27.

6
Singapore in the Early 1830s

GEORGE WINDSOR EARL
1832–1834

In 1827, as a 14-year-old midshipman, George Windsor Earl sailed from England aboard the East Indiaman Lady Holland *for India. After the return voyage he resigned from the East India Company's service, and in 1829 emigrated with his elder brother to western Australia. Three years later he sailed from Fremantle aboard the brig* Monkey *bound for Jakarta, and he was employed on other ships in South-East Asian waters before he was given his own command at Singapore of the small schooner* Stamford *on a trading voyage to Borneo. After playing a key role in the unsuccessful attempts to found a British settlement at Port Essington in northern Australia, he set up as a law agent and advocate in Singapore, and was appointed a magistrate in 1857. In the following year he was made third Assistant to the Resident Councillor, and afterwards served as Police Magistrate in Province Wellesley and Assistant Resident at Penang. Earl's book,* The Eastern Seas, *was published in London in 1837, and contains an account of his early adventures in the Malay Archipelago as well as an informed account of Singapore in the early 1830s.*

THE commercial portion of the town is on the west side of the river's entrance, the part nearest to the sea being occupied by the European merchants. A range of houses, fronted by wharfs, extends along the bank as far as the bridge, a distance of about three hundred yards, the principal streets running at right angles with the river. With the exception of the commercial square, these streets are occupied exclusively by Chinese, Klings,* and other natives, who are chiefly merchants or shopkeepers.

The houses, which have only one upper story, are fronted by wide piazzas, which screen the passengers from the rays of the sun, and shelter the goods exposed for sale by the native occupants. The houses in the principal streets are built of brick, but those in the outskirts of the town are composed of wood and thatch. The former are plastered with mortar of such an excellent quality, that it retains its smoothness and whiteness for a long time, and gives the streets a light and handsome appearance. Many of the dwellings recently erected by some of the European merchants are very fine buildings, and are not excelled by any in Eastern India.

On the opposite side of the river, a smooth road runs along the shores of the harbour to Campong Glam, a village a mile and a half from Singapore, occupied by about four thousand Chinese, Bugis, and Malays. From this, the road strikes a short distance into the country, and returns with a sweep to the town. On the road side, fronting the sea, are the villas of the principal Europeans (few of whom reside in the town), large and handsome buildings, fronted by green verandahs and venetian blinds. The Circular road forms the evening drive of the inhabitants; but it is not available for those who dwell in the town, as the wooden bridge has become so ruinous that, to prevent accidents, it has been reduced so greatly in width that it can only be crossed by foot passengers.

The town can boast of no Government buildings of any importance, with the exception of the jail, a square white building erected in a swamp at the back of the town, and a small stone hospital, situated near the Circular road. The court-house was constructed for a dwelling by an English merchant, from whom it is rented by the Government.

*Natives of (western) India.

The Government-house, the residence of the chief functionary in the settlement, is erected on the top of a hill at the back of the town, from which there is a fine prospect of the straits and the neighbouring islands.... The sides are composed of rough poles, the interstices being filled up by boards and venetian windows, and the roof is covered with attops [attap], or reed thatch, in the intricacies of which crickets, lizards, and all sorts of creeping things, sport unmolested. It is withal so unsubstantial, that after a Sumatra squall has passed over the town, inquiring glances are cast up by the inhabitants, to discover whether the house still remains in *statu quo*, or has disappeared from the top of the hill, and taken refuge from the storm in the valley on the opposite side. At the foot of the hill lies the botanical garden, which is now overrun with weeds, though several nutmeg-trees, planted by the founder of the settlement, flourish and bear fruit without any care or cultivation.

In the centre of the *marina*, close to the seashore, are the ruins of a large building called the Singapore Institution, and being an object which generally catches the eye of a stranger on entering the harbour, many are inclined to doubt that the settlement can be so young as it is represented. This edifice was founded by Sir Stamford Raffles soon after the establishment of the British on the island, in the fond hope that, by means of natives educated therein by European teachers, whom it was proposed to appoint, knowledge and civilization might be widely disseminated throughout the Further East. The building was nearly completed on his final departure from India, and negociations were in train for embodying with it the members of the Chinese College of Malacca, but when the master-mind was gone, the institution and its objects were neglected, and the building fell into decay....

The ground at the back of the town is laid out in gardens by the Chinese, who grow large quantities of fruits and vegetables for the supply of the inhabitants. On the bank of the creek are many plantations of pepper and gambier, also cultivated by Chinese, and on the coast of the island to the eastward of the town, and also on the little islets off the harbour, are small agricultural settlements of Bugis and Javanese, who, from their known bravery, are less liable to attacks from the roving Malay pirates, than the more timid Chinese would be, if similarly situated....

The interior of the island is almost unknown to the Europeans, but there is a small independent Chinese settlement a few miles distant from the town, which is said to be very populous, and as considerable quantities of produce are brought thence to the town for sale, their plantations must be extensive. No European has yet visited them....

The European mode of life, as far as regards the general routine of occupations, is precisely similar to that of Batavia, but there the resemblance ends. At Singapore there exists no political bar to social intercourse; no dread that private conversations may be reported to a jealous and unforgiving government; indeed, the contrast altogether is so great, that I have often felt surprised that a British resident of Batavia who visits Singapore on commercial business, or for the recovery of his health, can ever prevail upon himself to return to that pestilential and misgoverned city.

Amusements of an active nature in which the gentlemen engage, consist chiefly of boat-sailing and shooting, and the former, so decidedly British, is carried to a greater extent than in any other part of India. Sailing and rowing matches between the sailing-boats of the merchants, and also between the sampans of the Malays, occur almost daily, the native boat-men taking quite as much interest in them as the Europeans.

Those who delight in field-sports find ample amusement in the low lands at the back of the town, which abound in snipes and plovers, or in the creeks on the east side of the harbour, where flocks of pigeons assemble every evening from all parts of the island, to roost on the trees in the little detached islets, where they are free from the attacks of the smaller beasts of prey. Wild pigs and deer are to be met with in the wilder parts of the interior, but the jungle is too thick for the chace. Tigers occasionally visit the island from the Malay Peninsula, there being no difficulty in crossing the narrow strait; but as they resort to the neighbourhood of the settlement in quest of food, they are generally caught soon after their arrival by the Malays, who are very skilful in entrapping them....

Among the amusements of the Europeans may be included the paper warfare carried on by individuals through the medium of the two public journals, and a single glance will shew to what an extent it prevails. 'Libertas' inserts a letter in the Free Press concerning some grievance, probably a decision of the Court, and his arguments and assertions are refuted in the next Chronicle by 'Philo Le': 'Agricola', and 'Agricola Secundus', maintain a discussion concerning the agricultural capabilities of the island; and the letter of 'A Tory' is speedily answered by 'Anti Humbug'. As the parties are generally those best acquainted with the subjects under review, this exchange of opinions is found both amusing and instructive, for the inhabitants are enabled to see both sides of the question, and may therefore judge for themselves....

Singapore contains an epitome of the population of the whole Archipelago, and indeed of Continental India also. Chinese, Malays, Bugis, Javanese, Balinese, natives of Bengal and Madras, Parsees, Arabs, and Caffrees, are to be found within the circuit of a few miles, each people forming a separate community, and retaining its customs as completely as if it had never been transplanted.

An early walk through Campong Glam will serve to give a stranger a good idea of the habits and occupations of the different classes. Near the residence of the Sultan he will meet with Malays, lounging about near the doors of their houses, chewing betel, with their sarongs, which usually hang loosely about the waist, wrapped round the body to shelter the wearer from the cool morning breeze. The main street, however, will have a very different appearance. There Chinese mechanics will be busily employed forging iron-work, making furniture, or building boats; and the level green near the sea will be occupied by Bugis, who have landed from their prahus to mend their sails, or to twist rope and cables from the materials which they have brought with them. In a portion of the back part of the campong, natives of Sambawa, a far distant island to the eastward of Java, will be found chopping young trees into billets for fire-wood, and making hurdles for fencing; and in another, Bengali washer-men hanging out clothes to dry, and dairymen of the same nation milking their cows to supply the breakfast tables of the Europeans. On the roads Klings will occasionally be en-countered conducting tumbrils drawn by buffaloes cased in mud and dirt; the creaking of the wheels almost drowning the voice of the driver as he bawls to the animals, in his harsh and discordant jargon. Each nation, indeed, is found pursuing avocations which best accord with its tastes and habits....

Of the native population of Singapore, the Chinese are the most numerous and the most important, indeed their industry and perseverance have mainly contributed to the present flourishing state of the settlement.

The Malacca-born Chinese hold more direct intercourse with the European merchants than the others. Many of these are born of Malay mothers, but, as they always adopt the manners and mode of dress of their fathers, they are scarcely to be distinguished from the actual natives of China, and although they are probably less active and energetic than the latter, they are more enlightened, and make better merchants. Many of this class who have been educated at the Malacca college speak English tolerably well, and, from their constant communication with Europeans, they have acquired in some measure their general habits and mode of transacting business, which renders them more agreeable to the latter than those who have not enjoyed similar advantages. They are all employed in commerce, many as independent merchants, and some are engaged as cashiers and under-clerks in the offices of Europeans....

The commercial activity of the Chinese is seen to the greatest advantage during the annual visit of the junks from the Celestial Empire; these remain in the harbour from December until June, and, throughout the whole period, boats filled with Chinese are continually passing and repassing among the shipping, giving to the roads the appearance of a floating fair....

From five thousand to eight thousand emigrants arrive annually from China, of whom only forty or fifty are females. About one-eighth of these people remain at Singapore, and the others scatter themselves over the Archipelago. The majority proceed to the tin mines near Malacca, and on the island of Banca, to the pepper plantations on Bintang, and to the gold mines at Pahang, and on the western coast of Borneo....

To avoid persecution, every Chinese finds it necessary on his arrival to become a member of one of the secret societies, all of which have the object in China of overthrowing the present dynasty, while they are at Singapore rendered subservient to the national propensity for plunder, as one member will always screen another from detection. The different sects, however, hate each other cordially; therefore the peaceable inhabitants do not suffer so much from their aggressions as if they formed a united body.

It is to be expected that many bad characters arrive, among such considerable numbers of the lower classes of a people by no means famed for their morality; indeed, a fair proportion of the emigrants consists of those who prefer living by ways and means, to gaining an honest subsistence by labour. Great facilities are afforded to these, as their countrymen term them, 'disorderly planners of lucky and extraordinary means of gain', the independent village in the interior forming an excellent receptacle for stolen goods, and affording a safe refuge for those delinquents who are sought after by the authorities.

The houses in the outskirts of the town are often attacked by bands of Chinese robbers from the interior, but fortunately they are such arrant cowards that they retreat on the slightest opposition....

A few hundreds only of the Malays established in Singapore are natives of the island, the remainder being emigrants from the Malay Peninsula and Sumatra. The former are chiefly the dependants of the two chiefs who reside at Singapore; and the pernicious example set by these nobles and the wretches about them, greatly retards the improvement of the rest of their countrymen. The Malays in the vicinity of the abodes of these grandees and their satellites are generally idle in the extreme, while the settlers from the other states, who are not under the control of the chiefs, form the most industrious portion of the Malay community.

The emigrants are chiefly those who have flocked to Singapore to find employment, or to take refuge from the anarchy and confusion consequent on the frequent recurrence of political commotions in the Mahommedan states. They are not remarkable for their industry, but are so far superior to those found in the misgoverned and oppressed districts, under the controul of native chiefs, as to make it evident that the dissolute mode of life for which the Malays are famed is, in a great measure, the result of the circumstances under which they are placed...

The Malay pirates absolutely swarm in the neighbourhood of Singapore, the numerous islands in the vicinity, the intersecting channels of which are known only to themselves, affording them a snug retreat, whence they can pounce upon the defenceless native traders, and drag them into their lairs to plunder them at their leisure. Square-rigged vessels are generally allowed to pass unmolested, for the pirates, who are as cowardly as they are cruel, rarely attack craft of this description, unless they have received authentic information from their spies at Singapore that they may be taken with facility....

There are twenty European mercantile houses in Singapore, seventeen British, one Portuguese, one German, and one American: there are also three extensive Armenian mercantile establishments, and to these latter-named firms we are indebted for the re-opening of the trade with Borneo Proper. The British merchants are chiefly commission agents, who receive consignments of goods from merchants in Great Britain, and make returns in oriental produce purchased in the settlement. They rarely engage in commercial speculations with the islands in the Archipelago. The Europeans have very little direct commercial intercourse with the traders who visit the port, as their goods are purchased by the Chinese, who have a better acquaintance with the natives, and have patience enough to go into all the necessary details of bargaining and weighing the goods. When an European merchant wishes to make a shipment of produce to England, he visits the *bazaar*, and purchases the articles he requires from the Chinese, in exchange for others which have been consigned to him....

By the commercial reports it appears that the trade of Singapore is not on the increase: the opening of the trade between Great Britain and China has given a slight check to the commerce of the settlement; but as Great Britain has derived much benefit from its direct intercourse with China, the falling off at Singapore becomes of little consequence.

G. W. Earl, *The Eastern Seas, or Voyages and Adventures in the Indian Archipelago, in 1832–33–34, Comprising a Tour of the Island of Java—Visits to Borneo, The Malay Peninsula, Siam, &c.; Also an Account of the Present State of Singapore, with Observations on the Commercial Resources of the Archipelago*, W. H. Allen and Co., London, 1837, pp. 347–53, 357–70, 373–4, 384, 415–17.

7
A Visit to Sultan Husain

GEORGE BENNETT
1833–1834

George Bennett left England for Ceylon when he was 15 years old, and later visited Australia. He returned there in 1832, and in the following year sailed from Sydney to Jakarta, China, and Singapore, where he stayed for a month in November 1833. He subsequently settled in Sydney, and was described on his death in 1893 as the 'greatest of the physician-naturalists of Australia'. He had already visited Singapore in 1830, when he had an audience with Sultan Husain at Kampong Glam. His description of the Malay ruler is not flattering, but it accords with other contemporary accounts, including that of Munsyi Abdullah bin Abdul Kadir, who in his Hikayat *describes him as being obese, with a round face, squinting eyes, button nose, wide mouth, and raucous voice. The British had concluded another treaty with him and Temenggong Abdul Rahman on 2 August 1824, by which they alienated their rights and titles to Singapore forever in return for lump sum payments and monthly stipends.*

THE town is erected upon the banks of a salt-water creek, more commonly named the Singapore river: one side contains the warehouses, offices, stores, &c. of the merchants and shopkeepers, as well as the native streets, bazaars, &c.... The Commercial Square contains some very good buildings, used as offices, shops, and residences; the most conspicuous of which, for elegance, is the building used as offices and warehouses by the firm of Rawson, Holdsworth, and Co. The river, at the lower part of the settlement, always presents an animated scene, from the arrival and departure of native boats, with fruit, vegetables, and live stock, as well as from the number of neat sampans plying for hire, or attending upon the commanders of vessels, who employ them, in this sultry climate, in preference to exposing their crews to a tropical sun: many native boats lie waiting or delivering cargoes of the various productions of the fertile islands in the vicinity. At night, the flickering and brilliant lights from the numerous boats upon the river, make an animated appearance....

The settlement and island of Singapore is considered very salubrious. The small-pox, however, has lately been committing great and deadly ravages among the native residents; of these, however, there were none upon whom vaccination had been performed. Many have been surprised at the healthy state of Singapore as a residence, when it is so near the equator, and the town surrounded by swamps, and even built upon a swamp....

The European burial-ground is situated in rather a conspicuous spot, on a part of the declivity of the Government-hill; one part is planted with bamboos, which have a tasteful appearance, and the gloomy nature of the spot would be diminished if the fence of these trees was continued the whole way round the cemetery.

On riding or driving in the vicinity of the settlement, the character of the country and soil appears well calculated for the cultivation of coffee, sugar, cotton, pepper, and other tropical productions, as well as of the vine....

A pleasant evening drive, or promenade, is obtained upon the winding road leading to the Government-hill, which passes close by what was formerly, and even still retains the name of, the Botanic or Experimental Garden. Many of the hedges on this road are formed by an elegant small leaved bamboo, with its pendent branches drooping in graceful tufts, the tree itself not attaining the elevation usual with other more useful but less ornamental species: this bamboo forms a very beautiful, as well as compact fence. On attaining the gentle and gradual rise of the hill, the view that expands itself is both extensive and grand; embracing a wide portion of this splendid island, and causing feelings of regret in the mind of the spectator, that so much fertile land should be permitted to lie waste. Turning our eyes in another direction from the gloomy mass of forest scenery and undulating land, extending to the horizon, a more animated and pleasing scene is spread before us. Neat white houses and elegant mansions are seen on the open plain, or peeping above the dense vegetation when constructed upon a gentle rising hill....

Excellent roads are forming in the vicinity of the settlement, and there is one commenced to extend directly across the island. The road-gangs are composed of convicts from India....

I made an excursion into the interior of the island, for the purpose of viewing the plantations of Gambir, Pepper, &c. as well as for the purpose of investigating its natural productions. Most of the residents, deeply engaged in mercantile pursuits, find but little leisure or inclination to explore the island, or ascertain its real capabilities, or the picturesque scenery and fertile soil it contains, their rambles being merely confined to evening drives, or walks, in the immediate vicinity of the settlement....

The situations selected by the Chinese in this undulating country, for their farms and plantations were upon, or close to the sloping hills; and these places are selected for the Gambir and pepper plantations, the lower land proving too swampy. The pepper harvest had commenced, and the vines had the appearance of being very productive this season, being covered with a profusion of clusters of the pepper-berries, large, and of fine quality. Some had even attained maturity, having changed from a dark-green to a vivid red. From the latter, the berry being in a ripe state, the white pepper is made; some of very excellent quality was shown us by a Chinese planter who had prepared it....

The Gambir plantations were very numerous, as well as those of pepper; and it surprises me, that from the great and general demand for the latter production, both in the China and European markets, it is not an article of more general cultivation. Some persons have asserted that the soil of Singapore is not calculated for the production of pepper; but if in the numerous plantations I have seen, large clusters of fine berries, excellent both in appearance and flavour, is a sufficient denial of the assertion, I can readily make it, and hope its cultivation will be encouraged. Two or three thousand peculs of pepper are collected annually at Singapore....

One evening, accompanied by several gentlemen resident in the settlement, I went to pay a visit to the rajah of Johore. During a former visit to this settlement, in 1830, I had an interview with this exalted personage, of whom at that time I penned the following description:—'Being near the village of Kampong Glam, I observed a poor-looking bungalow, surrounded by high walls, exhibiting effects of age and climate. Over the large gateway which opened into the inclosure surrounding this dwelling were watch-towers. On inquiry, I found this was the residence of the rajah of Johore, who formerly included Singapore in his dominions. The island was purchased of him by the British government, who now allow him an annual pension. He is considered to have been formerly a leader of pirates: and when we saw a brig he was building, it naturally occurred to our minds whether he was about to resort to his old practices. We proposed visiting this personage; and, on arriving at the gateway, were met by a peon,* who, after delivering our message to the rajah, requested us to wait a few minutes, until his *Highness* was ready. We did not wait long, for the rajah soon appeared, and took his seat, in lieu of a throne, upon the highest step of those which led to his dwelling. His appearance was remarable: he appeared a man of about forty years of age—teeth perfect, but quite black, from the custom of chewing the betel constantly. His head was large; and his shaven cranium afforded an interesting phrenological treat. He was deformed; not more than five feet in height, of large body, and short, thick, and deformed legs, scarcely able to support the ponderous trunk. His neck was thick and short, and his head habitually stooped; his face bloated, with the lower lip projecting, and large eyes protruding, one of them having a cataractal appearance. He was dressed in a short pair of cotton drawers, a sarong of cotton cloth came across the shoulders in the form of a scarf, and tarnished, embroidered slippers, and handkerchief around the head, (having the upper part exposed,) after the Malay fashion, completed the attire of this singular creature....

The buildings of his highness and followers were now in some degree improved, being surrounded by a neat chunamed wall, and the entrance was by a gateway of brick, which had been only recently completed. Since my last visit his highness had caused a house to be constructed after the style of the European residents at Singapore, and it was situated exterior to the old boundary of his domain. We were ushered into the new house, the rooms of which were furnished after the English style, with wall-lamps, bookcase, (minus books,) tables, chairs, &c.; ascending to the upper

*A footman, orderly, or messenger.

room, chairs were placed for our accommodation, and the punka* was caused to be moved to cool our frames. When we were all seated, a yellow painted armed chair was placed at the head of the room, as a regal seat for his highness; his prime minister came to us, and, as we thought, seemed puzzled for what so large a party of Europeans could require an audience....

Society at Singapore is extremely agreeable to a visitor—for only as one can I judge of it. Whether in intercourse among themselves they are divided into the mechanical and aristocratical party, I cannot say, having only heard a whisper to that effect. I have found, during two visits to the little settlement, unbounded hospitality, and every attention to my scientific inquiries, of course some taking more interest in my researches than others.

G. Bennett, *Wanderings in New South Wales, Batavia, Pedir Coast, Singapore, and China; Being the Journal of a Naturalist in those Countries, during 1832, 1833, and 1834*, Richard Bentley, London, 1834, Vol. II, pp. 130–1, 137–41, 177–83, 213–15.

8
Christian Missions

HOWARD MALCOLM
1837

The founder of the American Tract Society, Howard Malcolm, was dispatched from Boston in September 1835 to examine the state and working of the Baptist missions in South and South-East Asia. After visiting Burma, Calcutta, and Madras, he arrived at Singapore on 19 April 1837 aboard the East Indiaman Thames, *and stayed for a little more than a month before sailing for Thailand and China. Malcolm recorded some useful factual information about Singapore in his account, but he was primarily interested in the activities of the Protestant missionaries in the island.*

*A large fixed swinging fan suspended by a rope from the ceiling.

THE present population of Singapore amounts to 30,000, of which there are only 7,229 females. Of Europeans there are 105 males and 36 females; Malays, 5,122 males, 4,510 females; Chinese, 12,870 males, 879 females; Klings, 2,246 males, 102 females. The rest are Bugis, Balinese, Bengalese, Negroes, Javanese, Arabs, &c.; with a few Indo-Britons, Armenians, &c. I saw one or two of the Papua, or negro race of the Indian islands....

The striking disproportion of females, who are but about one-fourth of the population, is owing partly to the laws of China, which forbid the emigration of women, and partly to those circumstances which make the male sex preponderate in all new colonies, and purely commercial places.

In going through one part of the town, during business hours, one feels himself to be in a Chinese city. Almost every respectable native he sees is Chinese; almost every shop, wareroom, and trade, is carried on by the Chinese; the hucksters, coolies, travelling cooks, and cries common in a great city, are Chinese. In fact, we may almost call Singapore itself a Chinese city; inasmuch as the bulk of the inhabitants are Chinese, and nearly all the wealth and influence, next to the British, is in their hands. A large part of the Klings and Bengalese are hostlers, servants, washermen, &c., to Europeans; and the Malays and Bugis occupy portions of the city by themselves....

From the first settlement of Singapore by the British, operations for the moral and religious improvement of the natives have been carried on. Translations into Malay, and the printing and distribution of tracts and Scriptures, engrossed most of the time of early missionaries. In this department a good deal has been done; but, so far as can now be seen, with very little success. Great efforts have been made also in the way of schools; not only by the missionaries, but by the British residents, and the government. The latter has allowed, from the public treasury, 100 dollars per month. Several Chinese schools, and still more Malay ones, have been constantly maintained. The principal authorities have at times exerted their influence to induce the people to send their children, and even gone from house to house to procure scholars. A multitude of children have been in the schools, first and last; and some hundreds have received more or less instruction. But it has been found impossible to secure the attendance of scholars for more than a few months; and almost none have learned to read....

Not a single Malay in Singapore has made even a nominal profession of Christianity, nor are there any hopeful catechumens. For a long time past, no one competent in the language has resided here; so that the only missionary efforts are the distribution of tracts, and some unpromising schools. Indeed, this has been very much the case from the beginning, as previous missionaries were chiefly devoted to these labours and to authorship, and very little has been done in the way of direct preaching. The history of this mission, now twenty years old, is an item of consequence, in our reasoning upon the modes of missionary labour.

The Catholics have two churches here—a French and a Portuguese; with several priests. They not only take charge of those of their faith who reside here, but have brought over a number of Malays, Chinese, and others, and have full audiences on Sundays. Popish missionaries through India, so far as I could learn, are men of good morals. They live far more humbly than any other missionaries, and mix much with their people. Their stipend, in all cases which came to my knowledge, is 100 dollars per annum. Their converts are taught, from the first, to contribute to the support of religion, and their teachers, being unmarried, have few wants which these cannot supply.

The Singapore Institution, founded by Sir Stamford Raffles in 1823, has maintained a feeble existence, but is now likely to be put on a footing of vigour and expansiveness. A new building, large and commodious, has been prepared for it, to which it will soon be removed, after which its course of study will be more collegiate, and the number of its pupils increased.

Singapore has, from the first, been a station of the London Missionary Society. It became a station of the American Board of Commissioners in 1834, and is now occupied by Messrs [I.] Tracey, [J. T.] Dickinson, [M. B.] Hope, Travelli, and [A.] North, from that society—the three former giving themselves to Chinese, and the others to Malay. Mr North is a practical printer, and has charge of a well-built and amply furnished printing-office. These missionaries have all been here so very short a time, that their chief occupation has been the acquisition of language. They have, however, a Malay and a Chinese school, and superintend the labours of a large number of Chinese printers, who have been constantly employed on the revised Chinese New Testament, and various tracts, by Mr [K. F. A.] Gutzlaff and others.

The Church Missionary Society have recently made this a station for the Chinese, and the American Baptist Board are about to do the same. The Rev. Mr [E. B.] Squier, from the former society, has been here a few months. While China remains inaccessible, missionaries for that country must prepare themselves in other places. Great commercial emporiums must be considered common ground to all persuasions of Christians, in their operations for the heathen; and in several instances, such as Calcutta, Bankok, Smyrna, &c., the missionaries of various sects live together in harmony and good understanding. In such places property is safe, the press free, workmen plenty, and exchanges easy, while uncertainties and delays in procuring paper and transmitting books are avoided.

H. Malcolm, *Travels in Hindustan and China*, W. & R. Chambers, Edinburgh, 1840, pp. 28–30.

9
United States Warships at Singapore

FITCH W. TAYLOR
1839

As with the previous author, the subject of Christian missions in Singapore was uppermost in the mind of Fitch W. Taylor, Chaplain to the United States squadron of ships, the frigate Columbia, *and the sloop of war* John Adams, *which arrived at Singapore in February 1839. The squadron was under the command of Commodore George Campbell Read, who had orders from the Secretary of the Navy to take action against piracy on the west coast of Sumatra, which was adversely affecting the American pepper trade. In the month prior to the squadron's arrival at Singapore, the American ships had bombarded the Sumatran village of Muki, which was then destroyed by American marines. The squadron remained at*

Singapore until 27 March before sailing for China, and eventually across the Pacific to complete the circumnavigation of the world.

WE anchored off the city of Singapore, February 5th, 1839, among the little fleet of vessels now lying near us....

I was happy to find, at this station, quite a number of the American missionaries: with them my sympathies lie. Besides the gentlemen and ladies regularly stationed here, some six or eight have taken up their temporary residence, with their brethren, at Singapore....

Singapore presents an inviting position for a town, destined ere long to become of considerable extent, as the result of its fine commercial situation. While riding through its different sections, to wait on the several families of the mission, many of the houses already constructed presented themselves on a scale of spaciousness, and considerable elegance and taste in the adaptation of extensive verandahs and airy rooms to meet the circumstances of the climate, in wooing the sea-breeze from the ocean, and to court the land-zephyr from the groves of the nutmegs and the palms. Many of the sites of the residences are commanding, and the houses are very generally surrounded by spacious grounds....

Since the arrival of our ships at Singapore, I have several times called upon the missionary families, now resident at this place. On the 13th dined with Rev. Mr A. Stronoch [Stronach] of the Scotch mission. Scotland and the Scots have always possessed an interest in my associations. The Scots however cease to please when they begin to forget their own highland and lowland associations, and manifest their preferences in commending the English, to the neglect of their own more peculiar characteristics....

There are two brothers here, who are attached to the London Missionary Society. They appear to be very worthy men, and their wives greatly esteemed. The ladies have just enough of the Scotch in their accent to render their conversation of deeper interest to me than it would have been without it. It reminds one that he is conversing with one of Scotia's daughters, from that land which we have learned to love for its intellect, and worth, and story, and song.

The Rev. Mr [E.] White, the English chaplain at Singapore, is a gentleman of great mildness of character, and has the reputation of some cleverness in the natural sciences. He seems to be fond of them, at least. He is a Cambridge scholar, and all Cambridge students seem particularly fond of their alma mater. Indeed all the English chaplains whom I have met in the East, do credit to the service to which they are attached, so far as their general intelligence is concerned, and in most instances have exhibited the practical effects of the principles of the religion which they teach, in their Christian action and pious lives. The chaplains in the Indian service are allowed to return home, at their pleasure, after having spent a certain number of years, and retire upon a pension of about two thousand dollars per annum during their lives, after leaving the service. Their salary while in the Indian service, in most instances, is five thousand dollars, and upwards, per annum. The residence occupied by the Rev. Mr W. is a commanding one—the whole sheet of beautiful water, expanding itself in full view from the verandah, dotted over by the huge and nondescript Chinese junks—the Cochin-China yellow-sided war-ships, bearing the merchandise of the king—the yet better-looking ships of the king of Siam—the finer specimens of naval architecture, as seen in the French, English, and American merchant-men—and still further out and beyond them all, our own two gallant cruisers, in the beauty of their squared yards and tall spars, and graceful and perfect hamper, symmetry, and order, filling up the picture, and presenting to the view of the gazer a charming nautical scene....

The time was now arrived when the ships were ordered to be in readiness for sea. Word had been passed that the succeeding Wednesday would be the day of sailing for our ships. All officers were to be on board, Tuesday evening, and no boat or officer afterwards to leave the frigate. Yet a few days would intervene. One, therefore, I devoted to a ride to Bookitima [Bukit Timah], said to be the highest ground on the island of Singapore, and distant some six or seven miles from the town. I had already ridden to most of the plantations in the neighborhood, marking the growth of pepper, gambir, coffee, cloves, and nutmegs. A fine smooth road has been cut quite to the top of Bookitima; and to avoid the necessity of walking up any part of the hill-steep in the sun, I procured an additional horse to serve me in case the first I drove should give out. The road lies along the level through the plantations in the low grounds for a few miles, until you reach the commencement of the ascent, formerly not attempted by horses, but since the road alluded to has been constructed, and but lately finished by the government's convicts, it is practicable to ascend to the hill-top, *provided* you have a horse that is good for aught but being led by a half-robed syce* over a level surface. No sooner had we reached the commencement of the ascent, before the horse protested against any change of olden customs and all new innovations. Stay he would, any how, as usual, at the foot of the hill. . . .

We ere long reached the top of Bookitima. Before us now lay field, forest, plantation, and the outlines of the whole island of Singapore, the distant water, like narrow lakes, meeting the eye on every side but one, designating the extent of the island. But a single view was enough. The prospect has nothing to attract with interest, as the view extends into the blue distance, to one who has gazed on richer landscapes, and mountain-scenery, and ocean stretching from the foot of the lofty mountain-side for leagues in the distance to sea. It is, however, a pleasant ride, when pleasant friends accompany you, like sweet solitude, when at your side you have a friend to whom you may whisper, how sweet is solitude, as some Frenchman has hinted, who was no less correct in his remark than another of his penetrating species, who defines gratitude to be a keen zest for favors that are to come.

F. W. Taylor, *A Voyage Round the World, and Visits to Various Foreign Countries, in the United States Frigate Columbia; Attended by her Consort the Sloop of War John Adams, and Commanded by Commodore George C. Read*, D. Appleton & Co., New York, 1847, Vol. II, pp. 10–13, 29–30, 74–6.

*A horse groom or driver of a horse-drawn carriage.

10
Whampoa and José d'Almeida

SURGEON EDWARD H. CREE
1840–1844

After studying medicine at Dublin and Edinburgh, Edward Cree served as a surgeon in the Royal Navy for 32 years, ten of them, between 1840 and 1850, in Asia. He first visited Singapore for a fortnight in May 1840 aboard HMS Rattlesnake, *and he returned for a similar brief stay in September 1844, when he was invited to attend a musical party at the house on Beach Road of the well-known Portuguese apothecary and merchant, Dr José d'Almeida, who had himself been a surgeon in the Portuguese Navy before settling at Singapore. Cree also refers to visits he made at this time to his fellow Edinburgh student, Dr Robert Little, who became equally well known through his medical and public work in Singapore, and to Whampoa. He confuses the father with the son, Hoo Ah Kay, the best known and most liked Chinese in the Straits during the nineteenth century. Whampoa got his name from his birthplace, Huangpu, near Canton, and he succeeded his father in running the firm of Whampoa & Co., provisioners and ship chandlers to the Royal Navy, in the store at the corner of Bonham Street and Boat Quay. He was one of the few Chinese at the time who spoke English fluently, rather in the manner of naval officers and seamen with whom he consorted, and this gave the firm a decided advantage over its competitors. Later the firm also set up a large bakery in Havelock Road, but was less successful in establishing a shop selling ice imported from America. At his bungalow two and a half miles along Serangoon Road, Whampoa built, with the help of horticulturists from Canton, a beautiful flower garden, incorporating orchards, hanging plants, Dutch walks, an aviary, and a menagerie. His hospitality to British naval officers and other travellers to Singapore was legendary, and even those travellers who were not fortunate enough to enjoy his hospitality felt it obligatory to visit his gardens, which were regarded as one of the sights of Singapore. Whampoa was Consul in Singapore for Russia, China, and Japan, and he was appointed one of the first Unofficial Members of the Legislative Council and later an extraordinary member of the*

Executive Council. Two years before his death in 1880 he was made a CMG. Cree's account is somewhat garbled in first referring to Whampoa's father, and then mistakenly stating that Hoo Ah Kay was educated at Edinburgh University.

1840

WENT on shore with [Captain] Call to have a look at the place, which is quite novel to me and very amusing—a sort of mixture of Indian and Chinese. There are good quays and warehouses on each side of a small river, which does not smell very sweet from the amount of drainage running into it. The houses are mostly of two storeys, with the upper one projecting beyond the lower. The windows are closed with wooden shutters. Some of the houses are Chinese looking, turning up at the corners and altogether put me in mind of the pictures on an old china plate of the willow-pattern....

Call and I went on shore and took a stroll about the place. Visited a new josshouse or Chinese temple, not of great size but gaudily painted and ornamented with fantastic porcelain dragons, &c., some beautiful carving on the pillars and screens with birds, flowers, &c. Two lions at the gateway carved in hard stone. In the mouth of each is a round stone, movable, but not to be taken out of the mouth. A Chinese artist was painting the outside with a little camel-hair brush. The doors being shut, we could not see the inside except through the carved windows.

On our way back we visited the stores of a well-known Chinese merchant, Whampoa [Senior], whose son [Hoo Ah Kay], who now manages the business, was educated in Edinburgh, at the University, and is a very intelligent man and well read in English literature. Major Dillon joined us and we went to the French hotel and ordered dinner of M. [G.] Dutronquoy, which was good and consisted of pork chops, curried fowl, roast duck, ham, cheese and potatoes for a dollar each and gave us good beer, madeira and claret.

We remained at Singapore till May 30th. I went on shore frequently, strolling about, the shops affording lots of amusement. Chinese articles for sale tempt one to spend money. Most of the things are reasonable in price, notwithstanding the number of officers now about the place. Chinese silks of all sorts, very beautiful birds, pictures, &c. Dutronquoy's hotel is comfortable, the landlord is a civil, amusing fellow, once an actor but who lately had a situation in Borneo. He signs French songs; has a couple of good billiard tables. His is a place of general resort for officers. I met many old friends and acquaintances there. The seamen and Marines are frequently on shore for exercise and have sham fights, to the astonishment of the inhabitants. A band played every evening on the parade where all the beauty, not much, and the fashion of the place assembled. Very few English ladies, but Dutch and Portuguese half-castes, some going about in smart equipages, buggies and palanquin carriages. The country round is hilly and pleasant and pretty well cleared and planted for a mile or two. Beyond is all jungle, where tigers and other wild beasts abound. Good roads are cut through the jungle in various directions. The Governor's House on a hill above the town is a pretty bungalow and has a pleasant view. There are many spice plantations, principally nutmegs and cloves. The tigers frequently carry off a coolie or two at work at the edge of the jungle. A reward is given by the Government for every tiger's head brought in, as they are so destructive to cattle as well as men. There are no elephants, so the tigers are not hunted here.

The harbour presents a busy scene, filled with ships of all sorts: six men-of-war, four steam vessels, thirty or forty transport and store-ships, twenty or thirty Chinese junks, the oddest looking craft I have seen. The latter will soon be leaving for China, as they only make one voyage a year, with the monsoon each way....

1844

A week in Singapore gets tedious, not much amusement—playing billiards at Dutronquoy's hotel, sketching a little, too hot to walk much. At the Singapore church only about a hundred people there, a sleepy sermon from Mr [E.] White, the Government Chaplain, whose daughter I was introduced to, a pretty black-eyed girl with a tinge of the black blood, but said to have a fortune of a lakh or two of rupees in nutmeg plantations, which would certainly make the black blood spicy. The fortune is said to come from the grandmother, who is not far removed from the jungle breed, but

Miss Church is nevertheless the prettiest girl in Singapore, and accomplished. The church has a vinegar bottle spire. The perpetual swinging of the punkahs tends to make one close his eyes, during Mr Church's not over-lively sermons....

In the evening walked along a good road through pretty country with plantations recently cleared of jungle. Saw many of the natives taking their evening bath in a little stream at the side of the road. Met a couple of drunken Englishmen driving in a gig, quarrelling and ending in a fight by the roadside, which terminated by their both tumbling into the ditch and the horse quietly going home with the empty gig. Old Quin is a patient of mine, whom I visit at the hotel every day....

Lunched with Dr [R.] Little, who is in private practice here. He is an Edinburgh man and an old fellow-student of mine....

Went out with Whampoa [Hoo Ah Kay], the Chinese merchant, to his nutmeg estate a few miles in the country. There was a great dinner there to some of the other Singapore merchants, very good and very lively with good wine. In the evening we were entertained with a native dance by Malays in costume with the music of tom-toms, cymbals and native songs. Whampoa gave us a specimen of a Chinese song in a monotonous high pitch, anything but musical, like the cat on the tiles. But the scene, by lovely moonlight and torches, with the background of jungle, made a wild one. Well into midnight before we got back to the town. It is not a usual thing to hear a Chinaman quote passages from Shakespeare and Byron, but Whampoa recited long passages from both and put the proper emphasis on the words....

Went to a musical party at Dr José d'Almeida's, a Portuguese merchant who lives on the Campong Glam and has a large family of daughters—and sons too, I believe, but they are kept in the background. They are all very musical and get up delightful concerts in their house, twice a week, to which some of us have a general invitation. The ladies are not good looking—Portuguese seldom are—and they also have a palpable mixture of the Malay, which does not add to their beauty, but they sing and play various instruments divinely. There are ten daughters and four sons. We were received by an old priest, the father confessor of the family. Old José introduced us separately and individually to each member of the family, a formidable affair, and lastly to the

Madam, a leaden coloured, fat old Malay woman who informed us 'Me no speekee de Englezee.' Some of her relations, Malay rajahs, were there and treated us to a hornpipe—one played on a fiddle some native airs, monotonous enough. It was a lovely moonlight night and the large room open to the veranda all round made it cool, so we were able to enjoy the quadrilles and waltzes—with a little flirtation.

E. H. Cree, *The Cree Journals. The Voyages of Edward H. Cree, Surgeon R.N., as Related in His Private Journals, 1837–1856*, ed. M. Levien, Webb & Bower, Exeter, 1981, pp. 49–51, 129–32.

11
The United States Exploring Expedition

LIEUTENANT CHARLES WILKES
1842

The four ships of the United States South Seas Exploring Expedition arrived at Singapore between 22 January and 19 February 1842, and sailed on 26 February for the Cape of Good Hope and New York. They had left Hampton Roads, Virginia, in August 1838, and they reached New York in June 1842, after sailing more than 80,000 miles exploring the islands of the south Pacific, Australia, New Zealand, Hawaii, the Oregon territory, and California, and collecting more than 2,000 birds, 150 mammals, 1,000 crustaceans, 50,000 plants, and 5,000 objects of human manufacture, including a Javanese kris which was presented by Captain Lewis of the barque Java *during the Expedition's stay at Singapore. Also at Singapore it was found that one of the Expedition's ships, the 96-ton pilot schooner* Flying Fish, *had a weakened frame, and she was sold locally, renamed the* Spec, *and ended her days in the Asian opium trade. The Expedition was under the command of the 44-year-old Lieutenant Charles Wilkes, who later during the American Civil War caused an international incident when he seized two Confederate commissioners sailing aboard the British mail packet* Trent. *During his stay in Singapore Wilkes visited the 1,000-acre sugar estate of the American Consul, Joseph Balestier, two miles along*

Serangoon Road, which was known locally as Balestier Plain. The American Consul was very popular in Singapore after being officially recognized by the Government in 1836, but his heavy investment in sugar led to bankruptcy, and his estate was auctioned in 1848 to pay off his creditors.

THE stranger, after anchoring in the roads, is not long ignorant how large a concourse of various races is here assembled. Our ship was crowded from an early hour with tailors, shoemakers, washer-women, and venders of curiosities. The latter brought shells, birds of Paradise, monkeys, parrots, corals, and mats. Without-board there were innumerable bumboats, bringing for sale fresh bread, eggs, milk, chickens and ducks, both alive and cooked, fish, fruit, and vegetables. All sued piteously for permission to come alongside, and made a prodigious clatter. The features, dress, and language of the venders were as various as the articles they had to sell; and they agreed only in the common character of a dark skin. The specimen thus presented of the population of Singapore prepared us for the sight of the motley group we were to meet on shore.

At Singapore I had the pleasure of renewing my acquaintance with Mr [J.] Balestier, our worthy consul. To him, his lady, and his son, we are under many obligations for their kind treatment and attention. Mr Balestier is so well known among men of science in the United States, it would be needless for me to say that from him I derived much interesting information relative to the place, its commerce, &c., for which I here offer my acknowledgments. He was extensively engaged in the cultivation of sugar, on a plantation of one thousand acres, within two miles of Singapore, nearly half of which was under cultivation. This extent of ground he has by his exertions reclaimed from the jungle, and it bids fair to repay the labour and expense he has incurred in clearing and bringing it into cultivation. He is the first person who has attempted the cultivation of sugar at Singapore, and for his success he was awarded the gold medal of the Calcutta Agricultural Society.

On reaching the mouth of the river, as was to be expected, the crowd thickened, and the way became more and more obstructed, until we were fairly jammed among the sampans, with their crowded population. The river does not exceed two hundred and fifty feet in width. It is shallow at its mouth, and passes through the centre, or rather divides the old from the new town; these are connected by a wooden bridge. As far up as the bridge, which is about one-third of a mile from the entrance, the river is of various widths, and its banks have been carefully built up with stone, having steps occasionally for the convenience of landing from the boats. A large population is on the river, dwelling in the sampans, which are all crowded with men, women, and children, the latter naked, and frolicking in and out of the water at pleasure. These boats are ranged in rows on each side of the passage towards the bridge, and are confined by stakes stuck in the bottom. As may be well imagined, there are frequent accidents and misadventures, that call for the exercise of the lungs of this crowded multitude, yet during the many opportunities I had of viewing them, both by day and night, I have seldom seen a set of people apparently so contented.

We landed at the bridge, near which is the office of our consul, in a large quadrangular building, one side of which faces the river. The terms of old and new town promise a difference of architecture as well as inhabitants, which they amply fulfil. The former occupies the south-west or left-hand side of the river, and exhibits along the quay a fine row of stuccoed or chunamed warehouses. The lower story of the greater part of these is an arcade supported by pillars at short distances. They are only two stories high, devoid of architectural ornament, but are convenient buildings for the trade. On the right are to be seen the buildings appropriated to the government offices. These are situated on an extensive parade-ground, studded with a few fine trees. The houses having extensive porticoes, and being adorned with flowers in large vases, have rather an elegant appearance, but this is in part dissipated on a nearer approach. They are usually enclosed with low walls, surmounted by iron railings, within which are small flower-gardens, that do not, however, display much taste.

The bridge which connects the two towns is by far the most attractive place in Singapore, for the constant passing and repassing across this thoroughfare makes it particularly amusing to a stranger. The consul's rooms were so situated as to command a free view of this moving panorama. The number of Asiatic nations that frequent Singapore is said to be twenty-four, consisting of Chinese, Hindoos, Malays, Jews, Armenians, Parsees, Bugists [Bugis], besides Europeans. The variety of costume exhibited may therefore be easily imagined, and afforded opportunities for inquiry as well as amusement. The bridge was particularly thronged during the first day of our visit, for it was a holiday, both with the Chinese and Mohammedans of Hindostan.

The trades, as is usual in the East, are carried on in the streets; and carpenters, blacksmiths, tinners, butchers, bakers, tailors, barbers, crockery and opium sellers, and coffin-makers, are to be met in succession. Money-changers are to found here and there, and large well-supplied shops are not wanting, although their narrow and contracted fronts give no reason to anticipate their existence. That of Whampoa, our comprador, was one of the largest, and it gave a better idea of Noah's ark than of anything else, presenting a mixture of living animals, with everything that is required for the artificial wants of the shipping. In front were all the varieties of ship stores that China and Europe could furnish; and in the rear were poultry, pigs, sheep, and pigeons, in pens and cages; with various parrots, cockatoos, and monkeys, while quantities of geese and ducks were accommodated beneath with pools of water. Between the live stock and the groceries were large quantities of vegetables and fruit, besides lots of bread, flour, and dough ready for the oven. The noise occasioned by the cackling, bellowing, crowing, and bleating, with the accumulation of filth, surprised as well as disgusted; for although it was reached at every tide by the water, yet there was ample necessity for the use of brooms and shovels. The Chinese, though cleanly in their persons, are far from being so in their general habits, if we may judge from those that I have met in the places we have visited....

The number of spoken languages is such as to recall the idea of Babel, and to excite a desire to learn the cause of such a collection of nations. This is partly to be found in the favourable commercial site of Singapore, but chiefly in the fact of its being a free port in every sense of the word. All are allowed to visit it without any question being asked; pirates of any nation may refit here, and no doubt frequently do, without any molestation, so long as they keep the peace.

I was much struck with the apparent absence of either police or military force; but after some inquiry, I was satisfied, by the order and general quiet of the multitude, that there must be a controlling power within reach, and found the policemen under the semblance of Persians, easily distinguishable by their neat and cleanly appearance. They are generally better dressed than the body of the inhabitants, and are to be known by their red and black sashes and turbaned heads. Without the precincts of the town, a regiment of Sepoys, six hundred strong, and officered by Europeans, is stationed. These are to be seen habited like English soldiers, in close-bodied red coats, than which a more inappropriate dress in such a climate as this can scarcely be imagined....

The ride outside of the town to the hills is pleasant, passing through plantations loaded with fruit, and the air at an early hour of the morning is filled with a spicy fragrance. The vivid green of the woods and grass is also remarkable, and continues throughout the whole year, for scarcely a day passes but a refreshing shower falls. The roads are thus kept free from dust, and at all times in good order. The usual mode of conveyance is in a palanquin, which is capable of containing two persons. The cooley, or Hindoo who attends his horse, usually runs by the side of the palanquin, and seldom tires. The charge for one of these conveyances is a dollar, whether for a whole or a part of the day, and a douceur is paid to the cooley according to the time he has been employed. The palanquin is a very convenient vehicle, and its use is absolutely necessary during the heat of the day, to shield the stranger from the burning rays of the sun. These cooleys will run all day through it without any inconvenience. They are principally from the neighbourhood of Madras, and are generally about the middle size, thin, and muscular.

We found, on our arrival, the whole of this motley population engaged in a festival. With the Chinese it was that of the New Year,... The Chinese, on such occasions, give themselves up entirely to gambling; their quarter of the town might be considered as a vast gambling-shop. During this holiday they are allowed to gamble as much as they please.

The extent to which gaming was carried by the Chinese could not fail to astonish any one who had not been brought up to it. It was extraordinary to see all engaged in such an exciting vice. Gaming was going on in every shop; under the colonnades, in the bazaars, and at the corner of almost every street, a variety of games were playing. Of several of these I had no knowledge; some were performed with cards, and others with dice. The stake seemed generally to be in small copper coin, called pice, about five hundred to the dollar, each of which is valued at three cowries; but although this was the usual betting coin, the stake was sometimes silver, and at times to a considerable amount....

The Chinese is at all times to be found industriously employed, except when gambling; and were it not for this latter propensity, and his desire of cheating foreigners, has probably as few vices as exist in any other race. Wherever he is found, peace and quietness seem to dwell; he moves, and has been moving for ages in the same path, and prefers all his own ways to those of the rest of the world. We saw the Chinese in some pleasing lights, and were much struck, on these festival occasions, by their attention towards their children, and the fondness and invariable kindness with which they were treated....

The convicts sent to Singapore are employed upon the public works; and a large prison in the suburbs of Singapore is provided for their safe-keeping at night, or when not at work. I was not able to ascertain their exact number, but I believe it amounts to some fifteen hundred.

The market was well filled with venders, so much so, indeed, that the passages through it are rendered narrow and tortuous; the principal article for sale was fish, fresh and dried, and prawns....

The bazaars form the general resort of those who frequent the market. Every avenue, arcade, or veranda approaching it is filled with money-changers and smallware dealers, eager for selling European goods, Chinese toys, and many other attractive curiosities. It is necessary to be careful in making even the smallest offer, for although it may be but half or a fourth of what is asked, it is instantly accepted....

The Malay population dwell chiefly in the suburbs, or what are termed the Malay villages. The Malays seem to bear the palm for idleness among the common people, and are rarely found engaged in any steady employment, preferring those that are either light or of a roving character. They engross the occupation of the drivers of palanquins, are strong and active, and will run a great length of time and distance, in a hot and oppressive day, seemingly without inconvenience. Those of the latter sort who are more wealthy, indulge in many luxuries, particularly in dress. They usually wear mustaches, which are always neatly kept, and occupy no small portion of their attendance and time; and, contrasted with the white turban, with its band of scarlet and gold, has a particular pleasing effect, with their swarthy skins. On holidays they are to be met with in their snow-white raiment, thrown over a richly-embroidered coloured vest, fitting tight to the body, with loose trowsers, tied just to meet their embroidered slippers at the ankle.

The most distinguished men as to looks are the Armenians. Although few in number, yet they have much influence from their wealth; they are an exceedingly handsome race, dress after the English fashion, and generally speak English or the Portuguese fluently. Some of them, that I had occasion to visit, were extremely courteous, but spoke of the inhabitants of Singapore generally as of a low class. The Armenian church is one of the finest buildings in the place.

Parsees are not numerous at Singapore, but they rank among the most wealthy of its inhabitants. They are dressed partly after the Eastern and partly after the European fashion. They excited our attention as being worshippers of fire, which they venerate as emblematical of the Deity. They are of various shades of colour, and generally more robust and portly than the other races. Many of them speak the English language.

Arabs from the east coast of Africa were also pointed out to me, and individuals of the Caffre tribe were also met with....

The opium shops are among the most extraordinary sights in Singapore; it is inconceivable with what avidity the smokers seek this noxious drug at the shop windows. They then retire to the interior, where a number of sickly-looking persons, in the last stage of consumption, haggard, and worn down with care, are seen smoking. The drug is sold in very small pieces, and for ten cents enough to fill a pipe once is obtained. With it are furnished a pipe, a lamp, and a couch to lie on, if such it may be called. The pipe is of a peculiar construction, and is in part of metal, having an interior or cup just large enough to contain a piece the size of a pea. The opium is difficult to ignite, and it requires much management in the smoker to obtain the necessary number of whiffs to produce intoxication in one habituated to its use. The couch is sometimes a rude bench, but more often a mat on the floor, with a small raised bench; and, in the frequented shops, generally occupied by a pair of smokers who have a lamp between them.

C. Wilkes, *Narrative of the United States Exploring Expedition, during the Years 1838, 1839, 1840, 1841, 1842,* Ingram, Cooke, and Co., London, 1852, pp. 287–9, 291–2, 294–6, 299.

12
Indian Convicts

FRANK S. MARRYAT
1843–1846

The author was the fourth and youngest son of the popular maritime novelist, Captain Frederick Marryat, who wrote Mr. Midshipman Easy. *He sailed as a 17-year-old midshipman aboard HMS* Samarang *(Captain Sir Edward Belcher) during a surveying voyage in the Malay Archipelago between 1843 and 1846 (see Passage 13). His description of Singapore is a composite of his three visits there during those years. He reminds us that at this period Indian convicts formed part of the population, having first been transported from Bencoolen (Bengkulu) in west Sumatra to Singapore in 1825. There were 1,500 convicts in the colony in Marryat's time, but transportation was stopped in 1860, and the remaining Indian convicts were removed 13 years later. Marryat himself died in 1855 before he was 30.*

FROM the anchorage the town of Sincapore has a very pleasing appearance. Most of the public buildings, as well as some of the principal merchants' houses, face the sea. The church is also close to the beach, I presume to allow the congregation the benefit of the sea breezes. It has no architectural beauty to recommend it, being a plain building with a spiral steeple, surmounted by a cross. The interior is fitted up with more regard to neatness than elegance. It has an organ, and is supplied with a host of young choristers from the academy.

Between the beach and Government Hill is a delightful upland, which is generally attended by all the beauty and fashion of Sincapore in the cool of the evening. A canal or small river divides the town into two parts. On the western side of it, stand all the stone houses of the merchants, and it is here that all commercial business is transacted. It is densely populated with Armenian Jews, Chinese, and people from every part of India, each nation residing in its own quarter, in the houses peculiar to and characteristic of their country. Indeed, one of the first things that strikes the stranger in Sincapore is the variety of costume; Chinamen, Malays and Indians, Armenians and Jews, all mingle together in every variety of picturesque costume, giving you an idea of a carnival. The palanquins resemble an omnibus on a small scale, they are drawn on four wheels, have a door on either side, and seats for four people. They are very high, and drawn by one horse. The conductors, however, are not perched up on high, but run by the side of the horse, as do all the syces in India.

There are two hotels, the proprietors of which are of course rivals. One is kept by an Englishman, the other by a Frenchman; both are equally attentive, but the Frenchman's house has the preference, in consequence of its superior locality, facing the esplanade, and looking upon the sea....

Sincapore, like all new settlements, is composed of so mixed a community, that there is but little hospitality, and less gaiety. Every one is waiting to ascertain what is to be his position in society, and till then is afraid of committing himself by friendly intercourse; moreover, every body is too busy making money. The consequence is, but few parties are given, and a ball is so rare that it becomes the subject of conversation for months. There are some good-looking girls at Sincapore, but it is only at church or on parade that a stranger obtains a glimpse of them. Prudery is at present the order of the day, and this is carried to such an extent from non-intercourse, that at a farewell ball given to the Cambrians, the women would only polka and waltz with each other....

Sincapore being the penal settlement of India, there are a large number of convicts here, who are chained, and work at the roads and bridges. One night I visited the gaol, and was taken over it by an overseer. We first visited the Chinese department. Two long benches ran along the room, on which were stretched some thirty men. As the overseer passed he struck each man with his rattan, and in a moment they were all sitting up, rubbing their eyes, and looking as innocent as possible. They were all confined for murder, and were a most rascally-looking set. From this room we proceeded to another, fitted in the same manner, and filled with Indians. Many of them were branded on the forehead with 'Doomga', which signifies murder; and in some cases the brand was both in Hindostanee and English. Leaving them, we entered a small room close to the gates of the gaol, and guarded by a sentry. In this room were confined the most reckless characters. They were but eight in number. Parallel to the bench ran a long iron rod, and to this they were shackled, both hands and feet. The first man among them pointed out to me by the overseer was a fine-looking grey-bearded Indian, of great stature, and with the eyes of a tiger. He had been formerly a rich shipowner at Bombay; but having been convicted of insuring his vessels to a large amount, and then setting fire to them, his property was confiscated by the government, and he was sentenced to work for life in chains. It is said that he has offered a million rupees to any man who will knock off his irons. His son carries on the business at Bombay, and it was reported that a vessel was always lying at Sincapore ready to receive him in case he should effect his escape; but of this there does not appear to be the slightest chance, as he is particularly watched and guarded.

The next culprits pointed out to us were two of the heads of the secret society of India. So much has already been said of this extraordinary association, that I need not discuss it here. There is, however, a society in Sincapore of a similar nature, composed of all the lower orders of the Chinese. It is said to amount to 15,000; and the police is much too weak to prevent the robberies, although some check is put to them by the presence of the military. It must not be supposed that because there are 15,000 in the society, that there are that quantity of robbers: such is not the case....

The richest Chinaman at Sincapore is Whampoa: he supplies the navy with stores, and has a thriving business. His country house is a favourite resort of the naval officers, and he gives excellent dinners, and very agreeable parties. His champagne is particularly approved of.

There is little or no amusement at Sincapore. During the

afternoon every body is asleep. In the cool of the evening half a dozen palanquins, and perhaps a few gigs, may be seen driving on the parade: these proceed at a steady pace round the grass-plot for about an hour: and this is the only exercise taken. Fashion is very drowsy here, and only wakes up occasionally, that she may sleep the longer afterwards. From the want of hospitality, the evenings are passed by strangers at the hotels, playing billiards, smoking, and drinking. The hotels are very good, in consequence of the steamers from Bombay to Hong Kong touching here; they are fitted up with an unusual degree of comfort; and the charges are, of course, not very moderate.

F. S. Marryat, *Borneo and the Indian Archipelago, With Drawings of Costume and Scenery*, Longman, Brown, Green, and Longmans, London, 1848, pp. 93–4, 213–17.

13
Ethnic Divisions of Singapore

CAPTAIN SIR EDWARD BELCHER
1846

Captain Sir Edward Belcher was appointed to command HMS Samarang *in November 1842 to survey the coasts of China, but the ending of the war between Great Britain and China led to a change in plan, and he was instructed to survey the coasts of Borneo and the adjacent islands, as well as parts of Japan and Korea. The ship sailed from Spithead in January 1843, and the voyage was completed four years later. Belcher's description of Singapore is contained in his* Narrative of the Voyage of H.M.S. Samarang, During the Years 1843–46 *(London, 1848), when the ship returned there on its final visit in May 1846, but it is informed by knowledge gained on his earlier visits, including that made on his voyage round the world in HMS* Sulphur *in 1840.*

SINGAPORE, as regards its local advantages, has undergone considerable improvement since I first became acquainted with it, under the government of

Mr [S. G.] Bonham, in 1840. The lines of streets, then only marked out by slight poles with rags, or causeways, or embankments, inclosing certain portions of barely cleared marsh, were now finished, solid ground filled in in many spots, and blocks of houses had been erected. The river-lines had been completed in stone, good roads formed, and several substantial and well-designed bridges spanned the stream at various points. In spite, however, of these improvements, due to the energetic mind of Mr Bonham, the former Governor, and who was deservedly a great favourite with all classes, the place itself had lost much of its interest, as well as attractions. The present excellent Governor, Colonel [W. J.] Butterworth, was equally esteemed; but the changes which had necessarily occurred in the mercantile prosperity of the place, between the periods alluded to, had now materially diminished the society, as well as, by the transfer of much of the capital to Hong-Kong, the means of supporting the marked hospitality which we experienced at the former period. Singapore, as we now found it, deprived of its worthy Governor, absent at Penang, was dull indeed; even the bustle consequent upon the crowded anchorage, where European and Chinese craft seemed to shut out the town from the passing voyager, was now considerably changed. Very few Junks (in comparison to the date alluded to) now visit Singapore. The Chinese find it more convenient, as well as to their advantage, to exchange their cargoes at the nearer mart of Hong-Kong, and thus avoid the dangers of the China Sea. Still, dull as it was, commercially, it was hailed by our crew as a most acceptable change after our solitary cruize since quitting the lively scenes of Manila. As regarded excitement, or 'Life', in the lower classes, the same din prevailed; offers of all kinds were eagerly pressed. Dubashes* for supplies; others with cards for the hotels; dealers in marine stores, from a pot of jelly to a pot of blacking, anchor, or guns. Chinese tailors and shoe-makers using every artifice to attract, and willing to suit your fancy, even to following up minutely the defects or repairs which they may discover in former garments, which they invariably ask for as *muster* (or pattern)....

*An (Indian) interpreter, often attached to a mercantile house.

The town of Singapore may be considered as separated into three distinct divisions. The western, Chinese; central, English; and eastern, Malay (or Kling, Chinese, and Malay). The western, is separated by the stream, and although it contains the counting-houses and stores of the English merchants, still their private habitations are mostly in the central division. The Chinese principally occupy, and reside in, the western division, and here may be procured any article desired, either from Europe, India, or China. Any article of which *a pattern* can be produced, will be imitated by the Chinese. Nothing is considered by them beyond their capacity, they will make the effort, and in general succeed in a marvellous manner. Care, however, must be taken, to point out any defects, or they will most assuredly be copied.

The central portion of the town is entirely set apart for public offices, church, official and private residences, and hotels, reserving ample space between the sea and the houses for parade, and carriage drives, which, in 1840, was generally well attended, between the hours of five and seven. On the east, are the shops of the Klings and Malays. This part of Singapore has been very much improved of late, and several excellent bridges now render the villages, on the opposite side of the stream, more accessible, having rescued them, in a considerable degree, from the filthy condition, which formerly prevailed there. The eye is naturally attracted to the general fabrication of arms in this region, and to those conversant in the examination of the Pirate boats of these seas, the question naturally suggests itself: Are these swords, parangs, knives, muskets, bell-mouthed blunderbusses, &c., intended for Pirates? There cannot be the slightest hesitation in the reply: They are; and the Pirate, 'emissary prahu', her Nakoda* and crew, are gazing on you, dressed in gaudy attire, and only await their chance of evading the gun boats, to rejoin their associates, with fresh supplies of arms and ammunition....

The utter want of defence against the smallest cruizer, which an enemy might send to levy contributions on Singapore, or to capture the merchantmen laden with most valuable cargoes, has, at length, excited attention, and plans and estimates have, I believe, been forwarded to the proper

*Master of an Asian vessel.

department, at the India house, there to remain and be debated upon; during which delay, this place may be wrested from us by the first state which may happen to make war.

Sir Edward Belcher, *Narrative of the Voyage of H.M.S. Samarang, during the Years 1843–46; Employed Surveying the Islands of the Eastern Archipelago; Accompanied by a Brief Vocabulary of the Principal Languages*, London, 1848, Vol. II, pp. 179–85.

14
A Chinese Burial

IDA PFEIFFER
1846

The Austrian woman traveller, Ida Laura Pfeiffer, began her lone travels in 1842 in a journey to Palestine and Egypt. Three years later she travelled to northern Europe, and in 1846 undertook her first round the world journey, in the course of which she visited Singapore between 3 September and 7 October. A second journey round the world by a different route was undertaken in 1851, when she again visited Singapore, as well as Borneo and Java. She died in 1858 after undergoing terrible hardships in a journey to Madagascar two years earlier. In her account of Singapore, she mentions her visit in September 1846 to the mercantile firm of Behn, Meyer & Co., which had been founded there five years earlier by the Hamburg-born, Theodor August Behn and Valentin Lorenz Meyer. At the time of Ida Pfeiffer's visit, August Behn had only recently married Caroline Meyer, a sweet-faced, large-eyed young woman, with cropped hair, and it was she who extended such warm hospitality to the Austrian world traveller.

ON the 3rd of September we ran into the port of Singapore; but it was so late in the evening that we could not disembark.

On the following morning I paid a visit to the firm of Behn and Meyer, to whom I had letters of introduction. Madame Behn was the first German lady I had met since my departure from Hamburgh. I cannot say how delighted I was at forming her acquaintance. I was once more able to give free vent to my feelings in my own native tongue. Madame Behn would not hear of my lodging in an hotel; I was immediately installed as a member of her own amiable family....

The Europeans lead pretty much the same kind of life at Singapore that they do at Canton, with this difference, however, that the merchants reside with their families in the country, and come to town every morning for business. Each family is obliged to keep a large staff of servants, and the lady of the house meddles very little in domestic matters, as these are generally altogether entrusted to the major-domo.

The servants are Chinese, with the exception of the *seis* (coachmen or grooms), who are Bengalese. Every spring, whole shiploads of Chinese boys, from ten to fifteen years old, come over here. They are generally so poor that they cannot pay their passage. When this is the case, the captain brings them over on his own account, and is paid beforehand, by the person engaging them, their wages for the first year. These young people live very economically, and, when they have a little money, return generally to their native country, though many hire themselves as journeymen, and stop altogether....

The whole island is intersected with excellent roads, of which those skirting the sea-shore are the most frequented, and where handsome carriages and horses from New Holland [Australia], and even from England, are to be seen. Besides the European carriages, there are also certain vehicles of home manufacture called palanquins, which are altogether closed and surrounded on all sides with jalousies. Generally there is but one horse, at the side of which both the coachman and footman run on foot. I could not help expressing my indignation at the barbarity of this custom, when I was informed that the residents had wanted to abolish it, but that the servants had protested against it, and begged to be allowed to run beside the carriage, rather than sit or stand upon it. They cling to the horse or vehicle, and are thus dragged along with it.

Hardly a day passed that we did not drive out. Twice a week a very fine military band used to play on the esplanade close to the sea, and the whole world of fashionables would either walk or drive to the place to hear the music. The carriages were ranged several rows deep, and surrounded by young beaux on foot and horseback; any one might have been excused for imagining himself in a European city. As for myself, it gave me more pleasure to visit a plantation, or some other place of the kind, than to stop and look on what I had so often witnessed in Europe....

A few days before my departure from Singapore, I had an opportunity of witnessing the burial of a Chinese in easy circumstances. The procession passed our house, and, in spite of a temperature of 113°, I went with it to the grave, which was three or four miles distant, and was too much interested in the ceremony to leave until it was concluded, although it lasted nearly two hours.

At the head of the procession was a priest, and at his side a Chinese with a lantern two feet high, covered with white cambric. Then came two musicians, one of whom beat a small drum at intervals, and the other played the cymbals. These persons were followed by the coffin, with a servant holding a large open parasol over that part of it on which the head of the deceased lay. Alongside walked the eldest son or the nearest male relative, carrying a small white flag, and with his hair hanging in disorder over his shoulders. The relations were all dressed in the deepest mourning—that is to say, entirely in black; the men had even got white caps on, and the women were so enveloped in white cloths that it was impossible to see so much as their faces. The friends and attendants, who followed the coffin in small groups without order or regularity, had all got a white strip of cambric bound round their head, their waist, or their arm. As soon as it was remarked that I had joined the procession, a man who had a quantity of these strips came up and offered me one, which I took and bound round my arm....

The coffin, which consisted of the trunk of a large tree, was covered with a dark-coloured cloth; a few garlands of flowers were suspended from it, and some rice, tied up in a cloth, was placed upon it. Four-and-twenty-men bore this heavy burden on immense poles: their behaviour was excessively lively, and every time they changed they began quarrelling or laughing among themselves. Nor did the other personages in the ceremony display either grief or respect; they ate, drank, smoked, and talked, while some carried cold tea in small pails for the benefit of such as might be thirsty. The son alone held himself aloof; he walked, according to custom, plunged in deep sorrow, by the side of the coffin.

On reaching the road that led to the last resting-place, the son threw himself upon the ground, and, covering up his face, sobbed very audibly. After a little, he got up again and tottered behind the coffin, so that two men were obliged to support him; he appeared very ill and deeply moved. It is true, I was afterwards informed that this grief is mostly merely assumed, since custom requires that the chief mourner shall be, or pretend to be, weak and ill with sorrow.

On arriving at the grave, which was seven feet deep, and dug on the declivity of a hill, they laid the pall, flowers, and rice on one side, and then, after throwing in a vast quantity of gold and silver paper, lowered the coffin, which I then for the first time perceived was of the finest workmanship, lacquered and hermetically closed. At least half an hour was taken up by this part of the proceedings. The relations at first threw themselves on the ground, and, covering their faces, howled horribly, but, finding the burial lasted rather long, sat down in a circle all round, and, taking their little baskets of betel, burnt mussel-shells, and areca-nuts, began chewing away with the greatest composure....

The grave was at last filled in, when the relations set up a most dismal howl, but, as far as I could remark, every eye was dry....

On the following day I witnessed the celebrated Chinese Feast of Lanterns. From all the houses, at the corners of the roofs, from high posts, &c., were hung innumerable lanterns, made of paper or gauze, and most artistically ornamented with gods, warriors, and animals. In the courts and gardens of the different houses, or, where there were no courts or gardens, in the streets, all kinds of refreshment and fruit were laid out with lights and flowers, in the form of half pyramids on large tables. The people wandered about the streets, gardens, and courts, until nearly midnight, when the edible portions of the pyramids were eaten by the proprietors of them. I was very much pleased with this feast, but with no part of it more than the quiet and orderly behaviour of the people; they looked at all the eatables with a scrutinizing glance, but without touching the smallest fragment....

I must remark that Singapore will shortly become the central point of all the Indian steamers. Those from Hong-

Kong, Ceylon, Madras, Calcutta, and Europe arrive regularly once a month; there is likewise a Dutch war-steamer from Batavia, and in a little time there will also be steamers running to and fro between this place, and Manilla and Sidney [Sydney].

I. Pfeiffer, *A Woman's Journey Round the World, from Vienna to Brazil, Chili, Tahiti, China, Hindostan, Persia and Asia Minor*, The Illustrated London Library, London, 1851, pp. 118–27.

15
Wild Game Hunting

GENERAL DOUGLAS HAMILTON
1846

Having been gazetted to the 21st Regiment of Madras Native Infantry, the author was posted with his regiment to Singapore in 1846, when he was able to indulge his passion for wild game hunting. Curiously, he was unable to track down a tiger, which by all accounts were numerous in the island, causing many deaths, mainly among the Chinese and Malay cultivators (see Passage 25). Hamilton later accompanied his regiment to Labuan to replace the Marines, and he remained there for some months before returning to India. He took a great interest in conservation in India, and retired in 1871 after 35 years' service. He was promoted General in 1888, three years before his death.

SINGAPORE with its valleys, plains, grand trees and undulating hills, is very beautiful. In 1846 a great portion of the settlement was covered with jungle so dense that it was almost impenetrable and sport was hopeless. There were some deer, muntjack or barking deer, and wild hog on the island, and we managed after many a blank day, to kill a few of these. I was fortunate in shooting the only stag of any size that had been killed on the island for a long time, and the advantage of not wearing any conspicuous color when out after game was very manifest on this occasion. We were posted by the side of the high road where the forest had been cleared and a scrub jungle had grown up. I saw the stag suddenly appear on some rising ground above the road and deliberately take his bearings. Now as all my companions had something white about them which made them very conspicuous, and I had nothing of the kind visible, he came straight down to where I was standing, and on his coming within shot got the contents of both my barrels which turned him back severely wounded, and he fell dead after proceeding a short distance; a fine beast, 13 hands at the shoulder with small but very thick antlers. They tell me that the deer on the island never have very large antlers. My sporting friends after this event, took great pains to hide every scrap of white in their dress, but no more stags came to be shot. There was said to be a great number of tigers on the island and some hundreds of Chinamen were reported to be killed each year by them, but as the Chinamen belonged to secret societies who were in perpetual feud and always ready to kill each other, I am afraid many a murder has been falsely attributed to the 'gentleman in stripes'. In respect to this, I was told rather an amusing story of a very knowing Chinaman. The stems of the large cable-like creepers that twine about the forest trees like huge snakes, are valuable on account of their variety of colour and beauty of grain, for wood veneering; the above mentioned individual having found a spot where these valuable creepers abounded and fearing that others might reap the harvest, adopted an ingenious plan to keep them away; he carefully carved a tiger's foot in wood and stamped the impression in every direction leading to this piece of jungle; after a time news was brought in by another wood cutter of these numerous tracks; on first visiting the ground there appeared to be little doubt as to its being much frequented by a tiger, but on carefully inspecting the foot prints, it was discovered that they were *all made by one foot.*

I offered large rewards to get a shot at a tiger, but though I often sat up for one I never once had a chance. There was however some very fair snipe shooting to be got in the cultivated grounds.

D. Hamilton, *Records of Sport in Southern India Chiefly on the Annumallay, Nielgherry and Pulney Mountains Also including Notes on Singapore, Java and Labuan from Journals Written between 1844 and 1870*, R. H. Porter, London, 1892, pp. 52–4.

16
A KCB for Rajah Brooke

CAPTAIN THE HON. HENRY KEPPEL
1848

Captain The Hon. Henry Keppel, later Admiral of the Fleet, and Queen Victoria's 'beloved little Admiral', commanding the 44-gun frigate HMS Mæander, *arrived at Singapore on 20 May 1848. On board was the Rajah of Sarawak, James Brooke, newly appointed Governor of Labuan and HM's Consul-General for Borneo, together with his entourage, which included the Lieutenant-Governor of Labuan, William Napier, to whom the Queen's warrant regarding Brooke's KCB was addressed. The investiture took place in the ballroom of the Public Assembly Rooms in Singapore on 22 August before 240 seated spectators, with the Royal Marines of HMS* Mæander *ranged along one side, and the band of the ship in the gallery. Three chairs were placed on the dais, the middle one representing the Queen. To the amusement of the onlookers, Napier, who because of his swaggering walk was known locally as 'Royal Billy', sat down on the royal throne to an exclamation from Admiral Collier said to have been 'more vigorous than polite in its language'. A large number of guests attended the Ball given by Napier the same evening, which was marked by the Governor, Lieutenant-Colonel Butterworth, losing his watch and his wife all her jewellery, stolen from Government House. The account given by Keppel of the omission of an invitation to the Editor of the* Straits Times, *Robin Carr Woods, if accurate, many explain the origins of the hostile campaign he mounted in his newspaper against Brooke's anti-piratical measures in Borneo.*

ON the 20th May we arrived at Sincapore, after an excellent passage of three months and five days, including stoppages at Madeira and Rio....

On the 22nd our passengers landed, Mr [J.] Brooke being received with all the honours due to a governor; and on the following day preparations were commenced for establishing the new colony. An office was opened in Sincapore, and contracts received for the frame-works of the temporary residences to be erected for the Government functionaries....

The June mail, which arrived on the 7th August, brought our new commander-in-chief, Sir Francis Collier, as well as the gratifying intelligence that Her Majesty had been pleased to confer the Order of the Bath on Mr Brooke—of which he was made Knight Commander,—and the Lieutenant-Governor of Labuan was directed to invest Sir James accordingly. The ceremony was performed on the 22nd of August, a very great event in Sincapore, Mr [W.] Napier representing Her Majesty with becoming dignity: the whole business was more amusing than imposing, and finished in the evening with a ball.

By some error, the representative of Majesty omitted to invite the too sensitive editor of a local journal, which oversight gave rise to a succession of amusing articles, supposed to be in disparagement of the new colony generally, and of the Royal Navy in particular: some of these subsequently found their way into an English paper, and, I am told, were alluded to in the House of Commons. Great indeed must have been the triumph of my little friend.

During our stay at Sincapore, the body of a large tiger was brought in by some Malays (a not unusual occurrence), to enable them to receive the reward given by Government. The Malays stated that, when they found this monster in a hole which had been dug to catch him, they threw quick lime into his eyes; and the unfortunate beast, while suffering intense agony from this cruel appliance, drowned himself in some water which was at the bottom of the pit, though not more than a foot deep.

The annual loss of human life from tigers, chiefly among the Chinese settlers, is perfectly fearful, averaging no fewer than 360, or one per diem....

There is a procession and much parade in bringing these tigers to the Government office. They are made to look as fierce as possible, propped up in a standing position by pieces of bamboo, the mouth open, and tail on end.

The Governor kindly presented me with this fallen monarch of the jungle, and I was astonished at the number of native volunteers for the service of denuding him of his skin, the only part I coveted, while they demanded the carcase for their trouble. But I found afterwards that they made a large profit by retailing the flesh, a belief being entertained by this people that the eating of it is not only a sovereign remedy for all diseases, but that it imparts to him who eats it the sagacity as well as the courage of the animal. A friend of mine belonging to the 21st regiment, M.N.I., who was slowly recovering from an attack of fever, finding some difficulty in masticating the food before him, questioned his servant as to the cause, when he discovered that the fellow had purchased a small piece of my tiger, which he had clandestinely introduced into his master's currie. When my friend got well, young Zaddie firmly believed that his remedy had effected the cure.

The Hon. Henry Keppel, *A Visit to the Indian Archipelago, in H.M. Ship Mænder, with Portions of the Private Journal of Sir James Brooke, K.C.B.*, Richard Bentley, London, 1853, Vol. I, pp. 6–13.

17
The Baneful Effects of Opium Smoking

DR J. BERNCASTLE
1849

The London medical practitioner, Dr J. Berncastle, sailed in October 1848 from Portsmouth aboard the ship Herefordshire *for Bombay. After staying there for three months, he embarked in May 1849 aboard the* Charlotte Jane *bound for China. The ship reached Singapore on 17 June, and Berncastle spent a week at Gaston Dutronquoy's London Hotel at the corner of High Street and the Esplanade, before sailing for Hong Kong. During his stay he visited his fellow medical student, Dr H. A. Allen, an active freemason, who later became well known as a stalwart of The Savage Club, which gave regular dramatic performances in Singapore for many years. Being a medical man, Berncastle was interested to see at first hand 'the baneful effects' of opium smoking on the Chinese, but in the Preface to his book he observed, fairly, that 'the* abuse *of* spirits *and* tobacco *at home is attended with evils quite as great to the health and morals of the people, as those arising in the East from the practice of opium-smoking'.*

WE soon found ourselves inside the spacious harbour, which appears almost land-locked by the different islands outside, looking not unlike a large lake, with the town in front, extending down to the water's edge. Ships of all nations were here, and a number of Chinese junks gave a finish to the Oriental aspect of the place. Earlier in the season of the monsoon, large fleets of these immense junks may be seen, going in and out of the harbour, there being a great trade, and also emigration of Chinese, from China to this place and back again.

We brought up, two miles from the shore, manned the gig with our dandy Lascars, with their flowing gold and silver turbans, and found ourselves, in half an hour, landed on the boat quay of Singapore. We went forthwith to Tronquoi's [Dutronquoy's] 'London Hotel', a splendid establishment, having most extensive accommodation, in the first style and at the moderate price of two dollars a day, wines not included. One peculiarity is, that you are charged the same, whether present at meals or not. The Hotel de Paris is another large house, but not on such a scale as the first.

Having heard quite accidentally, in the Straits of Malacca, that Dr [H. A.] Allen, whom I had known intimately as a medical student in Paris, in 1836, and who had emigrated to Australia, some years back, was now practising in Singapore, I called on him, and he was not a little surprised on recognising, by the voice only, so unexpected a visitor. I received, of course, the most cordial welcome, which, by the bye, one meets with at any time from one's countrymen in the East, where John Bull shakes off, soon after his arrival, his stiff, formal, distant style of manner, so habitual to him, and is really seen to great advantage. I was enabled to treat my friend to recent news from home, about some of his family I had met since he had heard from them.

Having given to each other a brief outline of our life, since the number of years we had been separated and steered such different courses,... he introduced me to his lady, whose personal attractions I had long ago heard of in England, which was well confirmed by her being considered one of the 'Belles' of Singapore, in fact, *the* 'Belle'.

The doctor acted as my *cicerone*, and we walked out in the evening, passing by the English Church, a very fine new building, the Theatre, Government House, and the Institution, built by Sir Stamford Raffles, the founder of the colony,...

In the Chinese quarter of the town, we entered a few opium-shops, but they were all empty, and we were told by the Chinamen to return in the evening about eight or nine, when they began to fill. Government farms out, for a fixed revenue per annum, the privilege of licensing a certain number of these opium-shops, which is a speculation to the man who takes it, and who is called the opium-farmer. We looked in upon a Chinese painter, and found him at work copying a portrait. This man has a reputation for taking good likenesses of many of the principal inhabitants....

At night, we returned to the opium-shops, and visited in succession ten or twelve. Each shop contains a bench about four feet broad, reaching from one end of the room to the other, on each side, leaving a passage between; these are covered with matting, for the smokers to recline upon, and have affixed to them, at equal distances between every two persons, a small lamp constantly burning, heat being required to be applied often to the pipe whilst smoking. Leading from this principal room are many smaller chambers, or recesses, concealed from view by a curtain. These contain nothing but a table and mats, upon which latter recline, out of sight, those smokers who are so far gone, that the eye would be shocked by the public exhibition of such depravity.

We met principally with common, half-naked Chinamen, of all ages, and in all the different stages of narcotism, some merely becoming gently exhilarated from their first pipe.... Many of them are not much injured by it, when not taken to excess, as their looks, and the number of years they had been addicted to it, sufficiently proved. I am not going to sanction the custom at all, but seeing much worse practices at home, we should be cautious how we blame these half-barbarous people, without religion, or the advantages of education and civilization....

This is the place of transportation for convicts from India, of whom there are about 1,500, who, by making roads and other public works, have done much to improve the island. A gang of fifty passed by, with chains to their legs, looking very contentedly and *nonchalant*. They were all natives, and one was munching a large pineapple as he dragged his chains along. This is the staple fruit for all classes, and food for many.

J. Berncastle, *A Voyage to China; Including a Visit to the Bombay Presidency; the Mahratta Country; the Cave Temples of Western India, Singapore, the Straits of Malacca and Sunda, and the Cape of Good Hope*, William Shoberl, London, 1850, pp. 6–29.

18
Singapore Hotels

CHARLES WALTER KINLOCH
1852

Charles Walter Kinloch, a civilian from Bengal, visited Singapore in 1852 on his way to Java, to recover his health. Singapore had early been a resort for invalids from India, but generally they stayed there, or more usually carried on to China. Kinloch was among the first of the travellers from India to try the climate of Java as a health restorative, and he set a fashion which became increasingly popular as the century progressed. He was not much impressed by the London Hotel, then the leading establishment in Singapore, kept by the Frenchman, Gaston Dutronquoy, who had opened his first hotel of that name in High Street shortly after his arrival at Singapore in March 1839. He transferred it five years later to the well-positioned corner of High Street and the Esplanade on the site formerly occupied by the Singapore Hotel. In the year before Kinloch's arrival at Singapore, Dutronquoy had opened a branch of the hotel at New Harbour, in the former house of James Guthrie, with the idea of attracting travellers landing at the recently erected P&O pier; but his affairs did not prosper, and he was declared insolvent in 1857, about the time he disappeared in somewhat mysterious circumstances. His wife and son opened a new London Hotel in Bonham Street in 1858, and it continued to be listed in the Singapore Directories during the 1860s. Dutronquoy's name is associated with the first daguerreotypes produced in Singapore.

THERE are several hotels at Singapore, the best of which is the London Hotel, kept by Mr Du Trouquoy [G. Dutronquoy], a native of Jersey; but even in this establishment, there is great room for improvement. The hotel consists of two upper roomed buildings, one of which is styled the Family Hotel. Neither house is comfortable; and the bath room accommodation is especially defective, the whole of the baths being public, and situated in a range of buildings altogether distinct from the hotel. Under the very windows of both hotels is a long tiled building, called a bowling alley. This pandemonium is lit up every night, and is filled with the townspeople and others, who play at bowls and drink brandy and water until a late hour of the night. The alley, as it is called, is very profitable to the proprietor; but it is a great nuisance to the inmates of the hotel. Both hotels face the sea, and command an excellent view of the shipping. But the houses on the beach are not considered the healthiest, and the residents at night time make a practice of closing their venetians in order to exclude the sea breeze, which they consider to be very injurious to health, especially during the prevalence of the southwest monsoon.

Considering the exorbitant prices of even the commonest necessaries of life, the hotel charges cannot be considered high. The charge for a single person breakfasting and dining at the public table being one dollar and a half per diem. The charge for families and parties occupying a private sitting-room, are proportionably higher. The only really objectionable charge in our bill was that for a bath, for which the proprietor asks half a dollar a day, a demand that is most unreasonable, seeing that water is abundant, and close at hand. There is only one boarding house at Singapore. It is kept by a lady of the name of Roberts, whose husband is secretary to the government. The house is spacious and well situated, and it possesses this great advantage over the hotel, that it is comfortably and even elegantly furnished, which is not the case as regards the latter establishment; with every disposition, however, to render her house agreeable to her different guests, truth compels us to say that the excellent lady of this establishment has hitherto failed to give general satisfaction. The table arrangements are very defective, a circumstance which we attribute to its being the practice of this house to provide wine and beer without making any separate charge for the same....

The charge for board and lodging is the same as at the hotel—viz., one dollar and a half per diem; but it must be quite evident that if wine and beer are included in this charge, it could not be possible to provide a suitable table. As we have heard a very high character of Mrs Roberts from our different friends, and as we should be really glad to hear of her success, we would suggest for her consideration that she forthwith discontinue the practice of allowing wine without an extra payment for the same. By adopting the plan here suggested, she will be enabled, we are quite sure, to provide a table superior to any at Singapore, without having to make any change whatever in her present scale of charges.

Between the Esplanade and the beach is an enclosed space, within which all the beauty and fashion of the place promenade daily, and enjoy the cool sea breeze. The scene is enlivened twice during the week by the regimental band, on which occasions the old women gather together to talk scandal, and their daughters to indulge in a little innocent flirtation.

The usual kind of carriage in use at Singapore is a kind of office jaun, here called a pàlki. The Syce runs at the pony's head, and neither he nor the animal he guides make anything of a matter of ten miles right an end, and frequently accomplished too, within the hour. These carriages are not particularly easy, and are only suited, therefore, to Singapore roads, which, it must be admitted, are super-excellent. The charge for a pony and palki varies from twenty to twenty five dollars the month. There are no places of public resort or amusement at Singapore; neither is there any society. The merchants, who form by far the largest section of the community, seem to look upon money making as the chief end and object of their lives, and their topics of conversation rarely extend to any other subject than that of nutmegs or the last price current....

The Indian visitor will very soon get tired of Singapore, for, setting aside the want of society and the absence of public amusement, the climate is too hot, and too depressing, to render a residence in this island agreeable beyond a period of a few weeks....

Housekeeping at Singapore is expensive and troublesome, and we would advise the Indian visitor, whether married or unmarried, to take rooms at the hotel, rather than attempt to

Singapore from the East Side of Government Hill, 1852, from [C. W. Kinloch], *De Zieke Reiziger; or, Rambles in Java and the Straits in 1852*. By a Bengal Civilian, Simpkin, Marshall and Co., London, 1853.

keep house for himself. Considering the large European society resident at Singapore, there seems no reason why supplies of every kind should not be as abundant there as in Calcutta; but, strange to say, no good beef or mutton is to be had on the island; a small, skinny, sickly looking animal, dignified by the name of a Bengal grain fed sheep, is slaughtered twice a week for the benefit of those who cannot dispense with their mutton chop, and is sold at a fixed price of two and a half dollars the joint. There is always a supply, however, of good fish in the market, and with that and Chinese pork, the residents are content....

[C. W. Kinloch], *De Zieke Reiziger; or, Rambles in Java and the Straits in 1852. By a Bengal Civilian*, Simpkin, Marshall and Co., London, 1853, pp. 11–18.

19
Excursions round Singapore

GEORGE FRANCIS TRAIN
1855

In 1853 the American businessman and world traveller, George Francis Train, sailed from Boston to Melbourne, where he established the firm of Caldwell, Train & Co. He stayed in Australia for nearly three years before sailing for Java on his way to England. From Jakarta he took passage in the steamer Queen of the Netherlands, *and arrived at Singapore in December 1855. During his brief stay he was accommodated at Dutronquoy's Hotel, where, in common with others, he found much to criticize about the standard of service. Later in England he made unsuccessful efforts to introduce street railways into Birkenhead and London.*

AFTER luxuriating in the fairy grotto scenery of Java, and grown fat on the good living and courteous treatment one may receive there,... the traveler (not an Englishman) who looks at Singapore as he lands in a fog, with a dozen Kling boatmen, as savage in appearance as fancy can picture, taking away your baggage, and talking and gesticulating like maniacs, an unintelligible jargon—while you jump into a gurry, with a stout runt of a horse, and see the syce (driver) rush off at a long, wolf-like trot, holding his galloping animal by a small rope, instead of mounting a coachman's seat, like a civilized being—when you get fairly settled down in that huge pile of ugly looking buildings, covering a good sized farm, and known as the London Hotel, and kept in a manner that would disgrace a landlord in the backwoods of Kansas, where your food looks uninviting, and is brought to you at the long, well ventilated and *puncah* cooling dining hall, by Asiatics and Islanders who always seem to me to have their hands upon their half-clad body, when you want a piece of bread, some Malay curry, or a pineapple; and when, perhaps, your sensitiveness makes you dainty—where your boots and books get mildewed, and your brown leather trunk resembles the skin of a Maltese cat, it has become so mouldy—where your cocoa nut oil lamp, manufactured out of a tumbler of water, on the surface of which a little piece of pith kept floating on the oil, by means of bits of cork, answers for wicking, burns dimly, and you cannot get a candle—where the bowling alley and billiard room are surrounded by the sons of the sun, and the natives, who laugh at costume—where the labyrinth of passages, show cases and rooms, require a man to have a compass, if he does not wish to lose his reckoning, and get out of his proper track—I say, when you think of your comforts and enjoyments at the Java Hotel, in Batavia, and then experience the annoyance and confusion at the London, you will come to the conclusion that in some things Java and Singapore are widely different.... But enough of this—for why lose my temper on what I cannot remedy, unless it is to recommend some enterprising American to come out and establish a hotel worthy of so fine a city as Singapore....

The rides about the city are most delightful, and the bamboo and rattan fence fill the eye with beauty. My excursion to Captain [H. T.] Marshall's beautiful residence—near the magnificent buildings erected by the steam company, which he has so long been connected with—and the inspection of the grounds over which fly the flag of the Peninsular and Oriental Company, will not hastily be forgotten. Our *syces* drove us directly through and about the several streets of the town, across the several bridges, around the esplanade, where the native band entertain the *élite* every Saturday afternoon with martial music; by the several go-downs, over to the Chinese burial ground...—passed the Malay washing ground, where these dark beggars tear your clothes to pieces, under the plea of getting them cleansed—we are arrived at the steam wharf, which five years ago was a marsh, but is now covered with the most capacious accommodations which this company possesses this side of England. The coal sheds have at present about 20,000 tons ready for use, and the store houses, the machine shop, the sail loft, the cooking rooms, the several piers and the large amount of ground do not appear to have cost so little as $80,000....

There are but few mercantile houses in the place, and those—some twenty-five or thirty in all—have been established for many years, and most of which are doing an extensive business. But, for a wonder, I find no American commission house managed by Americans! Messrs. Bousted & Co., have a large American trade, and manage their business well. An outsider, however, would find it, for a while, up-hill work in establishing a house where all the old firms would find it for their interest to work against him.

I believe that the European population will not exceed three hundred in all, but there are quite a number of half-and-half, whose color plainly shows the offspring of the native mother and the European father.

Many of the Chinese merchants are immensely wealthy. Wampoa is the millionaire of the place, and has a most elegant residence out of town. With him 'tis the old story—came into the place a beggar, and has walked steadily up the ladder of wealth till his riches make him noted. The Malays bring in their produce and sell to the Chinamen, and the Chinamen sells to the merchants, who fills the orders which the mail has brought him—a continual sale and barter; no brokers can be employed. The *prahus* of all the islands round about are pouring in at all seasons, but the Chinese traders come annually about Christmas time, and then such an excitement! The junks are surrounded by hundreds of boats, all anxious to trade and meet their friends; but the new comers decline to sell or talk business, till, with a praiseworthy trait of character, observed for ages, they have visited and repaired the graves of their ancestors, and spent a few hours at the Joss house in prayer.

F. Train, *An American Merchant in Europe, Asia, and Australasia: A Series of Letters from Java, Singapore, China, Bengal, Egypt, the Holy Land, the Crimea and its Battle Grounds, England, Melbourne, Sydney, Etc., Etc.*, G. P. Putnam & Co., New York, 1857, pp. 66–71.

20
The Bukit Timah Missionary

ALFRED RUSSEL WALLACE
1854–1862

In April 1854 the most famous of the nineteenth-century naturalist travellers in South-East Asia, Alfred Russel Wallace, arrived at Singapore in the P&O steamer Bengal. *His account of Singapore in his book,* The Malay Archipelago *(London, 1869), is, as he states, based on several visits he made between 1854 and 1862, but his stay with the French Roman Catholic missionary at Bukit Timah took place shortly after his arrival, between April and June 1854. In a letter written at this time he describes the French missionary as being a very pleasant man, able to speak English, Malay, and Chinese. He was talking of Father Anatole Manduit of Coutances in Normandy, who served in the mission for 15 years after his arrival at Singapore in 1844. He was Vicar of St Joseph's chapel for the Chinese, to which Wallace refers. It is not always recognized that it was in Singapore—at Bukit Timah—that Wallace commenced his momentous natural history explorations of the Malayan and Indonesian region that led to the co-formulation with Charles Darwin of the Theory of Natural Selection.*

FEW places are more interesting to a traveller from Europe than the town and island of Singapore, furnishing, as it does, examples of a variety of Eastern races, and of many different religions and modes of life. The government, the garrison, and the chief merchants are English; but the great mass of the population is Chinese, including some of the wealthiest merchants, the agriculturists of the interior, and most of the mechanics and labourers. The native Malays are usually fishermen and boatmen, and they form the main body of the police. The Portuguese of Malacca supply a large number of the clerks and smaller merchants. The Klings of Western India are a numerous body of Mahometans, and, with many Arabs, are petty merchants and shopkeepers. The grooms and washermen are all Bengalees, and there is a small but highly respectable class of Parsee merchants. Besides these, there are numbers of Javanese sailors and domestic servants, as well as traders from Celebes, Bali, and many other islands of the Archipelago....

By far the most conspicuous of the various kinds of people in Singapore, and those which most attract the stranger's attention, are the Chinese, whose numbers and incessant activity give the place very much the appearance of a town in China. The Chinese merchant is generally a fat round-faced man with an important and business-like look. He wears the same style of clothing (loose white smock, and blue or black trousers) as the meanest coolie, but of finer materials, and is always clean and neat; and his long tail tipped with red silk hangs down to his heels. He has a handsome warehouse or shop in town and a good house in the country. He keeps a fine horse and gig, and every evening may be seen taking a drive bareheaded to enjoy the cool breeze. He is rich, he owns several retail shops and trading schooners, he lends money at high interest and on good security, he makes hard bargains and gets fatter and richer every year.

In the Chinese bazaar are hundreds of small shops in which a miscellaneous collection of hardware and dry goods are to be found, and where many things are sold wonderfully cheap. You may buy gimlets at a penny each, white cotton thread at four balls for a halfpenny, and penknives, corkscrews, gunpowder, writing-paper, and many other articles as cheap or cheaper than you can purchase them in England. The shopkeeper is very good-natured; he will show you everything he has, and does not seem to mind if you buy nothing. He bates a little, but not so much as the Klings, who almost always ask twice what they are willing to take. If you buy a few things of him, he will speak to you afterwards every time you pass his shop, asking you to walk in and sit down, or take a cup of tea, and you wonder how he can get a living where so many sell the same trifling articles. The tailors sit *at* a table, not *on* one; and both they and the shoe-makers work well and cheaply. The barbers have plenty to do, shaving heads and cleaning ears; for which latter operation they have a great array of little tweezers, picks, and brushes. In the outskirts of the town are scores of carpenters and blacksmiths. The former seem chiefly to make coffins and highly painted and decorated clothes-boxes. The latter are mostly gun-makers, and bore the barrels of guns by hand, out of solid bars of iron. At this tedious operation they may be seen every day, and they manage to finish off a gun with a flint lock very handsomely. All about the streets are sellers of water, vegetables, fruit, soup, and agar-agar (a jelly made of sea-weed), who have many cries as unintelligible as those of London. Others carry a portable cooking-apparatus on a pole balanced by a table at the other end, and serve up a meal of shell-fish, rice, and vegetables for two or three halfpence; while coolies and boatmen waiting to be hired are everywhere to be met with.

In the interior of the island the Chinese cut down forest trees in the jungle, and saw them up into planks; they cultivate vegetables, which they bring to market; and they grow pepper and gambir, which form important articles of export. The French Jesuits have established missions among these inland Chinese, which seem very successful. I lived for several weeks at a time with the missionary at Bukit-tima [Bukit Timah], about the centre of the island, where a pretty church has been built and there are about 300 converts....

My friend at Bukit-tima was truly a father to his flock. He preached to them in Chinese every Sunday, and had evenings for discussion and conversation on religion during the week. He had a school to teach their children. His house was open to them day and night. If a man came to him and said, 'I have no rice for my family to eat today,' he would give him half of what he had in the house, however little that might be. If another said, 'I have no money to pay my debt,' he would give him half the contents of his purse, were it his last dollar. So, when he was himself in want, he would send to some of the wealthiest among his flock, and say, 'I have no rice in the house,' or 'I have given away my money, and am in want of such and such articles.' The result was that his flock trusted and loved him, for they felt sure that he was their true friend, and had no ulterior designs in living among them.

A. R. Wallace, *The Malay Archipelago: The Land of the Orang-Utan, and the Bird of Paradise. A Narrative of Travel, with Studies of Man and Nature*, Macmillan and Co., London, 1869, Vol. I, pp. 31–6.

21
An Early Singapore Photographer

JOHN THOMSON
1862

The Scotsman, John Thomson, travelled extensively in Asia during the 1860s, and wrote a number of books about his experiences. He was one of the most celebrated of the nineteenth-century traveller-photographers, and his Illustrations of China and its People, *published in four volumes between 1873 and 1874, is now regarded as a classic of early Asian photography. He arrived at Singapore on the P&O mail steamer* Emeu *in 1862, not 1861 as stated in his book, and set up as a photographer with his watchmaker brother in Beach Road. He led a largely itinerant life in pursuit of his profession, travelling in the Malay Peninsula, Thailand, Cambodia, and China, before returning in 1872 to England, where 14 years later he was appointed photography instructor to the Royal Geographical Society.*

WHEN I first saw the settlement in 1861 I was startled by the appearance of the European town, and since that time it has been yearly registering its substantial progress in steadily increasing rows of splendid docks, in bridges, in warehouses, and in government edifices. During these few years it has passed through strange vicissitudes of fortune. At one time the harbour and roads were crowded with square-rigged ships, Chinese junks, and Malay prahus. Now, were we to take these as the true indications of the trade of the port, we should at once conclude that its commerce had rapidly declined, for comparatively few sailing craft are to be seen there at any season of the year. But we must bear in mind that within that period the march of progress (though almost imperceptible to those who have dwelt continuously in these distant regions) has been rapid and startling in its results.

A submarine cable has brought Singapore within a few hours of London, while the opening of the Suez Canal, and the establishment of new steam navigation companies engaged in the China trade, have, to a great extent, done away with the fleets of clipper-built ships that formerly carried the produce from China and Singapore, by the long Cape route, to England. In the same way the absence of Chinese junks may be accounted for by increased facilities afforded to native, as well as foreign trade, through steam navigation in the China seas....

The trade of Singapore, save in times of unusual depression, continues steadily to advance, and since the transfer of the Straits Settlements to the Colonial Office, their commerce is reported to have increased twenty-five per cent.

In Commercial Square—the business centre of Singapore, where buyers and sellers most do congregate—the visitor will find men of widely different types, and a great variety of nationalities; among them all, perhaps, the most conspicuous is the dark statuesque-looking Kling from the Malabar coast, motionless beside his gharry, or darting out from the deep shade of the trees to present his active little pony and neat conveyance before some warehouse, which he has long been watching with a hawk's eye in the hope of a hire. Half-a-dozen at least of his fellow-countrymen crowd up as quickly to the spot as he, and vent their disappointment in noisy gabble, when one more lucky than they rattles down the road with the prize; a pleasure party, perhaps, arrayed in white, and making the most of the short time at their command in a survey of the beauties of the island, which are neither few nor far between....

Commercial Square is made up of buildings both old and new. There are the shops, the stores, the banking-houses, and the merchants' offices. There Europeans and Chinese pursue their various occupations. But the rows of new buildings, with their colossal proportions, cast a cool shade over the less assuming, antique, green-venetianed structures, erected in 'the good old days', in times when the residents might hear once in six months from home, and when two or three successful shipments of produce from the 'spice islands' might bring a princely fortune to their proprietor. 'Those were good times indeed,' said a worthy but unfortunate old merchant to me. 'We lived then above our offices, a small but a very happy community. Now we might almost as well live in London as here; steam and telegraph bring us daily into communication with the old world. Our Sundays are not our own. By night and by day we are at work, writing for the mail.' His words fell little short of the truth....

Let us return for a stroll round the square, peeping as we pass through the open doors of the bank. Here our ears are almost deafened by the interminable jingle of dollars as they are rung and weighed, or counted by practised Chinese schroffs.* Further on is a huge store, and the name of its proprietor, 'Boon Eng', painted on an imposing array of signboards.

Boon Eng himself accosts you, and invites you to inspect his varied assortment of the choicest European wares. He suggests that you should be good enough to sample his sherry, or 'eau-de-vie', as they are of number one 'brands', while his stationery, hosiery, and saddlery, are, as he assures you, by the best English manufacturers.

A fine specimen of the Anglo-Chinese shopkeeper is Boon; tall, and portly withal; but while he courts your patronage, you find yourself instinctively turned towards the splendid carriage and pair which has just drawn up at his door; and your surprise is great when Boon Eng himself—for it is just closing time—lights a cigar, steps into the vehicle, and is driven swiftly off by his Malay coachman to some pleasant villa in the country....

In Singapore the Chinese far outnumber the Malays, and therefore they hold a more important position than in Penang, where the Malayan population is in excess. Were any serious outbreak to occur among the Singapore Chinese, I believe it could be suppressed most easily by arming the Malays, for they make first-class fighting men, or else by setting the members of one Chinese faction against the members of another. There are at the present time a number of Chinamen who fill responsible positions. One is an unofficial member of the Legislative Council, others are justices of the peace, and others again hold the opium and spirit farms. Many more own extensive tracts of cultivated land, or have

*Money changer or banker.

Chinese merchants, from J. Thomson, *The Straits of Malacca, Indo-China and China or Ten Years' Travels, Adventures and Residence Abroad*, Sampson Low, Marston, Low, & Searle, London, 1875.

large capital invested in commerce, and it is obviously the interest of such personages as these to promote peaceful and industrious habits among the lower orders of their countrymen.

If we knew nothing of Chinese clanship and Chinese guilds, we should think it strange that the wealthier Chinamen are rarely made the victims of the great gang robberies that, during my time, used frequently to occur. These robberies are perpetrated by bands of ruffians numbering at times as many as a hundred strong, who surround and pillage a house that is always the residence of a foreigner. Chinese thieves are thorough experts at their profession, adopting the most ingenious devices to attain their infamous ends. I recollect a burglary which once took place at a friend's house, when the thief found his way into the principal bedroom, and deliberately used up half a box of matches before he could get the candle to light. His patience being rewarded at last, he proceeded with equal coolness in the plunder of the apartment, not forgetting to search beneath the pillow, where he secured a revolver and watch. These Chinese robbers are reported to be able to stupify their victims by using some narcotic known only to themselves. I have no doubt this was done in the case just referred to, by the agency of the Chinese house-servants, who perhaps introduced the drug to my friend's bed....

The Singapore residents have devised many amusements for themselves. They have their clubs, their bowling-alleys and fives' courts, and their race-course. Picnics are numerous, and the frequent gatherings at private houses are pleasantly diversified by performances at the Theatre, and concerts in the Town Hall.

There used also to be a sporting club, and more than once I have been out tiger-hunting with its members, but I never encountered anything more formidable than a deer. Singapore has a great name for tigers; however, I never saw but one in its native jungle, during three years' residence on the island....

There are a few Malay workmen in Singapore. One of these, a certain 'Tukang Timbago', or worker in brass, whose shop I used to visit, was a maker of rice-bowls, teapots, and spirit-flasks. His mode of casting the brass was most ingenious, differing from any plan which I have seen employed elsewhere. His patterns were minutely made on an instrument resembling a potter's wheel; on this he placed a ball of beeswax, which, in a few minutes, he spun up with his fingers into the form of the vessel he was about to cast; by this time the material had become exceedingly thin. If the vessel was to have a narrow mouth, he made his wax model in two halves, which he afterwards joined together. This done, he next fixed on small cylinders of wax, designed to form ducts for the molten metal. After completing the wax model, he proceeded to cover it with a coating inside and outside of fine soft clay, which he followed up with a second coating when the first was dry, and by continuing this process the whole was at length enveloped in a mass of clay, which was then baked hard in an oven, and the whole of the melted wax model allowed to flow out of the ducts, leaving a most perfect mould inside the clay. A vessel cast by this method presents a wonderfully smooth surface, and is quite true, and ready for the wheel on which it is turned for use. The extreme thinness, trueness, and smoothness of the casting surpassed anything I had ever seen before....

J. Thomson, *The Straits of Malacca, Indo-China and China or Ten Years' Travels, Adventures and Residence Abroad*, Sampson Low, Marston, Low, & Searle, London, 1875, pp. 53–7, 64–5, 72, 75.

22
In Search of Health

WILLIAM WALKER
1864

William Walker arrived at Singapore aboard the P&O steamer Emeu *in April 1864 on his way from India to Java to recover his health. Unlike his predecessor, Charles Walter Kinloch in 1852 (Passage 18), he had visited Singapore many years earlier, shortly after it was founded, when he was an officer on the 12-gun brig* Nautilus*. He noted the changes, including St Andrew's Cathedral, which was erected between March 1856 and January 1862, when it was consecrated by Bishop Cotton of Calcutta. It was built with Indian convict labour to a design by Lieutenant-Colonel Ronald Macpherson of the Madras Artillery, who is said to have reproduced something of the character of Netley Abbey in Hampshire. A monument was erected to him in the compound of the Cathedral after his death in 1869.*

WE arrived here on the 30th April after a thirty-seven hours' run from Penang, in the P. and O. Co.'s good ship *Emeu*, Captain Eastly, and a better ship or captain I never sailed in or with. The last time I was in Singapore was in 1821, at which time it was a mere fishing village, and I do not recollect that it then had one pucka-built house. Now it rivals Bombay in its public buildings, and quite equals it in the commodiousness of its merchants' offices, excels it in the palatial style of its hotels, and extent of roads. But it owes much of its superiority in roads to convict labour.

I will, however, say something about its harbour, which is a deep bay, enclosed in a sweep of land to about three-fourths of a circle, with the town lying in the bottom of the bay. On the north side is a small detached island where ships can careen. Docks are about to be built. A little on the south side of the pocket of the bay is a small river navigable for cargo-boats for eight miles, but for smaller craft to a much greater distance. It is this little river which has had a large share in administering to the vast commercial prosperity of the place. The mouth of this river is protected by batteries; there is also an intrenched battery and barracks on the top of a hill

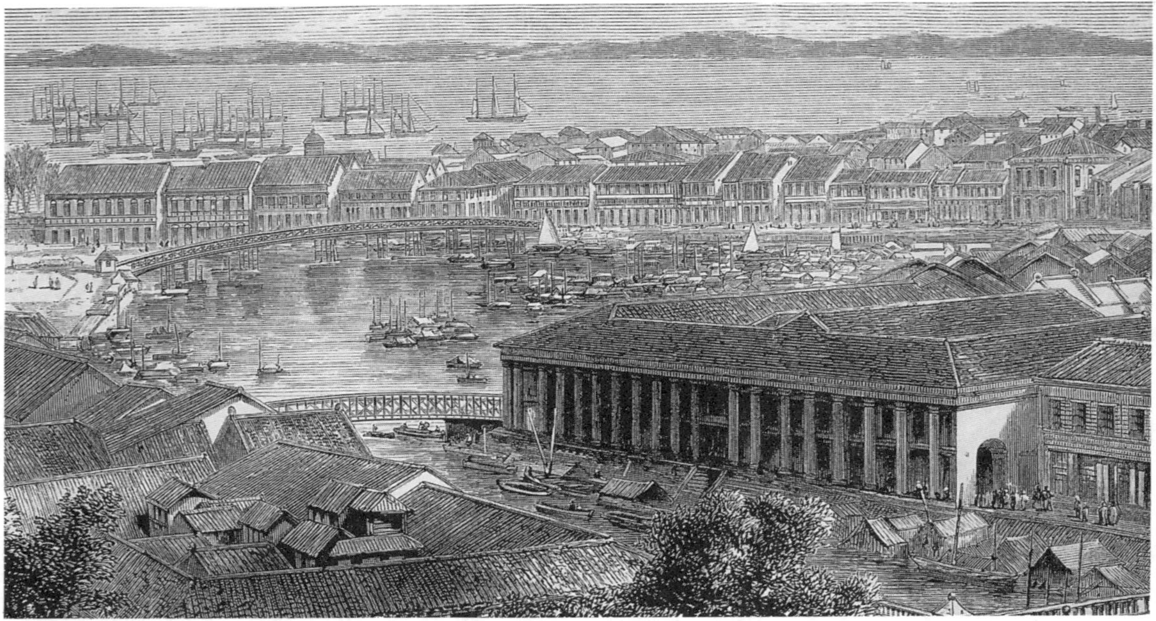

View of the Singapore River from Fort Canning, 1866, from Albert S. Bickmore, *Travels in the East Indian Archipelago*, D. Appleton and Company, New York, 1869.

immediately at the base of the town, on which is the mail signal-staff and night-light, for a clear entrance-guide into the bay. While I was at Singapore, there were in the roadstead generally about forty square-rigged sailing vessels and ten steamers. The batteries I have mentioned are about to be abandoned for other sites not likely to draw an enemy's fire on the town as those under reference would do....

It has been suggested that in the event of war, the whole mercantile marine of the port might lay in New Harbour in defiance of an enemy's fleet. This may be a good plan enough when the entrances to the Strait are defended by powerful batteries; otherwise, at present, two frigates might go into the Strait, with the wind northerly, and by setting fire to one end of the crowded mass of shipping, burn every one of them. Singapore, being a free port, has only a little chowky-looking place for a custom-house, and that even I never saw unlocked. Besides the mercantile houses along the banks of the river, there is a large place called Mercantile Square, around which are established all the principal houses of general business, and which the river pretty nearly separates from the private part, which lies on the north, or left bank. The communication across the river is by a wrought-iron box-girder bridge, which spans from side to side without intermediate support....

The most conspicuous of the public buildings is the new Town Hall, built close to the entrance of the river. It is in the Italian style, and has a most imposing appearance notwithstanding that the style is totally unsuited to this climate of fiery sun and beating squalls of rain. Its front is recessed back by advancing the side wings; the back face is flush with the entrance on the east side, where, to shut out the blinding sun and rain, a galvanized iron sloping portico or verandah has been put up. I got a peep through the Venetian doors of the principal hall, the ceiling of which was being decorated with considerable taste in compartments, with gilded pineapples at the intersections of the squares. Near it is the Courthouse, but which possesses no architectural feature. In front of these two buildings is a long enclosed strip of Esplanade facing, and close to the sea beach; it is a quarter of a mile long and one hundred yards broad, with a road on each side—that on the east following the curve of the bay, while the western road gives access to the hotels and other buildings which abut on this road. Among these is the Gothic Episcopalian Church of St. Andrew. The architect and builder is Colonel [R.] Macpherson, R.E., then Executive Engineer of the Straits Settlements, but who is now resident member of the Council of Penang (which means governor). If he had done no other service than the designing and building of this church, he would have well deserved the distinction of having left an imprint of usefulness to his generation....

Hotels are plentiful here, but their cookery is so filthy, oily, and greasy, that a man may starve before he touches a bit that is put before him. I put up at the Esperance Hotel, where I found this abominable cookery. The rooms are all nicely furnished, and the beds, although hard as a stone, are all very clean. I paid for the rooms four dollars a day, and my stay of twenty days produced a bill of 100 dollars less a few cents. This did not include board or wine. Although the charges are high for everything, the accounts are kept with scrupulous exactness and honesty. In a word, they don't follow the practice of *double entry.* This hotel has a stock-farm for the supply of their table, but I don't think it can be well-attended to, as the meat, with a few exceptions, is anything but good. The reader must understand that these lands, 'refreshed by frequent showers', and covered with green grass, cannot rear stock, and all (Ceylon, Penang, Malacca, Singapore, Java) have to import their bullocks and sheep. What is wanting in Singapore is an hotel where our countrymen can get their meals without being poisoned with grease in every dish put upon the table.

T. [Walker, W.] Cringle, *Jottings of an Invalid in Search of Health, Comprising a Run Through British India and a Visit to Singapore and Java*, Times of India Office, Bombay, 1865, pp. 158–61.

23
European Society

JOHN CAMERON
1865

In a strict sense, John Cameron was not a traveller to Singapore, but was the Editor of the Straits Times. *However, his account of European society in Singapore is so accurate and complete, that it has to be included to show the social order that the ordinary traveller encountered on his arrival in the mid-nineteenth century. Cameron had been a master mariner before he settled in Singapore in 1861, and he remained there until his death 20 years later. He took an active part in local affairs, and wrote the first local play to be produced in Singapore,* Boots at the Swan, *which was performed to great acclaim in 1861.*

SOCIETY may be said to be composed of the chief Government officials, the merchants and bankers with their assistants and clerks—the lawyers, the doctors, and the military—at least, any of those positions *prima facie* give the necessary social status. Unfortunately however, here as elsewhere, circumstances occasionally combine to render the best of these positions unavailing, and it is not always owing to the faults of those who are excluded, but sometimes to their misfortunes. One of the chief of these impediments appears to be an insuperable, though a somewhat over-sensitive objection taken to all who are descended in any way from the people of India, no matter how remote the descent; and it has happened more than once at a ball, that one lady has refused to dance opposite another because her *vis-à-vis* was slightly darker than herself in complexion. There can be no real necessity for such extreme sensibility as this.

It is to the merchants chiefly that Singapore is indebted for the introduction of its very expensive, though very pleasant style of hospitality. Their dinners are affairs of every week; they possess the charm of being at once magnificent and unrestrained, and they do much to maintain a spirit of emulation in household luxuriance. It is wonderful how perfect, too, is the knowledge possessed of the measure of hospitality of each house, and how soon new arrivals and visitors become acquainted with the comparative degrees of excellence in this respect. The discreet bachelor scarcely allows a week after his landing to pass by before he makes his calls upon the residents; and it is remarkable how closely they follow in the ascertained order of hospitality. The military, however, have the credit, and with every appearance of justice, of being the most accurate and rapid in their discovery of this desirable information. They scent the quarry from afar off, and come down upon it with singularly good success. In addition to household hospitality, picnics to various parts of the island are of frequent occurrence.... A few public balls, too, are scattered throughout the year—on the occasion of the races, of the opening of a public building, or the arrival or departure of some important personage.

But even the ordinary style of living in Singapore may be set down as luxurious, and this to a degree that could not well be indulged at home on similar means. Any distinction, too, in this respect between one class and another is merely of degree. All have alike that exemption from the necessity of positive exertion in domestic concerns, which a large supply of native labour gives. There is also an abundance of what at home would be termed rare delicacies, and with which even on the spot, the taste never completely palls. Neither are the substantials of the table so expensive as to render an economy of these necessary. The tables of the wealthiest are to be distinguished from those of the poorest, rather by the lavish supply of European preserves and condiments—and, of course, by a draft from a choicer and more extensive cellar, than by any greater abundance or variety of dishes. Again, every one has his stable—though the poor man may have but one steed, and the rich man a dozen.

To give a correct idea of the everyday life of the European it is necessary rather to distinguish between the unmarried and the married, than between the man of narrow and the man of extended means. Most of the bungalows, as I have before mentioned, are about two miles from town; nearly all, at least, are within hearing range of the 68-pounder gun on Fort Canning, the discharge of which each morning at five o'clock ushers in the day. This is the accepted signal of all old residents to start from bed, the younger however, usually indulge in an extra half-hour's slumber. Still, six o'clock generally sees all dressed and out of doors, to enjoy a couple of miles walk or ride through the lovely country roads, in the delicious coolness of morning, before the sun's rays become disagreeably powerful....

On coming home from these morning rounds, the custom is to get into loose, free and easy attire, generally baju* and pajamas. A cup of coffee or tea, with biscuit or bread-and-butter and fruit, is then consumed, and the next two hours spent in reading, writing, or lolling about in the verandahs which front each apartment of a house. I have said reading, writing, or lolling about; but, more correctly speaking, the time is devoted to a combination of the first and the last. In the daily avocation of most, the pen is pretty actively handled; and unless at mail times, or by those of a literary turn of mind, it is seldom taken up out of office. Reading is generally accomplished in the extremely reclining posture for which the verandah chairs of Singapore are so admirably adapted; and no doubt a deal of 'quiet contemplation' must be gone through in the same attitude, in fact, perhaps, more than is generally conceded. The 'dolce far niente' has its charms here as well as elsewhere, and what is more, it has a good excuse.

At half-past eight the breakfast dressing gong or bell is sounded. A gentleman's toilette in this part of the east is not an elaborate one, and half an hour is ample time for its completion. The bath is its chief feature. Attached to the dressing-room of each bedroom in almost all houses is a bath-room, with brick-tiled floor, containing a large bathing jar holding about sixty or seventy gallons of water. The orthodox manner of bathing is to stand on a small wooden grating close to the jar, and with a hand bucket to dash the water over the body. This is by no means such an unsatisfactory method as to the uninitiated it may appear. The successive shocks to the system which are obtained by the discharge of each bucketful of water, seems to have a much more bracing effect than that of one sudden and continued immersion. Every gentleman has his native boy or body servant, whose sole duty it is to attend upon him personally. While bathing, these boys lay out their master's apparel for the day; so that on coming from the bath a gentleman has little trouble to

*A loose fitting coat usually opening down the front.

get himself attired. As to shaving the process is generally performed by itinerant Hindoo barbers, who for the small charge of a dollar or a dollar and a half per month come every morning round to the residences of their customers. The charge is so small, and the saving in trouble so great, that almost all avail themselves of the convenience.

The universal breakfast hour is nine o'clock, and when the bell then rings the whole household assemble, and should there be ladies of the number this is the first time of their appearance. Singapore breakfasts, though tolerably substantial and provided with a goodly array of dishes, are rarely dwelt over long, half an hour, being about the time devoted to them. A little fish, some curry and rice, and perhaps a couple of eggs, washed down with a tumbler or so of good claret, does not take long to get through and yet forms a very fair foundation on which to begin the labours of the day. After breakfast the conveyances drive round to the porch or portico and having received their owners hasten in to town. No matter how many may reside together, each bachelor has generally his own 'turn-out'; and for half an hour every morning the two bridges leading across the river into town present an endless string of these rather motley vehicles—by no means an uninteresting spectacle. On the whole both the private conveyances and horses of Singapore are creditable to it, though the same cannot be said for the miserable pony hack-gharries that are let out on hire. A large number of horses are brought up from Australia, not less I should say than 100 each year, and all find a sale at what must be remunerative prices. None are ever exported again, and where they all go to it is difficult to conjecture, for the European population who chiefly make use of them increases but slowly, and yet horseflesh is not subject to greater mortality here than elsewhere. The climate seems to agree well with them; they grow fat and sleek and live long, though they can scarcely go through the same amount of work as in their native country; each horse has its groom and grass-cutter, and probably the additional attention they receive compensates for the exhausting temperature.

Arrived in town, ten minutes or a quarter of an hour are usually spent in going the rounds of the square to learn the news of the morning. These commercial square gatherings are quite a characteristic of the place and of the community, and whatever channels they may open to the flow of local gossip, or it might even be scandal, yet they are so far useful that they serve the purpose of an open air and non-commercial exchange. Differences of position are in most cases left behind in office, and all meet here on a footing of equality, or if there is any ascendancy at all it is that which is obtained by the readiest wit or perhaps by the greatest measure of self-assurance. As scarcely a day passes without the arrival of a steamer with news from England, China, India, or from some interesting point in the neighbourhood, there is always ample material for an animated exchange of ideas and information on leading topics, whether they be European politics, the war in America, the position of affairs in China, the combined action at Japan, the affairs of India, Java, Borneo, the administration of the local Government, or the condition and prospects of the adjacent markets.

This sort of congress takes place between the first arrival in town and ten or half-past ten o'clock. At that hour business has commenced and continues in full force till tiffin time, or one o'clock; and certainly it is gone through in quite as smart and active a manner as at home. The climate, though it may produce a greater languor in the evening, has apparently no such effect during the day. There is not much out-of-door bustle; but still when occasion requires the folks post about the square under the midday sun at a lively pace and with apparent impunity.

Tiffin time does not bring the luxurious abandonment to the table which it does in Java; people in Singapore are more moderate in their indulgence, yet some show of a meal is in most cases made; a plate of curry and rice and some fruit or it may be a simple biscuit with a glass of beer or claret. Half an hour's relaxation too is generally indulged in, and as the daily newspaper comes out about this hour, there is a goodly flocking either to the exchange or the public godowns in the square for a perusal of it.

Two o'clock is the exchange hour, and though I do not think there is really much intercommunication on commercial subjects, yet as a rendezvous and a place where the leading men of the mercantile world can have an interchange of ideas even on irrelevant matters, it has the good effect of promoting and maintaining a more general intimacy than might otherwise prevail. Unlike the chamber of commerce, from which it is distinct, the exchange as a body assumes no political influences, and is thus no doubt saved many a humiliating experience which it has fallen to the lot of the former body to encounter. The exchange is rather distinguished for its hearty and mixed co-operation in all that tends to ameliorate or enliven the condition of life in the settlement.

Business hours are not particularly severe, and by half-past four or five o'clock most of the mercantile houses have got through their work. But only a few proceed direct home at this hour; the greater number, at least of the younger members of the community, resort to the fives-court or the cricket-ground on the esplanade. The former is an institution of long standing in Singapore; as far back as thirty years ago it was erected, and at no time since then has the interest taken in the game subsided. On the contrary, about two years ago it was found necessary to build another court out at Tanglin about two miles from town in the vicinity of the residences, so greatly had the number of members increased. The game is well-known at home, and I need not describe it further than to say that it is a kind of rackets, but that the hands instead of bats are used to play up the ball and that consequently the exercise is much more severe. It is really surprising, in a temperature seldom ranging at the hour the game is played below 82°, to see those who have gone through a fair day's work at the desk come here and doff their vests, coats, and shirts to an hour or an hour and a half of about the most severe exercise in which it is possible to engage; and this too in an unroofed building with the rays of the sun if not directly beating down, at least reflected in fierce glare from the whitewashed walls. And yet medical men attribute the extreme good health of the residents to this continued exercise indulged in, begun by the morning walk at sunrise and ending with cricket or fives at sunset. Cricket is of course precisely the same game in Singapore as it is at home.

But there are two evenings in the week when the whole European community may generally be seen upon the esplanade, whether or not they be fives or cricket-players, and these are band evenings, generally Tuesdays and Fridays. The band, which is that of the regiment on the station at the time, or from one of the men-of-war which occasionally visit the port, plays on a raised mound on the centre of the

The Padang, or Esplanade, by John Turnbull Thomson, 1851. (National Museum, Singapore)

esplanade green. The chains which protect the green on ordinary occasions are on these evenings let down, and carriages, horsemen, and pedestrians are alike admitted to the greensward. Gathered round the band in a tolerably broad circle are the beauty and fashion of the place. The ladies, to whom almost all the other outdoor amusements are denied, partake at least in this, and though the ruddy glow of the colder latitudes has fled from most cheeks, still there supervenes a languid softness which is more interesting and perhaps more beautiful. The pretty pale-faced European children too may on these occasions be seen tripping about in playfulness a little less boisterous, but quite as cheerful as is witnessed at home. The band plays from half-past five till half-past six, at which hour it is all but dark, when the carriages make for home in a long string, gradually falling off one by one as the various residences are reached.

Except on band nights however, most of the commercial and all of the official world retire home a little before six o'clock. Arrived there, probably a glass of sherry and bitters will anticipate the refreshing process of dressing for dinner. A slight difference as to dinner-hour prevails; some dine at half-past six, some at seven; the former however is the time most commonly adopted. There is one advantage here which is too seldom to be found in other parts of the world. Whatever may be the hour, a clock-work regularity and punctuality is observed, and this not with respect to dinner only, but with respect to all other meals. No doubt this regularity also has its share in the maintenance of the good health of the European community.

Dinner in Singapore is not the light airy meal which might reasonably be imagined from the nature of the climate; on the contrary, it is quite as substantial a matter of fact as in the very coldest latitudes. The difference is not that the substantials are fewer, but that the luxuries are more numerous. Indeed the everyday dinner of Singapore, were it not for the waving punkahs, the white jackets of the gentlemen, and the gauzy dresses of the ladies, the motley array of native servants, each standing behind his master's or mistress's chair, and the goodly display of argand lamps, might not unreasonably be mistaken for some more special occasion at home. Soup and fish generally both precede the substantials, which are of a solid nature, consisting of roast beef or mutton, turkey or capon, supplemented by side-dishes of tongue, fowl, cutlets, or such like, together with an abundant supply of vegetables, including potatoes nearly equal to English ones grown in China or India, and also cabbages from Java. The substantials are invariably followed by curry and rice which forms a characteristic feature of the tables of Singapore, and though Madras and Calcutta have been long famed for the quality of their curries, I nevertheless think that those of the Straits exceed any of them in excellence. There are usually two or more different kinds placed on the table, and accompanying them are all manner of sambals or native pickles and spices, which add materially to the piquancy of the dish.

During the progress of the substantials and of the curry and rice, the usual beverage is beer, accompanied by a glass or two of pale sherry. The good folks of Singapore are by no means inclined to place too narrow restrictions on their libations, and it has been found in the experience of older residents that a liberality in this respect conduces to good health and long life. Besides this the American Tudor Company keeps up a tolerably regular supply of ice, and as it is sold at three cents, or less than $1\frac{1}{2}$*d.* per lb., it is within the reach of all, and is an invariable adjunct to all beverages.

To curry and rice succeeds generally some sort of pudding or preserve, but sweets have not the same temptation here as at home. Very good cheese however is obtained in fortnightly supplies by the overland steamers, and, as good fresh butter is always to be had, this part of dinner is well enjoyed, accompanied as it is by no illiberal allowance of excellent pale ale. But it is in the luxuriance of the dessert perhaps more than anything else that the tables of Singapore are to be distinguished, and it is little wonder that it should be so; for there is no season of the year at which an abundance of fruit cannot be obtained. Pineapple may be considered the stock fruit of the island, and one or two splendid specimens of these generally adorn the table. There are plantains, ducoos, mangoes, rambutans, pomeloes, and mangosteens; the latter fruit is peculiar to the Straits of Malacca and to Java, and so great is its fame that to India or China no present or gift from Singapore is more acceptable than a basket of them. It is of a somewhat singular genus; it is round, of the size of a small orange, is covered with a thick woody purple bark in place of rind, which has to be cut or broken off, and inside are the snowy-white cloves of the pulp, sweet and with a very delicate but delicious flavour, unlike anything else I know of. But though dessert generally makes a finer display than any other part of dinner, it is not that to which most attention is directed. A cigar and a glass or two of sherry after the ladies are gone, and dinner is over.

Many of the residences have billiard-rooms attached, in which case the usual custom is to retire there after dinner. Where no billiard-room is within reach, a chat in the verandah, a little meditation, or perhaps a book passes the hours pleasantly enough until bedtime. And as dinner is seldom over before eight o'clock, and the usual hour for rest is ten, it is not a very long interval between them that has to be disposed of.

As I have remarked before I think it is to be regretted that the people of Singapore so determinedly set their faces against every sort of entertainment which does not include a dinner. I am quite sure that much of the after-dinner time, that is under the present system in a manner thrown away, might be more agreeably, and at the same time more profitably spent, if the custom were to set in that people should meet occasionally after dinner, and pass their evenings in the same sort of social intercourse as is usual at home, and in most other parts of the world.

Such is the everyday life at Singapore.

J. Cameron, *Our Tropical Possessions in Malayan India: Being a Descriptive Account of Singapore, Penang, Province Wellesley, and Malacca; Their Peoples, Products, Commerce, and Government*, Smith, Elder and Co., London, 1865, pp. 287–303.

24
Chinese Poor Taste

CHARLES CARELTON COFFIN
1867

The American journalist, Charles Carelton Coffin, was correspondent for the Boston Journal *during the American Civil War, and the Austro-Prussian War of 1866. In that year he and his wife began a journey round the world, leaving New York for London aboard the Cunard steamer* Persia, *and taking the Messageries Impériales Company's steamer* Euphrates *at Marseilles for Alexandria. After travelling overland to Suez they boarded the P&O steamer* Baroda *bound for India, and from Calcutta they sailed in the steamer* Clan Alpine *for Singapore, where they spent a few days before sailing to China, Japan, across the Pacific to California, and then overland to the eastern seaboard. During their two and a half years' circuit of the world, Coffin sent weekly letters for publication in the Boston* Journal, *and it was from these that he compiled his popular book,* Our New Way Round the World, *which contains a mine of information for others intending to travel round the world.*

IT is early morning when we steam into the harbor, feeling our way slowly along a passage that winds among numerous small islands. The main channel is farther south, but this up which we pass to the new harbor, though narrow, has deep water, and is navigable for large steamers....

Emerging from the network of islands, and making a wide sweep to avoid a coral reef, we have an opportunity of seeing the crescent-shaped harbor, filled with English and American vessels, which have stopped here for fresh supplies on their way to or from China. Several steamers are at anchor. One iron screw, just in from Manila, is taking in coal for her long stretch across the Indian Ocean round the Cape of Good Hope, and thence to Liverpool, under contract to make the distance between Manila and the Mersey in seventy days, or forfeit five dollars per ton for every day exceeding the time specified. Another steamer has its flag flying at the peak, as a signal for departure, and a few hours hence will be running down the coast of Sumatra for Batavia, three days distant.

The harbor is alive with boats,—junks just in from China, and Malay craft such as formerly were manned by pirates, ever on the watch for ships passing through the straits. Many a noble vessel lies beneath these waters, captured by them in years gone by. But piracy has been entirely suppressed in these seas, and this once dreaded section of the Indian Archipelago is now as free from the sea-rovers as the Atlantic....

The streets of the town are wide and straight; the houses and shops mainly of two stories, covered with tiles. The signs are in Chinese characters, and nearly every person we meet has a pigtail. The scenes are new and strange;—men with hats three feet in diameter, the crown running up to a point like a cupola, others tunnel-shaped, others like reversed wash-bowls; men, with a strip of blue cotton cloth round the loins, trip past, walking briskly, carrying buckets and baskets, tubs and pails, suspended from a light, springing bamboo laid across their shoulders. These are the market-men. Looking into the shops, we see all crafts and trades. There are shoemakers, joiners, carpenters, washermen, bakers; and opium saloons, reeking with sickening odors. We drive into the square where Europeans principally congregate, and find it laid out with shade-trees, flowering-shrubs, and gravelled walks, and surrounded by ware-houses. Young men from England are here to make their fortunes in trade. They are dressed in white pants and black jackets,—the orthodox business costume for this climate....

The public square is a pleasant business place, though business does not seem to be very lively. No one moves with vigor. The climate takes all energy out of a European in a short time. The merchants gather in groups beneath the grateful shade, and talk business and take things easily. In the side streets are numerous dram-shops for the sailors. The 'Jolly Tar', the 'Sailors' True Home', display the Stars and Stripes close beside the Cross of St. George....

The grounds around the English residences are tastefully laid out, and adorned with shrubs and flowers in great variety. Nowhere have we seen such profusion and richness of vegetation. It flourishes with such vigor that it is almost impossible to keep the gravelled walks and flower-beds free from grass and weeds.

'Don't fail to see the Chinaman's garden,' is the injunction of a gentleman on the steamer. Taking a carriage, we ride through the town, past the government buildings,—large and imposing edifices, looming grandly from the bay,—past two very pretty churches, and residences of merchants, surrounded by well-kept grounds, shaded with tropical trees, and beautified by gorgeous flowers of every hue. Upon the road we meet crowds of Chinese, going to or returning from market; some halting at the tea-shops to drink their favorite beverage, or at the opium saloons to whiff the fumes of the stupefying drug.

Never rode we through an avenue so beautiful as that leading to the 'Whampoa Gardens'. Stately palms, wild almonds, tall, feathery bamboos, and trees of unknown name, line the roadway, spreading out their branches overhead, their trunks wreathed with creeping plants. Orchids and wild heliotrope bloom in the thick hedges: shrubs, plants, vines, in endless variety, broad and narrow leaved, ovate, heart-shaped, trifoliate,—leaf and flowers filling the air with odors new and strange, and almost overpowering.

A ride of about two miles brings us to the residence of a Chinaman who has made a large fortune by trade at Singapore, and who, instead of returning to his native land, as most of his countrymen are in the habit of doing, has made this his permanent home. He loves floriculture, and has spent a great deal of money in fitting up his residence and the grounds around it. A tall fellow, with thin face, lantern-jaws, long pigtail, wearing a blue cotton tunic and flowing trousers and Chinese hat, escorts us through the grounds, to which we have free admission. The proprietor is sick, otherwise he would himself show us the rare tropical plants and flowers.

The grounds are not laid out in accordance with the rules of landscape gardening given by English and American florists. The premises contain a dozen acres,—gardens within gardens,—with arbors, tea-houses, and canals, and tanks stocked with goldfish. There are straight paths, winding walks, and labyrinths, a wonderful variety of tropical vegetation,—a place where the florist or botanist might find unspeakable pleasure. Our conductor brings us to a section of the grounds where dogs, dragons, hobgoblins, and crocodiles, with great goggle eyes, stare at us,—fashioned from a twining shrub, that is hedged in and clipped off, trained on wires, and thus tortured into fantastic shapes.

Passing through one of the tea-houses, we find that the proprietor has Italian vases, French clocks, Japanese carved work, windows of German stained glass, floors of English encaustic tiles, flower-pots from the potteries of his native land, arranged with little taste or order. A Chinaman's ideas of the artistic are grotesque. The pictures which we see on China-ware are excellent representations of Chinese art. They have not advanced beyond the child's plain surface drawing, and have no comprehension of the rules of perspective....

C. C. Coffin, *Our New Way Round the World*, Frederick Warne & Co., London, 1883, pp. 234–40.

25
Malays, Indians, and Chinese

CUTHBERT COLLINGWOOD
1866–1867

The author occupied the Chairs of Botany in the Royal Infirmary Medical School in Liverpool and Biology in the School of Science. He was also senior physician to the Liverpool Northern Hospital. In 1866–7 he undertook, with the sanction of the Admiralty, a scientific voyage for the study of marine zoology, especially sea and reef fauna, during the course of which he visited China, Formosa, Borneo, and Singapore. In his account of the island he refers to a subject which fascinated nineteenth-century travellers to Singapore—deaths caused by tigers. The first such death recorded was in 1831, and during the middle decades of the century many deaths occurred, mainly among Chinese and Malay cultivators, sometimes within a mile or two of the town. The Government offered financial rewards for every dead tiger brought in, ranging from $20 to $100, and it was claimed that the number of tigers in the island increased proportion-

ately to the reductions that the Government made in these rewards. The newspapers of the time are full of stories of tigers, true and exaggerated, but there is little doubt that they constituted a menace. Collingwood's reported allegation by officers at Fort Canning that murders by Chinese were sometimes disguised as attacks by tigers, was made as early as 1855 in a Calcutta newspaper, but it was dismissed in Singapore as being largely nonsense.

A Malay village is a common but picturesque and interesting feature of the neighbourhood of Singapore. Its situation and surroundings cannot fail to strike a stranger, and to be a matter of interest to the observant. These villages are always built upon platforms raised on wooden piles, either on the margin of the sea, or more commonly of rivers and creeks, or over mangrove swamps; and the water in all cases, at some period of the day, flows underneath their dwellings. It might be supposed that such damp situations would be unhealthy in the extreme; but such are always chosen by these people, who build clusters of wooden houses called *kampongs*, which are either approached in boats, or by a pathway of earth, raised above the

A Malay village, New (Keppel) Harbour, from *The Cruise of Her Majesty's Ship* Bacchante *1879–1882*, ed. J. N. Dalton, Macmillan and Co., London, 1886. (Antiques of the Orient, Singapore)

level reached by the rising water. A background of cocoanuts and bananas often adds beauty to the scene, and the dusky forms and faces moving about among the rickety dwellings, on the platforms, or paddling about in canoes, give it a curious semi-savage aspect. All the litter and dirt of the establishment is simply swept through the open cracks in the floor, and without further trouble is thus washed away by the tide; an arrangement which well suits the character of the indolent Malays, who lazily lie upon their backs on the platform, while the little naked children make dirt-pies, or paddle about in minute cock-boats; the women, meanwhile, listlessly shambling about on their household duties. Such a village has a wild and uncivilised appearance, and yet there are not unfrequently curious and incongruous signs of luxury visible. Outside some of these houses may be seen vases of flowers, well cared-for; and I have noticed here and there cushions laid out apparently for airing, whose ends were daintily embroidered....

The foreign (Eastern) residents in Singapore mainly consist of two rival races, widely different in dress, habits, and religion—viz., Klings, from the Coromandel coast of India; and Chinese. I say rival races, because they are both active and industrious, and compete with one another in the chief industrial occupations by which a livelihood can be obtained. The Klings are, indeed, the only people who can contest the field with the Chinese, and they do so notwithstanding many disadvantages....

The Kling women are dark beauties, finely made, and dressed in flowing robes, which conceal the whole figure down to the feet, but leave the arms bare to the shoulder. Their dress sits on them gracefully, and their ornaments give them an air of barbaric splendour. Armlets of gold are worn above the elbow, and bracelets of gold upon their arms; golden rings encircle their ankles, and several finger-rings glitter on their hands; heavy ear-rings hang pendent from their ears, and one side of the nostril is pierced to give passage to a gold nose-ring, more or less chased in front. These ornaments are not unfrequently all worn by one woman, and it appears to be a common practice to invest their money in these trinkets, so that a Kling woman carries a small fortune upon her person. But cases are not wanting in which this ostentatious display of wealth has excited the cupidity of miscreants who have murdered the woman for the sake of what she carries, and have ruthlessly torn the rings from her ears and nose, and wrested the armlets and anklets from off her limbs; and the wonder only seems to be that this does not more frequently happen. The little black Kling children of both sexes dispense with all clothing more commonly than the Malays.

The Klings are universally the hack-carriage (gharry) drivers, and private grooms (syces), and they also monopolise the washing of the clothes of the dressed community. The Singapore Dhobies, as they are termed, who are nearly all men, certainly produce whiteness in linen, but sadly at the expense of material. Standing in a stream beside a large flat stone, they rinse and soap the clothes, and then, instead of rubbing them in the fashion of Western laundresses, they dash them over their head repeatedly with great force, and with a loud sough, upon the stone, which, however rough it may be at first, is soon worn smooth by the contact of the unfortunate linen.

But besides this class, there are Klings who amass money as tradesmen and merchants, and become rich. I visited their silk shops, in the busy part of the town, kept by men who from their scanty and poor attire were scarcely distinguishable from coolies, but nevertheless had a balance at their bankers', and were in the habit of buying goods to the amount of thousands of dollars at a time from the merchants with whom they deal. One was pointed out to me who had just purchased for 5,500 dollars a small cocoa-nut plantation, which he was anxious to possess, simply because, since it adjoined his own property, he did not wish another to hold it. . . .

The Chinese inhabitants of Singapore have all the characteristics of Chinese elsewhere. They are the busy working population, who hive together like bees, performing the artizan duties necessitated by a large community, and other essential operations, of a nature which the more scrupulous Klings would disdain to lend their hands to. Street after street is crowded with these active and energetic Celestials, who here, as in China, have the spirit of centralisation and co-operation. One street contains none but blacksmiths toiling over their forges—another resounds with the saws and chips of a crowd of carpenters—a third with the dull blows of the stone-masons' mallets, &c. Each devotes itself to its own craft, and admits no interlopers, while all the inhabitants are busily engaged in effecting one common end,—and that is, to hoard up enough money to enable them to *cease work*, and return to their native district in China, there to pass the remainder of their days in a comfortable independence among their own people, and especially amidst their own family.

Besides these there are, in certain parts of the town, considerable numbers of Bugis people from Celebes, &c.,—tall and strong, wild-looking fellows, wearing a pair of short drawers and a rough cloth flung over the left shoulder like a plaid. They belong chiefly to the *prahus* or crafts which lie at the east side of the harbour, and may be generally seen loitering about at this end of the town out of mere curiosity, and strongly reminded me of the Lancashire operatives wandering about Liverpool, open-mouthed, on a holiday. Their vessels are ugly-looking, two-masted craft, with black and white longitudinal stripes, which trade with Singapore from all the islands of the Archipelago. Formerly there were many more of them, for while Singapore was a free port, all the Dutch ports required dues and levied imposts. The Dutch, however, learning wisdom, though late, freed their ports; and since then they have diverted great numbers of the Bugis prahus from the Singapore market, to which those which still repair thither bring gold-dust, tortoise-shells, ambergris, pearls, birds'-nests, turtles' eggs, sharks' fins, trepang, mother-of-pearl shells, and other curiosities of Eastern commerce.

The bungalows or residences of the European population are generally set in the midst of gardens or small plantations—pleasant habitations, surrounded with Betels and Bananas. They have, for the most part, an imposing look, for people in the East can not, or will not, live in small houses; and the open verandahs which nearly always run round the outside, make them look larger than they really are. For the most part such residences are exclusively occupied by Europeans, neither Malays nor Klings live in such expensive style; but certain wealthy Chinese exceptionally make a great show, and entertain in a style of costliness and refinement not surpassed by the most opulent English. Of these Mr Whampoa, who contracts with the Government for the supply of stores and provisions to Her Majesty's ships, is *facile princeps*. He is well known for his choice and elegant entertainments, and his mansion is surrounded with extensive gardens laid out in true Chinese style....

The native streets of Singapore consist of two-storied houses, with an arcade running along in front, narrow and more or less dilapidated, and blocked up with merchandise. In these the Chinese and Klings live side by side, the houses of the latter being usually less looked after and more ruinous. In their shops are often exposed European articles of the commonest kind and poorest quality, which, however, find a ready sale. In the outskirts of the town and less built-up streets the scene is interesting and picturesque. Tall and graceful Betel Palms, spreading Bananas and Cocoa-nuts, dense and feathery Bamboos and Casuarinas, bushy Screw-pines (Pandanus), handsome-leaved Bread-fruit and Jack trees (Artocarpus), Durians and Mangos, and other fruit-trees constitute the leading features of the vegetation. Mangroves twine their long, rib-like roots in marshy spots, and Melastomas, Heliotropes, sensitive plants, and luxuriant ferns characterise the drier spots. Amid these scenes the variously-costumed people are a never-ending study: the Chinese, generally ugly and dirty, with scanty clothing usually of a dirty colour, and nearly always with a load upon their shoulders,—the women, and often little girls, carrying an infant astride upon the hips; the Klings, erect, handsome, and picturesquely clad in bright and graceful garments; Malays, in many-coloured patterns, chewing betel-nut, and walking as though bound on a pleasure excursion; Hadjis, who have made the pilgrimage to Mecca, with yellow turbans on their heads; the crowds of little children nearly or quite naked, of all shades of colour, and grotesquely shaven; the half-castes, with a sprinkling of Europeans, altogether constitute an *ensemble* which the traveller from temperate climes cannot fail to regard with intense interest.

A great deal is said of the number of tigers which are supposed to infest Singapore. A recent writer estimates the deaths from these animals at 365 per annum, chiefly among Chinese cultivators of the Gambier plantations in the interior of the island. Residents at Singapore, however, always assured me that there was no danger whatever from them, and that they are never seen now. Indeed the officers at Fort Canning expressed their belief that many of the instances of disappearance of Chinese which were attributed to the ravages of tigers, were really cases of murder by other Chinese; and truly it would not be difficult in distant and secluded plantations for one man to secure the disappearance of another to whom he owed a grudge....

The Gambier plantations are very thick, the plants being placed very close together, and growing to the height of five or six feet, so that they form a jungle in themselves; and there is abundance of rank grass, which affords ample cover for tigers; but were so many persons killed as asserted, no Chinese could be induced to go and work in them. A very old resident in Singapore told me that he had long been in the habit of rambling about the jungle for weeks together, often penetrating five or six miles from the government roads, and yet he never saw or heard a tiger, though he has seen their tracks in his plantation. It is difficult to conceive what can induce tigers to cross over to Singapore; for although there are a few deer and plenty of pigs in the island, there is a much greater variety of game in the Johore peninsula. Can it be a taste for human flesh, which is more plentiful in the island?

An old guide-book stated that so numerous were the tigers that on the arrival of the steamers the passengers might see them come down to the water's edge to drink (salt water, of course). And it was a common statement that the island was *infested* with tigers. But, at the present day at least, one might walk all through the island without seeing a trace of them; and the *roads*, at all events, are perfectly safe, not only from tigers, but also from robbery or violence.

C. Collingwood, *Rambles of a Naturalist on the Shores and Waters of the China Sea: Being Observations in Natural History During a Voyage to China, Formosa, Borneo, Singapore, Etc., Made in Her Majesty's Vessels in 1866 and 1867*, John Murray, London, 1868, pp. 243–7, 249–54.

26
A Young American Traveller

FRANK VINCENT
1871

In 1871 the young American, Frank Vincent, began a series of travels that took him during the next 15 years to various countries of Asia, northern Europe, South and Central America, and Africa. He described his adventures in a number of books, and his travels in Asia in the most popular of his works, The Land of the White Elephant: Sights and Scenes in South-Eastern Asia *(New York, 1874). His initial contact with South-East Asia was Burma in April 1871, after which he travelled to Penang, Malacca, and Singapore, before going on to Thailand and Cambodia.*

WE engage a Malay *prow* to take us ashore, and are landed near the *Hotel d'Europe*, to which our good captain has recommended us. This hotel we find to be very large and comfortable, situated in the midst of beautiful gardens, facing 'the green', and commanding a fine view of the straits, the large island of Bintang in the distance, and the Chinese junks and foreign shipping in the harbour. Attached to the establishment, which is kept by a German, is that 'peculiar institution' an American bar-room, where California mixed drinks are served, and there is besides a 'regular down east' Boston Arctic soda-water fountain; a billiard-room; and a reading-room, where one will find papers and journals, in four or five languages, from New York, London, Bombay, Calcutta, Batavia, Hong Kong, Shanghae, Yokohama, and San Francisco....

During our stay at Singapore we received every kindness and attention from the American Consul, Dr Jewell, of Washington, D.C., who lived with his wife in the same hotel. Dr J. and his family are Mississippians by birth, education, and residence, but they remained faithfully loyal to the National Government during our late terrible civil war. The Doctor has been seventeen years in Washington, connected, in various capacities, with both the Treasury and Post-Master General's Departments. He had lived a little more than two years in Singapore, and was both able and willing to give us much valuable information.

One day we visited Fort Canning to obtain a general view of Singapore. This fort, built upon a small pyramid-shaped hill, about 200 feet in height, and just back of the town, mounts, among numerous guns of smaller calibre, some few 68-pounders, and is garrisoned by 300 British and 700 Sepoy troops....

The Governor's house is a large brick and stucco building on the summit of a little knoll, perhaps half a mile inland from Fort Canning. Were it not for its immense cupola it would be mistaken for a Government department or office of some kind, and, as it is, the second storey, composed entirely of arches and Venetian blinds, and the upper storey formed of pillars and Venetians, present a very ugly appearance. There are few trees about the house, so that it receives the entire force of both sun and rain, and, excepting only when a strong breeze is blowing, it must be a very uncomfortable residence.

The large Chinese temple of Singapore is worthy of a visit. It is situated in one of the principal streets, and consists of a plain stone house with most fantastic and curious adornments, having a court-yard in front and around open sheds. Before the entrance are two large stone tigers, in whose mouths held by the teeth, may be seen and felt, perfectly round, loose stones, so cut out by an ingenious Chinaman. Then there are bas-reliefs, and inscriptions, and figures carved upon the front of the building, while its pillars are encircled by enormous dragons. But it is in the supporting of the roof that the most lavish ornamentation is to be seen—the wood carving of gods, and animals, and flowers, and arabesques, all painted and gilded, being something wonderful.

F. Vincent, *The Land of the White Elephant: Sights and Scenes in South-Eastern Asia. A Personal Narrative of Travel and Adventure in Farther India, Embracing the Countries of Burma, Siam, Cambodia, and Cochin-China (1871–2)*, Harper & Brothers, New York, 1874, pp. 102–7.

27
Garden Delights

MARIANNE NORTH
1876

The English botanical artist, Marianne North, then aged 46, reached Singapore in January 1876, after travelling by way of California and Japan. She stayed in the colony for about a month before proceeding to Sarawak. Half of her stay in Singapore was at Government House, with the Governor of the Straits Settlements, Colonel (later Major-General) Sir William Francis Drummond Jervois, of the Royal Engineers. During her world travels Marianne North made over 800 paintings of plants and flowers, and these are now housed in a gallery at Kew Gardens. It is interesting that she mentions in her account of Singapore her fellow botanical artist, the Dutchwoman Bertha Hoola van Nooten, whose magnificent folio volume of flowers and fruits of Java was published in Brussels in 1863. She also mentions briefly her meeting with the Maharaja (later Sultan) of Johore, Abu Bakar (see Passage 38).

TWO more days brought us to Singapore, where I landed on the 19th of January 1876. I could barely hobble from the office of the hotel to my rooms at the other end of the building, through its lovely garden; but how delicious that still warm air was, with exquisite blue sky, lilac shadows, and white lights! The figures which squatted under the verandah and portico had a grace about them which I had never seen before, and their rich dark complexions were the real thing, and not white turned brown or yellow by fading or scorching. Their turbans, sashes, and draperies of pure colour, and the sprinkling of gold and silver, were in such perfect harmony with their skins. Many of them were simple bundles of white calico. It was such a pleasure to look at these figures that I could not even scold when they persecuted me to buy a hundred things I did not want. I found a lemon-tree close to my room, covered with tailor-ants which had sewn up the leaves into most ingenious nests, the pretty flowers opening their sweet petals close to them.

One of my windows was quite blocked up by a great bread-fruit tree covered with fruit as big as melons, with leaves two feet in length, gloriously glossy, and I set myself at once to make a study of it. While at this work Mrs S. [C. Stringer], the banker's wife, and her father, Major MacN. [J. F. A. McNair], came to see me. The former insisted on my moving at once to her comfortable house outside the town. Like all the houses of Singapore, it stood on its own little hill, none of these hills being more than two hundred feet above the sea; but they were just high enough to catch the sea-breezes at night, and one could sleep with perfect comfort, though only three degrees from the equator. This house had belonged to the House of Guthrie for two generations, and was surrounded by every sort of fruit-tree. Of these there were perhaps more in Singapore than in all the rest of the world. The lovely Mangosteen was just becoming ripe, and the great Durian, which I soon learnt to like, under the teaching of the pretty little English children, who called it 'Darling Durian'.

No garden could have been more delighted in than that one was by me. Every day I was sure to find some new fruit or gorgeous flower to paint, Mrs S. working beside me all the hot day through in her deliciously airy upper rooms. Then we drove out among the neighbouring gardens in the late afternoon and evening, and went to bed soon after dinner; for Mr S. and the other gentlemen came home far too tired after their days in the hot bank in the town for playing at company or sitting up at night. They had a delightful little monkey called Jacko, who considered that all dogs were made to be teased; and it was strange to see how the big creatures submitted and humoured it. This monkey was a bad sitter, and seemed to have a malicious pleasure in throwing itself upside-down whenever I looked at it. Then if I scolded, it held out its paw to shake and be friends. There was also an ourang-outang who used to be led in by the hand by the Malay butler. They were exactly alike. Both had the most depressed expression, which the small one never varied. The big one grinned sometimes,—when he looked even more like a monkey than he was before....

I was taken to see a neighbouring lady one day, who told me that a few years ago she was sitting in her central room at work when the roof suddenly came down on her. The white ants had eaten the wood of the supporting beams all round the nails, till the whole gave way without warning and crushed the house; but she and her children were all dug out unhurt, having been under the gable or cone of the roof, which kept its shape. Houses at Singapore are generally built with a high central cone and a windowless room under it lighted from the other rooms, with no ceiling between it and the high-peaked roof, under which are more lights and ventilation. Those rooms were always too dark for painting in, and too airless for my taste. I prefer hot air to none, and could never get into the tropical habit of sleeping while the precious daylight lasted.

Mrs S.'s verandah was full of rare plants; orchids, caladiums, and other exquisite things. On one, *Ficus Benjamina*, were planted some score of phalœnopsis in full flower, like strings of white butterflies hovering in the air with every breath of wind. One day we went to have tea with Mr Wampoa, the famous Chinaman, whose hospitality and cordiality to the English have been so well known for half a century in the Straits. He showed us all his curiosities; but his garden was to me the great attraction, rare orchids hanging to every tree, and the great *Victoria regia* in full bloom in his ponds, as well as the pink and white lotus, and blue and red nymphæas. Many of his plants were cut into absurd imitations of human figures and animals, to me highly objectionable, but amusing to the children. He had also several live creatures and birds of great beauty. He showed us a tortoise from Siam with six legs. The hinder ones it only used when trying to get up a very steep bank or steps, propping itself up with them, while it struggled on with the four front ones. The Siamese cat was a remarkable little creature, coloured like a fox, and might possibly have been a mixture of the two animals originally. It had sky-blue eyes, and was very shy. Mrs S. had one which followed her about and slept in her room.

The Maharajah of Johore, a near neighbour and great friend of her husband's, came to dine and play at billiards with him in a black velvet coat with diamond buttons, worn over the usual Malay petticoat or Sarong. He wore a rich turban on his head, and spoke good English. After a fortnight I went to stay at Government House with Sir William and Lady Jervoice [Jervois]. It was a huge building with fine halls and reception-rooms, but very little bedroom accommodation. It stood on the highest hill of the district, and overlooked all the town of Singapore, its bay and islands, and miles of the richest country covered with woods and cocoa-nuts. Close under my window was a great india-rubber tree with large shiny leaves and fantastic hanging roots. In the front of the garden was a gorgeous tree of *Poinciana regia* blazing with scarlet blooms. I immediately begged a branch and hung it up to paint, but made a most absurd mistake. I placed it the wrong way up. It was stupid, but I was consoled afterwards when I found that that clever Dutch lady, Madame van Nooten, had actually published a painting of the poinciana growing in the same topsy-turvy way! Nothing approaches this tree for gorgeousness; the peculiar tender green of the acacia-like leaves enhances the brilliancy of its vermilion tints. The amherstia was also in great beauty in the same royal garden, with scarlet pods and delicate rosy-lilac young leaves. The beaumontia creeper was there too, with its white waxy bells and beautifully embossed leaves. It was curious to see how little the English people cared for these glories around them. Lawn-tennis and croquet were reigning supreme in Singapore, and little else was thought of after business was over. Lady Jervoice and her daughters were exceedingly kind to me, and played Mozart deliciously of an evening, while Sir William was a most genial host.

Marianne North, *Recollections of a Happy Life: Being the Autobiography of Marianne North*, Macmillan & Co., London, 1892, Vol. I, pp. 231–5.

28
Fruit, Fish, and Poultry Markets

ANNIE BRASSEY
1877

Annie, or Anna, Brassey was the wife of the wealthy Thomas Brassey, first Earl Brassey, who was for many years Liberal Member of Parliament for Hastings, Civil Lord of the Admiralty, Parliamentary Secretary to the Admiralty, and producer of The Naval Annual. *She assisted him in his political career, and accompanied him on cruises in their*

3-masted topsail-yard schooner Sunbeam, *in which they sailed round the world in 1876–7. They called at Singapore for three days in March 1877, during which the schooner filled her 80-ton bunker with coal at the Tanjong Pagar docks. Lady Brassey's book,* A Voyage on the Sunbeam, *which was published in London in 1878, was a best seller, and went through many editions. She died nine years later, aged 47, near Brisbane, Australia, while making a cruise for the recovery of her health.*

WE were off Singapore during the night. At 5 a.m. the pilot came on board and took us into Tangong Pagar to coal alongside the wharf. We left the ship as soon as possible, and in about an hour we had taken forty-three tons of coal on board and nearly twenty tons of water. The work was rapidly performed by coolies. It was a great disappointment to be told by the harbour-master that the Governor of the Straits Settlement and Lady Jervoise [Jervois] were to leave at eleven o'clock for Johore. We determined to go straight to the Government House and make a morning call at the unearthly hour of 8 a.m. The drive from the wharf was full of beauty, novelty, and interest. We had not landed so near the line before, and the most tropical of tropical plants, trees, flowers, and ferns, were here to be seen, growing by the roadside on every bank and dust-heap....

The town of Singapore itself is not imposing, its streets, or rather roads of wooden huts and stone houses, being mixed together indiscriminately. Government House is on the outskirts of the city, in the midst of a beautiful park. We found the Governor and his family did not start until 11.30, and they kindly begged us to return to breakfast at half-past nine, which we did. Before finally leaving, Sir William Jervoise sent for the Colonial Secretary, and asked him to look after us in his absence. He turned out to be an old schoolfellow and college friend of Tom's at Rugby and Oxford; so the meeting was a very pleasant one. As soon as the Governor and his suite had set off for Johore we went down into the town....

The north-east monsoon still blows fresh and strong, but it was nevertheless terribly hot in the streets, and we were very glad to return to the cool, shady rooms at Government House, where we thoroughly appreciated the delights of the punkah.

There are very few European servants here, and they all have their own peons to wait on them, and carry an umbrella over them when they drive the carriage or go for a walk on their own account. Even the private soldier in Singapore has a punkah pulled over his bed at night. It is quite a sight to meet all the coolies leaving barracks at 5 a.m., when they have done punkah-pulling.

At four o'clock Mr Douglas called to take us for a drive. We went first to the Botanical Gardens, and saw sago-palms and all sorts of tropical produce flourishing in perfection. There were many beautiful birds and beasts, Argus pheasants, lyre birds, cuckoos, doves, and pigeons more like parrots than doves in the gorgeous metallic lustre of their plumage. The cages were large, and the enclosures in front full of Cape jasmine bushes (covered with buds) for the birds to peck at and eat.

From the gardens we went for a drive through the pretty villas that surround Singapore in every direction....

At six o'clock this morning we visited the market. It is a nice, clean, octagonal building, well supplied with vegetables and curious fruits. The latter are mostly brought from the other islands, as this is the worst season of the year in Singapore for fruit. We tasted many fruits new to us—delicious mangosteens, lacas, and other fruits whose names I could not ascertain. Lastly, we tried a durian, *the* fruit of the East, as it is called by people who live here; and having got over the first horror of the onion-like odour, we found it by no means bad.

The fish market is the cleanest, and best arranged, and sweetest smelling that I ever went through. It is situated on a sort of open platform, under a thick thatched roof, built out over the sea, so that all the refuse is easily disposed of and washed away by the tide. From the platform on which it stands two long jetties run some distance out into the sea, so that large fishing boats can come alongside and discharge their cargoes at the door of the market.

The poultry market is a curious place. On account of the intense heat everything is brought alive to the market, and the quacking, cackling, gobbling, and crowing that go on are really marvellous. The whole street is alive with birds in baskets, cages, and coops, or tied by the leg and thrown down anyhow. There were curious pheasants and jungle-fowl from Perak, doves, pigeons, quails, besides cockatoos, parrots, parrakeets, and lories. They are all very tame and very cheap; and some of the scarlet lories, looking like a flame of fire, chatter in the most amusing way. I have a cage full of tiny parrots not bigger than bullfinches, of a dark green colour, with dark red throats and blue heads, yellow marks on the back, and red and yellow tails. Having bought these, everybody seemed to think that I wanted an unlimited supply of birds, and soon we were surrounded by a chattering crowd, all with parrots in their hands and on their shoulders. It was a very amusing sight, though rather noisy, and the competition reduced the prices very much. Parrakeets ranged from twelve to thirty cents apiece, talking parrots and cockatoos from one to five dollars. At last the vendors became so energetic that I was glad to get into the gharry again, and drive away to a flower shop, where we bought some gardenias for one penny a dozen, beautifully fresh and fragrant, but with painfully short stalks.

Lady Brassey, *A Voyage in the 'Sunbeam'*, Longmans, Green, & Co., London, *c.*1881, p. 56.

29
The Liverpool of the East

FREDERICK WILLIAM BURBIDGE
1877

In 1877 Frederick William Thomas Burbidge, a member of the editorial staff of The Garden, *and previously a gardener employed at the Royal Botanic Gardens, Kew, was commissioned by the Chelsea horticultural firm of James Veitch & Sons to collect ornamental plants from Borneo. He arrived at Singapore in July or August 1877, and in the latter month briefly visited Johore, before proceeding to Labuan and Sabah, where he spent a year hunting for plants. He returned to England, via Singapore, in 1878, and in the following year, until his death in 1905, he was Curator of the Botanic Garden of Trinity College, Dublin. Burbidge gives a highly evocative account of Singapore, recalling the bustling activity of Commercial Square, renamed Raffles Place 20 years earlier, and the firms of John Little & Co., founded in 1853 as provision dealers and general merchants, and destined to grow into one of the foremost retail businesses in Asia, and Katz Brothers Ltd., begun by Hermann Katz, a naturalized Englishman, and his brother, shortly before Burbidge's arrival, and soon to flourish as wholesale and commission agents after obtaining the contract to supply the Dutch army operating against Aceh in northern Sumatra from 1872. Burbidge also refers to the two well-known Singapore traders and ships' captains, John Dill Ross, Sr., and William Lingard, who inspired the character of Tom Lingard in Conrad's* Almayer's Folly, An Outcast of the Islands, *and* The Rescue. *It is remarkable to note that Conrad introduces Lingard in his first novel,* Almayer's Folly, *published in 1895, with words that echo Burbidge's description 15 years earlier, 'the acknowledged king of them all . . . he whom the Malays . . . recognised as the "Rajah-Laut"—the King of the Sea'. We also know from Conrad that the real life Captain Lingard patronized Emmerson's Tiffin Rooms, founded by the veterinary surgeon, Charles Emmerson, at the end of Cavenagh Bridge, near the Singapore River, 'a regular haunt of all and sundry, from the Tuan Besar down to the seafaring class'. Emmerson also established a hotel in two large houses at No. 1 Beach Road, the site in 1887 of the Raffles Hotel, which soon began to rival the Hotel de l'Europe, the successor of Dutronquoy's London Hotel, at the corner of High Street facing the Esplanade.*

THIS port, which is also the seat of the government of the Straits Settlements, has not inaptly been called the 'Liverpool of the East', and the applicability of that title soon becomes evident to the stranger from 'home', who finds himself on the landing-stage at Tanjong Paggar for the first time. Here is a range of warehouses or 'godowns' for the storage of goods, and coaling sheds for the supply of the mail and other steamers moored alongside. One is soon glad to get away from the heat, the noise of the steam winch, and the coal-dust; and a gharry or cab having been procured, the dusky Jehu springs to his seat on the shaft, from which 'coign of vantage' he uses both whip and voice in urging on at a gallop a plucky little pony, scarcely larger than a donkey, and most probably bred either in Sumatra or Pegu. You meet other little ponies in other little gharries coming full tilt down the road to the wharf, a string of buffalo-carts, or occasionally a neat little private carriage, and you soon become aware of the fact that Singapura, as it is still called, of the Malays is both hot and dusty. On you go, and the stuffy little gharry, even if it has no windows, soon becomes as hot as an oven, and the perspiration streams from every pore. By the time you reach the hotels the chances are that your shirt and collar are in the state best described as 'pulpy'; and if you are of a sanguine temperament, your face may be said to resemble 'the rising sun'. Of course you have kept your eyes open as you came along past the rough hedges on the right clothed with red lantanas, the neat police-station on the bank to the left, with those beautiful crimson and buff-flowered hibiscus bushes before the door. Then the rows of Chinese houses and shops, an elaborate Hindoo temple or two of white stone, and then street after street of whitewashed red tile roofed shops, until you reach the square, where you meet your agent, or to the hotels, nearly all of which are clustered around the tall spire of the cathedral, which you will have seen as the ship steamed slowly into harbour. The chances are you will have been recommended to one or other of the hotels by some knowing friend.

The Hotel de l'Europe is the principal one; but at the time I arrived in Singapore the *chef-de-cuisine* had such a bad name that I was recommended elsewhere. One is sure to be comfortable at any of the first-class houses at prices varying from two to five dollars daily, or less by monthly arrangement. For this sum one may secure a more or less comfortable bedroom or suite simply whitewashed, the floor covered with yellow rattan matting, which is both cool and clean. The walls, as a rule, do not boast of anything great in the way of pictorial embellishment; at night, however, lively little insect-eating lizards disport themselves thereon; and then, too, the hum of the hungry mosquito is heard. In the morning you rise soon after gun-fire (5 a.m.). It is daylight about 6 a.m.; and after partaking of a cup of tea or coffee, and the inevitable two bits of toast, you have a walk. Everybody nearly seems astir. While dressing, the chances are you will hear a gentle tap at the door, or hearing it opened very cautiously, you turn suddenly, and are startled by a dusky apparition in an enormous white turban. It is an itinerant Kling, or Hindoo Figaro, who seeing you are one of the new arrivals by yesterday's mail, would like to shave you, or cut your hair, at a charge of half a dollar.

Strolling outside into the main thoroughfares you see a strange motley crowd. The markets are full to overflowing with edibles of all kinds; meat, fish, vegetables, and fruit lie about in glorious profusion. Here a heap of fresh fish of the most vivid colours, there a pile of yellow pine-apples or bright scarlet chilies, oranges, pomoloes, mangosteen and rambutan, Chinese long beans, fresh green lettuces and young onions, tomatoes, and the hundred and one elements of native cookery, which are perfectly unintelligible to any but native eyes. Chinese coolies coming in from the interior of the island laden with fruit and vegetables, or other commodities. Sleek fat-faced celestials in black jackets, loose white trousers, and white European felt hats, taking their morning's stroll, and in every doorway gaunt-featured Chinese artizans of the tailor and shoemaker type sit or stand enjoying the cool fresh air and their morning's whiff of tobacco at the same time. The Chinese predominate, but you will find dusky spider-limbed Klings and the more compact little brown Malays fairly represented. You will notice gharries coming into town laden with Chinese traders, and other vehicles bring in the European storekeepers, agents, clerks, &c. You return about eight o'clock, and have a bath, and then dress for breakfast.

As you sit in the verandah or open basement awaiting the gong for breakfast being struck, various itinerant traders, generally Klings or Chinese, try to tempt you with their wares, for which they ask about five times as much as they are worth, or could be bought for in London. Japanese and Chinese fans, slippers, cabinets, lacquer ware, and carved ivory goods, all of second or third rate value, form their stock in trade in general, while some offer gold brocade worked for slippers or smoking-caps, crape handkerchiefs and shawls, or Indian embroidery, and even socks and white handkerchiefs of cheap European make.

Of course, to a new arrival, everything is strange, and not the least perplexing is the Babel of language on all hands. English, Dutch, German, Chinese, Javanese, Hindustani, Spanish, Portuguese, and Malay, the latter by far the most general—the lingua franca which all use in common. At last, bang! bang!! bang!!! goes the gong, and breakfast is ready exactly at 9 a.m. There is no ceremony. A little regiment,—an awkward squad rather,—of Chinese 'boys' hand the dishes in turn. As a rule, everything is well cooked, and there is variety enough for everybody. Beef-steaks and mutton-chops, one or two well-made curries and rice, eggs and bacon, cold ham, boiled eggs, salads, vegetables, and plenty of fresh fruit. Coffee or tea is not so much in favour here in the East as at home, bottled Bass, claret, or Norwegian beer, being preferred instead. After a long morning's walk, however, scarcely any beverage is so grateful as an accompaniment to the post-prandial cigar as is a cup of freshly-roasted coffee. Breakfast over, the real business of the day commences. All the large stores and godowns are opened at 8.30 or 9 a.m., and from 10 until 12.30 everyone is alert and busy. Gharries are whisking about in all directions. The fattest and sleekest and richest of Chinese merchants arrive in their more or less imposing carriages, boats and sampans are going to or returning from the shipping in the roads, buffalo carts ply between the godowns in town and those at the wharf, the sun pours down its heat and light from the zenith, and everybody seems intent on making their hay while it shines.

All the principal stores and shops are either in 'the Square' or its vicinity, and here you can procure home comforts of nearly every description, together with the latest books and home papers. You will procure the latest news at Little's Store, and will see many things there to interest you. Sale & Co.'s, and Katz's Stores, are also well worth a visit, and few of the Chinese shops will compare well with that of the late Hon. C. Whampoa, C.M.G., who was a most influential trader in the place. The 'Square' is an oblong plot of turf planted with various tropical trees, and one of these, although fast going to decay, is well worthy of notice, being completely enshrouded with rare orchids of various kinds. This stands immediately opposite the Singapore Dispensary, and owes its interesting appearance to Mr [R.] Jamie, who first planted it with orchids some years ago....

A morning in the 'Square' gives one a tolerably clear insight into the enterprise and trade of Singapore. You hear a good deal about the price of sago or gutta and rice, or about the chartering of steamers or sailing craft, or the freight on home or export goods. You are sure to meet two or three captains of trading steamers. Captain Linguard [W. Lingard], perhaps, after one of his trips to the Coti river away on the south-east of Borneo, and then you will hear something of the rubber-market, or of the pirates, of whom, perhaps, few men know more than this energetic 'Rajah Laut', or 'Sea King', as he is called by the natives.

Another maritime celebrity is Captain [J. D.] Ross [Sr.], a genial sailor, who owns the mail steamer 'Cleator', which runs between Singapore, Labuan, and Brunei, on the north-west Bornean coast. Captain Ross is well acquainted with the principal places in the whole Malayan Archipelago; and few residents have an equal colloquial knowledge of their languages. He has been attacked by pirates more than once in the old days, and is quite a nautical authority in every way. That tall, dark young fellow yonder, with the heavy moustache, is Captain Cowie, who ran the gauntlet of the Spanish gun-boats so successfully during the Sulu war, carrying rice, powder, and arms for the Sultan's people; and here one also meets 'old sea dogs' of nearly every nationality, but more especially English and Dutch.

One must of course look in at Emmerson's for tiffin, and a glance at the home papers and telegrams. Tiffin is much like breakfast, only nearly all the dishes are cold. The curries here are excellent; and a well-made salad of fresh green vegetables is a treat, when the temperature is 92° in the shade.

F. W. Burbidge, *The Gardens of the Sun: or A Naturalist's Journal on the Mountains and in the Forests and Swamps of Borneo and the Sulu Archipelago*, John Murray, London, 1880, pp. 14–19.

30
A Visit to Whampoa's Garden

WILLIAM T. HORNADAY
1878

The 23-year-old American zoologist, William Temple Hornaday, arrived at Singapore in May 1878 to begin his travels in the Malay Peninsula and Borneo in search of wild animals for American museums. In 1873, while a student at Iowa State

Agricultural College, he had been appointed assistant in charge of the zoological section of the College's museum, and in the following year he began to undertake expeditions to collect animals, initially in Florida, Cuba, and the Bahamas, then in South America, and finally in India and Malaya. On his arrival at Singapore he learned of the thriving trade in wild animals for museums and circuses, and having heard that Whampoa had a full grown orang-utan in the menagerie in his garden along Serangoon Road, he secured an invitation to visit him. Hoo Ah Kay was then 62 years of age, and he died two years later, in March 1880, leaving instructions that he was to be buried near Canton, where he was born.

ENTERING Singapore by way of New Harbor is like getting into a house through the scullery window. One's first impressions of the town are associated with coal-dust, mud, stagnant water, and mean buildings, and I found it required quite an effort to shake them off. This back-door entrance is by no means fair to Singapore, for under its baleful influence the traveller is apt to go away (by the next steamer usually) with a low estimate of the city, every way considered.

For the first stage out from New Harbor, the road is built through a muddy and dismal mangrove swamp. Here and there we pass a group of dingy and weather-beaten Malay houses standing on posts over the soft and slimy mud, or perhaps over a thin sheet of murky water. Delightful situation, truly, for the habitations of civilized human beings. Monkeys would choose much better. A Malay prefers to build over water; and, failing that, he builds over the softest mud he can find, usually on the bank of a river or lagoon. His house is quite in keeping with its location. The roof is made of palm leaves, and very often the walls also. The windows are mere slits across the wall near the floor, with clumsy wooden bars across; there is not a speck of paint or whitewash or colored paper visible anywhere, and the whole structure reminds one of an old crow's nest.

Farther on, we emerge from the swamp and pass a Chinese Joss house and cemetery on a hill-side, beyond which we have for a mile, on our right hand, a solid row of Chinese shops and dwellings, and on the other side of the road, a creek flowing mud and slime instead of water. Talk of malaria! It could be cut in that creek, in blocks a foot square, like ice in the Hudson. And the worst of it is that creek stinks—pardon, I mean sticks—by us until we are well into the city itself.

How odd the Chinese shops look with their huge red lanterns, wonderful signs, and flaming inscriptions in black on red paper pasted on the door-posts, lintels, and window-casings. How fat and sleek and hearty-looking are all the Chinese men and women, and how plump and saucy-looking are all their children. I am sure the Chinese are more fleshy, man for man, than any other people in the world....

The streets are wide, the shops are trim and orderly, and apparently filled to overflowing with their respective wares. What fine times we shall have loafing about these queer streets, and poking our nose into everything that is new!

Just now, however, it is pouring rain, so we rattle on through the Chinese bazaars, across an iron bridge, spanning a sort of inner harbor for lighters and small boats (Singapore River), and, without having passed a single European house or shop, we alight at a hotel just at the foot of Fort-Canning-on-the-hill.

Singapore is certainly the handiest city I ever saw, as well planned and carefully executed as though built entirely by one man. It is like a big desk, full of drawers and pigeon-holes, where everything has its place, and can always be found in it. For instance, around the esplanade you find the European hotels—and bad enough they are, too; around Commercial Square, packed closely together, are all the shipping offices, warehouses, and shops of the European merchants; and along Boat Quay are all the ship chandlers. Near by, you will find a dozen large Chinese medicine shops, a dozen cloth shops, a dozen tin shops, and similar clusters of shops kept by blacksmiths, tailors, and carpenters, others for the sale of fruit, vegetables, grain, 'notions', and so on to the end of the chapter. All the washerwomen congregate on a five-acre lawn called Dhobi Green, at one side of which runs a stream of water, and there you will see the white shirts, trowsers, and pajamas of His Excellency, perhaps, hanging in ignominious proximity to and on a level with yours. By some means or other, even the Joss houses, like birds of a feather, have flocked together at one side of the town. Owing to this peculiar grouping of the different trades, one can do more business in less time in Singapore than in any other town in the world.

Architecturally considered, Singapore has little to boast of except solidity and uniformity. With but few exceptions the buildings are all Chinese, and perfectly innocent of style. It is a two-story town throughout, solidly built of brick, plastered over, and painted a very pale blue or light yellow. There is a remarkable scarcity of the tumble-down, drunk, and disreputable old buildings so essential to the integrity of all other cities. Some of the Chinese shops and dwellings of the rich merchants are quite elaborately ornamented on the front with fancy tile and brick work, figures of apocryphal dragons and Chinese lions in high relief, and surrounded by beautifully kept gardens of tropical plants and shrubs. All of these impart a tasty and luxuriant air to the streets. The wealthy Chinamen take very kindly to European luxuries of all kinds except in matters of dress. They are lavish in the use of fine furniture, wines, and food, and their turnouts are really dazzling with their fine open carriages, matched horses, elegant harnesses, and liveried servants, though in dress they draw the line at the white stiff hat of English make. Their dress is cool and roomy, made of white silk or linen, and they wear no jewelry whatever....

The hotels of Singapore are all bad, and life in them is exceedingly dull. The liquor consumed in them, and the drunken men one sees almost daily, keep the abstemious traveller in a state of perpetual disgust. The extent to which intoxicating liquors of all kinds are drunk in the East Indies is simply appalling. The drinking habit is so universal, that, as a general thing, when you go to call on an acquaintance at his house, or to visit a stranger in company with other friends, the greeting is, 'What will you have to drink?' If you say you do not drink, or do not wish anything, you are urged most urgently to '*take something*', until it becomes positively disagreeable; and really the easiest way is to compromise by taking a glass of their beastly lemonade or abominable soda. Furthermore, when your new acquaintances, or old ones either, for that matter, call upon you at your hotel for half an hour's chat, you are expected to order drinks for the crowd, until the crowd is full of whatever it likes best. To omit this feature is to give positive offence in some cases, and even at the best to send your visitors away saying that you are uncivil and not worthy the acquaintance of gentlemen....

In due time, I called upon our consul, Major [A. P.] Studer, to pay my respects, little thinking that in him I would meet a 'fellow-citizen' from my own proud State, Iowa, and be received almost with open arms. Yes, that was my good fortune, and more than that, I had the pleasure of an early introduction to the Major's charming daughter, then Miss Studer, but now a lass no more, a genuine American girl—which is the highest praise I can bestow upon a young lady. It was a great treat to me all around, and their kind hospitality made my stay in Singapore, at the three different times I was there, far more endurable and free from social dulness than would otherwise have been the case.

I think Major Studer is one of the most efficient consuls with whom I have yet become acquainted. First, last, and all the time, he is uncompromisingly American, loyal to the backbone, and devoted heart and soul to the interests of the government he represents. In addition to this he has the stamina which such a position requires, and does his duty without the slightest fear of what those around him may say or do. I was not surprised to learn that his official acts have not always met the approbation of those most affected by them, for to my mind no consul can do his duty unflinchingly without making some enemies. From him I learned more of the political history of the Straits Settlements, and the Malay Archipelago, both inside and out, than I could ever have obtained elsewhere....

Had I been a showman or collector of live animals, I could have gathered quite a harvest of wild beasts in Singapore, at very small cost. I was offered a fine tiger at $150; baby orangs at $20 to $30, a fine pair of proboscis monkeys at $100; a pair of full-grown tapirs at the same price; manis and slow lemurs at $2; and a rhinoceros at $250. These were the asking prices, and it is quite certain that much smaller sums than those named would have purchased the animals in question. The greatest bargain I heard of, was the sale of a full-grown orang-utan (*Simia satyrus*), four feet two inches in height, to the Hon. H. A. K. Whampoa, for the ridiculous sum of $65, or $35 less than the price first asked. My desire to see this animal led me to pay a visit to the country seat of his owner, a very wealthy Chinese merchant, quite advanced in years and honors. I went by invitation, and the call was one to be remembered.

On one side of a quiet street in the suburbs, there is a wall enclosing a spacious garden. Passing through an open gate, the posts of which are very high and ornamented with carved figures of Chinese dragons, we drove through a well-kept garden, sighted a spacious but unpretentious white house, and drew up before the massive and finely carved front doors. A gardener, who was trimming a shrub close by, took my card and thrust it through the open carving. Presently the doors opened wide, and I saw Mr Whampoa coming slowly from the farther end of the wide hall to meet me. He was an old man with a low stoop in his shoulders, a large head, a very thin queue of white hair, small twinkling eyes with a very pleasant expression, perfect manners, and a very kind, unassuming smile. He speaks English as well as I, and has the honor to be Chinese Consul, Turkish Vice-consul, member of the Legislative Council, and the happy possessor of many, many dollars as the result of his labors.

My errand was to see the big orang-utan, but the contents of that lofty hall quite drove the charming creature out of my

Whampoa (Hoo Ah Kay) sitting in one of the gateways of his house in Serangoon Road, *The Graphic*, 12 June 1880. (Antiques of the Orient, Singapore)

mind. The first thing that caught my eye was a rounded gray stone about the size of a small coal-scuttle, lying upon the floor as if it were of small account. I scanned it idly, until my glance rested on a spot that had been polished, and I saw that it was jade! Value about three thousand dollars, a present from the owner of a mine for whom Mr Whampoa had once done some business. We passed through three large, square apartments, which formed a grand saloon, in which were tables for the reception of rare objects of virtu, and the walls and niches were quite filled with 'curios'. On a table stood a bronze elephant with a pagoda on his back, three feet high, Japanese work evidently, and exquisitely done. Near it hung a huge Chinese gong, four feet in diameter, on which were two dragons inlaid in gold. Above that, hung a huge—almost colossal—pair of stag-horns, on the massive branches of which were perched stuffed birds of paradise. Bronze storks stood upon the floor, and elsewhere were numerous dragons in bronze, elephant tusks, spears, etc. The furniture was all of ebony, exquisitely carved and lavishly inlaid with mother-of-pearl and ivory. On the walls and cornices were divers and sundry inscriptions in Chinese characters, painted very large and very red. I had hard work to repress the curiosity I felt, and the questions that rose to my lips at every step; but I did not wish to tire the feeble old gentleman, or make him regret my visit, so I held my peace.

W. T. Hornaday, *Two Years in the Jungle: The Experiences of a Hunter and Naturalist in India, Ceylon, the Malay Peninsula and Borneo*, Charles Scribner's Sons, New York, 1885, pp. 2–9.

31
Beautiful Indian Women

ISABELLA BIRD
1879

The famous British woman traveller, Isabella Bird, then 48 years old, arrived at Singapore in January 1879 from Hong Kong, aboard the steamer Sindh *of the Compagnie des Messageries Maritimes. She was on her way home after travelling in northern Japan, but she was persuaded to undertake a short tour of the Malay States of Sungei Ujong, Selangor, and Perak, before continuing her journey to England from Penang. She spent only three or four days in Singapore, which she describes as an hospitable place, but which was for her 'a mere halting-place,* en route *to the mainland'.*

IT is a drive of two miles from the pier to Singapore, and to eyes which have only seen the yellow skins and non-vividness of the Far East, a world of wonders opens at every step. Singapore is really the Charing Cross or Oban of the East. From it steamers start for Australia, China, Japan, England, France, Italy, Ceylon, India, Burmah, Sumatra, Malacca, and any number of small ports. Yet the only people who look thoroughly awake are the Chinese, who number 86,000 out of a population of 130,000. They monopolise many streets altogether, erect temples, club-houses, opium dens, and gaming-houses, are utterly unquelled by the heat, and are said to be gradually supplanting the smaller European merchants. They bring their clan feuds with them, and by means of their secret societies and an unlimited amount of false swearing, defy British justice, and constitute an element of danger as well as of prosperity. Their merchants, some of whom are very rich, sell everything, and as they are always able to undersell Europeans, their customers are of all races and classes. They are in such an enormous majority that one would suppose Singapore to be a Chinese town.

The city is all ablaze with colour. I can hardly recall the pallid race which lives in our dim, pale islands, and is costumed in our hideous clothes. Every costume, from Arabia to China, floats through the streets; robes of silk, satin, brocade, and muslin; and Parsees in spotless white, Jews and Arabs in dark rich colours, Klings (natives of Southern India) in crimson and white, Bombay merchants in turbans of large size and crimson cummerbunds, Malays in red *sarongs*, Sikhs in pure white, their great height rendered almost colossal by the classic arrangement of their draperies, and Chinamen, from the coolie, in his blue or brown cotton, to the wealthy merchant in his frothy silk *crêpe* and rich brocaded silk, make up a medley irresistibly fascinating to the stranger. Among these mingled foreign nationalities; the Klings, next to the Chinese, are the most numerous, and as there is no check on the immigration of their women, one sees the unveiled Kling beauties in great numbers. The Klings and Bengalees seem to do whatever the Chinese leave undone. In one place one sees hundreds of them round a piece of water not pre-eminently clean, unmercifully beating the delicate laces, gauzy silks, and elaborate flouncings of the European ladies on great stones, for they are the laundrymen of Singapore. Then they row boats, drive gharries, run as syces, lend small sums for large interest, sell fruit, keep small shops, carry 'chit books', and make themselves as useful as their mediocre abilities will allow, but never amass fortunes as the Chinese do. They are said to be harmless to their neighbours. The men are very fine-looking, lithe and active, and, as they clothe but little, their forms are seen to great advantage.

The Kling women are, I think, beautiful—not so much in face as in form and carriage. I am never weary of watching and admiring their inimitable grace of movement. Their faces are oval, their foreheads low, their eyes dark and liquid, their noses shapely, but disfigured by the universal adoption of jewelled nose-rings; their lips full, but not thick or coarse; their heads small and exquisitely set on long, slender throats; their ears small, but much dragged out of shape by the wearing of two or three hoop-earrings in each; and their glossy, wavy, black hair, which grows classically low on the forehead, is gathered into a Grecian knot at the back. Their clothing—or rather drapery—is a mystery, for it covers and drapes perfectly, yet has no 'make', far less 'fit', and leaves every graceful movement unimpeded. It seems to consist of ten wide yards of soft white muslin or soft red material, so ingeniously disposed when the wearer puts it on as to drape the bust and lower limbs, and form a girdle at the same time. One shoulder and arm are usually left bare. The part which may be called a petticoat—though the word is a slur upon the graceful drapery—is short, and shows the finely-turned ankles, high insteps, and small feet. These women are tall, and straight as arrows; their limbs are long and rounded; their appearance is timid—one might almost say modest—and their walk is the poetry of movement. A tall, graceful Kling woman, draped as I have described, gliding along the pavement, her statuesque figure the perfection of graceful ease, a dark pitcher on her head, just touched by the beautiful hand, showing the finely-moulded arm, is a beautiful object, classical in form, exquisite in movement, and artistic in colouring, a child of the tropic sun. What thinks she, I wonder—if she thinks at all—of the pale European, paler for want of exercise and engrossing occupation, who steps out of her carriage in front of her, an ungraceful heap of *poufs* and frills, tottering painfully on high heels, in tight boots, her figure distorted into the shape of a Japanese saké bottle, every movement a struggle or a jerk, the clothing utterly unsuited to this climate, or any climate, impeding motion, and affecting health, comfort, and beauty alike?

What may be called the native streets are crowded. The bazaars, which contain a medley of fruits, roots, Chinese edibles, old and new clothing of all nations, ironmongery from England and America, pottery from China and Staffordshire, native mats, and Eastern and Western stuffs of all colours and prices, create a perpetual twilight by hanging 'tatties' or other screens between themselves and the street, forming long dark alleys, in which buyers and sellers chaffer over the goods. The bustle and noise of this quarter are considerable, and the vociferation mingles with the ringing of bells and the beating of gongs and tomtoms—an intensely heathenish sound. And heathenish this great city is. Joss-houses, Hindoo temples, and mosques almost jostle each other, and the indescribable clamour of the temples and the din of the joss-houses are only faintly pierced by the shrill cry from the minarets calling the faithful to prayer, and proclaiming the Divine unity and the mission of Mohammed in one breath. This huge, mingled, coloured, busy, Oriental population bulks more largely in my eyes than the ruling race. The foreign merchants, hidden away behind jalousies in their offices, or dashing down the streets in buggies, make but a small show, and their houses are mostly roomy, detached bungalows, hidden by the bountiful vegetation of the climate, in which their wives lead half-expiring lives in deep twilight, kept alive by the efforts of the good-natured punkah-wallah. There is an hour at which they emerge and drive in given directions, and divert themselves with kettle-drums, dances, and other devices for killing time, with the mercury at 80 degrees! Just now the Maharajah of Johore, sovereign of a small State on the nearest part of the mainland, and much favoured and decorated by the British Government for unswerving fidelity to British interests, has a house here, and his receptions and other parties break the monotony....

But Singapore, to me, is a mere halting-place *en route* to the mainland, a kindly and hospitable one, for I had scarcely arrived at the hotel before a resident, to whom I had not even a letter of introduction, called and took me to his house. All the European houses appear to have very deep verandahs, large lofty rooms, punkahs everywhere, windows without glass, brick floors, and jalousies and 'tatties' (blinds made of fine grass) to keep out the light and the flies.

Isabella Bird, 'Sketches in the Malay Peninsula', *The Leisure Hour*, London, 1883, pp. 17–19.

32
The Singapore Chinese

AMBROSE B. RATHBORNE
1880

Ambrose Rathborne was an Australian surveyor who worked during the 1880s and early 1890s in the Malay States of Negri Sembilan, Selangor, and Perak as a partner in a firm of railway and planting contractors. The firm took an active part in planting coffee in the Malay Peninsula, and drew on Rathborne's own experience of his years in Ceylon, from where he arrived at Singapore in January 1880.

THE first circumstances that strike the traveller on reaching Singapore are the bustle and stir going on around, the busy Chinese hurrying hither and thither, the air of prosperity pervading all, and the rich greenness of the vegetation caused by the moist heat and the constant showers, for throughout the year there is but seldom any prolonged period of drought.

The houses are substantially built, and the godowns of the European merchants are fine; there are here not only many black races, but numerous white nationalities as well, each and all happy and flourishing under the British flag, which makes no difference between them, permitting all to trade and compete without distinction of race, to pay the same taxes, and to be in every way equal....

The lower classes of Chinese live closely crowded together, earning a livelihood by many forms of manual labour, and the celerity with which ships coal in the harbour is due to their work, for they follow one another in quick succession, a seemingly endless chain of men carrying baskets full of coal on their backs from the sheds to the ships, and returning with them empty in their hands for fresh loads. As a community they are hardworking and generally law-abiding, but should any rule or regulation be issued by the Government which is not to their liking, they become riotous and violent, making the occasion an excuse to satisfy their innate love of a row, to insult Europeans, and do a little looting on their own account. Those who take part in these tumults possess no houses or wives, have deposited their earnings in safe keeping, and have nothing to deter them from joining in the fun and fray, knowing that at most a broken head, which they do not mind, or a term of imprisonment in jail, where they have better food and are more comfortable than they are outside, is all that usually falls to their lot if they get within reach of the police, as directly severe measures for repression are taken these disturbances quickly cease. The better class of Chinese usually have nothing to do with these outbreaks, for there is an excellent and salutary law that provides for the deportation of any person not a natural-born subject of Her Majesty, who at any time may be proved to be associated with secret societies dangerous to the peace, or to be an instigator or participator in any riots or disturbances; so that those who have anything to lose think twice before intriguing and running the risk of being sent out of the country. They are hospitable and friendly, pressing their visitors to drink brandy and champagne instead of the ubiquitous tea. They are fond of reiterating emphatic expressions of their own opinions, and this appears to be their most popular form of argument. Many of them speak English, but Malay is the universal language of this part of the world, and forms the medium of conversation between the different races. The only master they recognize is superior force, and our system of administering justice is so different to what they have been accustomed to, that they are filled with delight to think that so long as they keep within the law, no one else can interfere with them, and this subject forms an oft-recurring source of conversation. They are fond of their children, and liberal in subscribing to local sports and amusements.

The suburban residences of the merchants are situate at some little distance from the town, and are good substantial houses, each one built on a portion of the many small hills which are so numerous on the island of Singapore. They stand sequestered in their own grounds amongst beautiful and shady trees and well-kept lawns, forming a pleasing and home-like prospect; and it is to these comfortable and attractive dwelling-places, with their cool, lofty rooms, that the merchant returns in the evening after his day's work is done, driving thereto along a smooth and well-watered road, passing beneath an avenue of trees which makes the way agreeable and shady even on the hottest days.

A. B. Rathborne, *Camping and Tramping in Malaya: Fifteen Years' Pioneering in the Native States of the Malay Peninsula*, Swan Sonnenschein & Co., London, 1898, pp. 2–6.

33
A Scarcity of Women

WILLIAM SPROSTON CAINE
1887

William Sproston Caine was a radical Member of Parliament for Scarborough from 1880, and for Barrow-in-Furness from 1886 till 1892. During his world tour between August 1887 and March 1888 he addressed a series of letters giving an account of his travels to the leading newspaper of his constituency, Barrow News, *and it was these letters, 'written during idle hours on board steamers', that formed the basis of his book,* A Trip Round the World in 1887–8, *which was published in London in 1888, and dedicated to his constituents and friends at Barrow-in-Furness.*

WE had a pleasant and uneventful passage to Singapore,... arriving on Sunday morning about noon. We moored alongside the coal wharves of the Pacific and Oriental Company, which are about three miles from the town. The heat was very great. Singapore being almost on the equator, the same temperature prevails almost all the year round, and although the sun had been clouded over all the morning the thermometer stood over 90° in the shade. After lunch we started off in a carriage to see what we could. The carriages are covered with a thick roof, and the sides and ends are open all round, with windows of open wood-work, which can be drawn up as a shield from the burning sun. It has long been one of my dreams to see the tropics, and I looked eagerly out of the carriage for plants and trees familiar to me as a horticulturist and cherished in hot-houses at home, which I longed to see growing in their native heat. The first hedge we came to contained a shrub and two creepers in bloom, which were familiar greenhouse friends, and every garden we passed was a mass of bananas, palms, pineapples, cactuses, and flowering plants. I have never seen such greenery....

We drove through the town to the botanical gardens, a park of some 300 acres, beautifully situated on the sunny slope of an evergreen hill, the most delightful garden imaginable, nearer to Eden than I could have believed anything on earth to be. Thence we repaired to the cathedral for evening service. We found it a very fine church, with a choral and processional ritual. It was strange to see three rows of huge punkahs or fans running down the whole length of the cathedral, waving back and forward all through the service over the heads of the congregation. I was glad to escape from the pompous cathedral service to a hearty little meeting of soldiers and blue jackets at the Sailors' Rest, a coffee house and recreation room established for their benefit by an excellent lady who lives in Singapore, Miss Cook [S. Cooke], to whom I was introduced after the service, which was conducted by Col. Cardew, who commands the regiment of infantry stationed at Singapore.

On Monday morning we again drove into the town, as the steamer was not to sail before four o'clock. Singapore appears to consist of three towns. The business or English town, Malay town, and China town. They are all connected by a wide esplanade facing the harbour, between two and three miles long. There are many fine buildings. The Post-office, the City Hall, the Police Barracks, the imposing Public Library, the Cathedral, and the Government Buildings are all handsome stone edifices of considerable pretensions. The town is full of open spaces, beautifully laid out, especially the Chinese park, a charming little garden of four acres in the middle of the most densely populated district. There is another pretty garden of ten acres, in the middle of the esplanade, facing the cathedral, covered with a green sward like velvet, and surrounded by magnificent trees. The esplanade itself for more than a mile is shaded by a double avenue.

The great business centre is Commercial Square, surrounded by banks, shops, and warehouses. Seven leading streets radiate from this centre, presenting the usual gay and lively scenes peculiar to an Eastern commercial city, in which the 140,000 inhabitants of Singapore swarm, clad in the brilliant and picturesque dresses of their twenty-five nationalities, relieved by the rich brown skins of those who wore no dresses at all. I suppose there is no place in the world where such a conglomeration of peoples is gathered together as appear in the busy streets of Singapore....

One is much impressed by the scarcity of women in the streets. Chinese women, however, do not leave their country readily, and although there are 72,000 Chinese males in Singapore, there are only 14,000 Chinese women; there is also but one Tamil woman to four Tamil men. The Malays, being the natives of the place, have their population pretty equally divided between the sexes.

W. S. Caine, *A Trip Round the World in 1887–8*, George Routledge and Sons, London, 1888, pp. 247–9.

34
Singapore Coachmen

JAMES HENRY CHAPIN
1887–1888

The American, James Henry Chapin, Professor of Geology and Mineralogy in St Lawrence University, travelled round the world in 1887–8. He arrived at Singapore after visiting Japan and China, and he later travelled to Ceylon, India, Egypt, Palestine, Malta, and Spain. His book, From Japan to Granada, *published in New York and London in the year after his return to the United States, is didactic in nature, with only occasional passages of light relief, as here in his account of his arrival at Singapore.*

A motley company of natives come streaming to the shore as the ship approaches, and nowhere else in all the Orient is there better opportunity to study the varieties of the human race, that commerce brings together. The jinrikisha of the Japanese is somewhat in use for conveying passengers to and from the town, three miles away, but the chief vehicle is a carriage of the milk-cart pattern, drawn by scrubby, vicious ponies, whose owners hold their impetuous spirits in check by keeping them on a low diet, so that the bony framework reveals itself at every point.

The coachman of Singapore has studied human nature and knows how to touch a tender chord in his customer. He does not hesitate to charge three times the fare the law appoints, and if you protest he points pathetically down his capacious throat, then presses his hand upon his stomach, in evident distress, as an indication of the straits to which he is reduced to get a living. Of course you do not want to see the man starve to death before your eyes, so you consent to be imposed upon, or at least effect a compromise. Whatever food may cost—and much fruit may be had for the gathering,—the Malay is not at great expense for clothes. The climate demands but little, and he is not concerned for what society enjoins. A strip of cotton cloth about his loins, a loose mantle of the same material when he goes upon the street, a little matting to protect him from the sun by day and rain at night, and he is provided for. High colors have an attraction when he affects some variety in costume, but these are among the luxuries and not the necessities. The dry-goods trade seldom profits largely by his presence. He can get along without much of any thing that it provides....

J. H. Chapin, *From Japan to Granada: Sketches of Observation and Inquiry in a Tour Round the World in 1887–8*, G. P. Putnam's Sons, New York, and The Knickerbocker Press, London, 1889, pp. 106–7.

35
A Service at St Andrew's Cathedral

FLORENCE CADDY
1889

In December 1888 Florence Caddy, then in her fifties, sailed from England to Singapore aboard the Duke of Sutherland's yacht Sans Peur. *She was the wife of a naval medical officer, and during the previous ten years had written a number of books, including novels, biographies, and books on household management and design. The* Sans Peur *reached Singapore on 6 February 1889, and sailed for Bangkok three days later.*

WHILE the inevitable coaling was going on, we went to the Raffles Hotel to lunch and read the papers, and learn what the world had been doing during our sojourn in the obscurity of Siam. We read just enough to keep abreast of the world, and then went off to do our shopping; passing with more interest than before the image of an elephant, erected in memory of the King of Siam's visit; the first time a Siamese monarch had ever left his own dominions. King Chulalonkorn went also to Ceylon and Calcutta, and all the chief sacred places of India.

The large town of Singapore appears so flourishing and enlightened, so advanced and well-governed, that, after seeing the quaint and crowded city of Bangkok, we feel as if we had come out of the theatre into the plain light of day....

I went to the cathedral service in Singapore. The church is very neat and nice inside, if you can call that inside which is open like a cloister on both sides. In the evening it is lighted with gas, lit too early, or rather turned up high too early, otherwise every precaution is taken to ensure coolness; the church besides being shaded by trees, is open all round, and has open cane seats set in dark wood. The sight of the thirty-two punkahs tugged by different strings by thirty-two Moormen, waving out of time in all directions towards nave and transept, and not at the same level, has a most bewildering effect. It makes some people feel sea-sick. The punkahs should be moved by one string as they are in large halls. The music is soft and sweet, and for the most part congregational, though there is a surpliced choir.

Major [W. R.] Grey, governor of the prison here, dined with us, and from him we learnt how much better and more humane our prison arrangements are than those of the Chinese or Siamese. His great aim is to lead the prisoners to a better life, and carefully to distinguish between hardened criminals and those capable of returning to be of use to society. Our government does not recognise the debt slavery often incurred through gambling. Gambling altogether has been prohibited in Singapore. Perhaps this is one reason why the Chinese look so flourishing and happy here.

Florence Caddy, *To Siam and Malaya in the Duke of Sutherland's Yacht 'Sans Peur'*, Hurst and Blackett Ltd., London, 1889, pp. 227–30.

36
A City of Orientals

HENRY NORMAN
1889

Sir Henry Norman was for many years a journalist on the editorial staffs of the Pall Mall Gazette *and* Daily Chronicle. *Between 1889 and 1893 he undertook an extensive tour of the countries of the Far East, during which he visited Malaya and Singapore. He retired from journalism in 1899, and between 1900 and 1923 served as a Member of Parliament. He was an acute observer of the political scene in Asia, but he was also a convinced believer in the benefits of British colonial rule.*

TO a casual observer ... Singapore does not present such striking features as many other places. The business town is two or three miles away from most of the private residences; these are not in groups but in units, each solitary in its own charming grounds; you cannot make a call under half an hour's drive, and until you have learned a little Malay it is a most difficult community in which to find your way about; and the Club is practically closed at seven o'clock, and if you make arrangements to dine there, your single lighted table only emphasises the surrounding darkness.

This evergreen island, almost on the equator, where neither Christmas nor Midsummer Day brings much change to the thermometer, and in whose tropical jungles the cobra and hamadryad live and a stray tiger is occasionally found, is the seat of a large number of very ticklish problems of government, and the visitor would be surprised indeed if he could see for a moment, through the eyes of the Governor of the Straits Settlements, the variety and responsibility of the questions requiring decision and action every day. It is a singularly complicated problem, to begin with, to govern the city itself, with its six thousand Europeans and Americans (including the garrison), its four thousand Eurasians, its four thousand Javanese, its sixteen thousand Indians, chiefly Klings (native of India, from the Coromandel coast), its thirty thousand Malays, its hundred and twenty thousand

Chinese and all its mixed mass of Bengalis and Bugis, Jawi Pekans and Boyanese and Burmese, Persians and Arabs and Dyaks and Manilamen. These native peoples are quiet enough when left alone, but a single unpopular ordinance is sufficient to bring them rioting into the streets. A few years ago Singapore was in the hands of a mob for two days—in fact, until the government gave way—because it was decided to make the causeways clear for passengers. The city used to be the headquarters of several of the principal Chinese Secret Societies, the most inscrutable and ruthless and law-upsetting organisations in the world. These were suppressed by formal enactment on the initiative of Sir Cecil Smith, four years ago, and a 'Chinese Advisory Board' created to deal with their legitimate work, but it may well be doubted whether a system to which the Chinese have an irrepressible tendency has not been made more secret rather than extirpated. Mr [G. C.] Wray, the 'Protector of Chinese', in his latest report, says that 'sporadic attempts are still made, and will always be made where Chinese congregate in large numbers, to start illegal organisations', but he believes, or perhaps one should say, hopes, that 'secrecy is impossible amid a heterogeneous society like ours, and incessant vigilance and prompt action on the part of the Chinese Protectorate are all that is necessary in such cases'. The chief societies were the Ghee Hin, the Ghee Hok, and the Hok Hin. The former was the original and the most powerful one, and when it was suppressed, after great difficulty and many disputes among its members concerning the distribution of its property, its membership in Singapore was thirty thousand and in Penang forty thousand. The other two have been 'registered' and permitted, as they are ostensibly only Chinese mutual benefit societies. There is still not the slightest doubt, however, that they stand between their members and the foreign law. Professional bailers attend the courts to bail out any member of their society, and they help their members in all sorts of ways to flee from justice. A chapter, and a most romantic one too, might be written about these societies. They have, for example, the most elaborate system of signs for mutual recognition. One of them bases its signs upon the numeral three. At table, a member wishing to make himself known to any fellow-member present places three glasses together in a certain way, or passes a cup of tea held peculiarly with three fingers.

A man fleeing from justice and praying for refuge, puts his shoes outside another's house, side by side, with the heels turned towards the door. If the owner turns one shoe over on the other, the fugitive knows he can take refuge there. In spite of the suppression, I fancy that *Hoan Cheng Hok Beng*—'Upset Cheng', the present Manchu dynasty of China, 'restore Beng', the former dynasty—still has a magic and compelling significance in Singapore, for these are the pass-words of the famous Triad Society, which honeycombs China and has more than once put the throne in terror. The Triad consists of the characters *Thien Tay Hoey*—'Heaven, Earth, Man'.

To appreciate Singapore as a city of Orientals, one must spend a day or two in the native quarters, and this is just what the ordinary visitor fails to do. From this point of view it is certainly one of the most astonishing communities in the world. To begin with, it is enormous. For days you may wander about without ever turning on your tracks, through miles upon miles of semi-native houses and shops, through crowded streets, in variegated bazaars, with all the merchandise of all the East spread out endlessly before you. Each race has its own quarter—there is 'Kampong Malacca', 'Kampong Kling', 'Kampong Siam', 'Kampong China'. In one spot you are dazzled with the silks of India; in another the *sarongs* of Java are spread out like a kaleidoscope; in another you are suffocated with an indescribable mixture of Eastern scents; in another an appalling stench meets you, strange rainbow-like birds utter raucous cries, and the long thin hairy arm of a gorilla is stretched out between bamboo bars in deceptive friendliness; in another there is such a packed mass of boats that you hardly know when your foot has left dry land. And all this mixed humanity exists in order and security and sanitation, living and thriving and trading, simply because of the presence of English law and under the protection of the British flag. Remove that piece of bunting from Government House, and all that it signifies, and the whole community would go to pieces like a child's sand-castle when the tide rises. Its three supports are free trade, fair taxation, and even-handed justice among white, black, brown and yellow, and these exist in the Far East under the British flag alone. At least, I have been almost everywhere else without finding them. Of course, in all this the Chinese enormously preponderate. The foolish opinion is sometimes heard at home that this Chinese community represents China—that it is a specimen of what China may become, a standing bond of union between ourselves and China. The very opposite is the case. This community has grown up and exists precisely because it is *not* China—because the conditions of its existence are precisely the antithesis of Chinese conditions. The Straits Chinaman would not exchange his British nationality for anything else in the world; he plays cricket, football, and lawn tennis; he has his annual athletic sports; the recreation ground, and indeed every open space, is covered in the afternoons with Chinese engaged in these games; he goes to the Free Library and he reads the newspaper; he attends a Debating Society and he carries off prizes at the Raffles School; he eats foreign food and imitates foreign vices. When he has prospered he drives through the streets in a carriage and pair with a European coachman on the box. He knows that he is the equal of the Englishman before the law, and considers that he is slightly superior to him in other respects. He looks upon the Civil Service as *his* servants, upon the Governor as *his* ruler, upon the forts as *his* protection, upon the whole place as *his* home. A Chinaman is one of the most influential members of the Legislative Council.

H. Norman, *The Peoples and Politics of the Far East: Travels and Studies in the British, French, Spanish and Portuguese Colonies, Siberia, China, Japan, Korea, Siam and Malaya*, T. Fisher Unwin, London, 1895, pp. 38–42.

37
Bathing at Raffles Hotel

COLONEL R. V. K. APPLIN
1890

Colonel Reginald Vincent Kempenfelt Applin arrived at Singapore in 1890 aboard the P&O steamer Oriana *as a recruit of the British North Borneo Company. Before he received his appointment as a Cadet he served briefly as a clerk in a British mercantile house in Makassar. He owed his cadetship to Admiral Sir Henry Keppel, who was a friend of his father, and when he went to the British North Borneo Company's offices in Leadenhall Street, London, he found the Admiral sitting in a chair at the foot of the stairs. 'Going to Singapore, eh? Wish I was young enough to go with you. Hot place, Singapore. They've got your name for the next vacancy upstairs. Well, good luck, young man. Hot climate. Keep your bowels open, and, and—your mouth shut, and you'll get on all right. Good-bye!' Applin served during the Mat Salleh rebellion in Sabah, but afterwards left the Company's service to pursue a military career. He served in the Boer War and in France during the First World War, when he was twice mentioned in dispatches. He commanded the 14th King's Hussars between 1919 and 1922, and two years later was elected a Member of Parliament.*

AFTER getting my letters from the Post Office I went to the Government Offices and presented my introduction to Mr Hornby. I found that he had just given up his bungalow and with his wife was staying at the Raffles Hotel. Here I engaged a room. I expected a night of sweet slumbers in a bed ashore, after over a month in a ship's bunk. I spent a painful and sleepless night under a large mosquito curtain which seemed to contain all the mosquitoes in the hotel, and they fully satisfied their lust for blood on the tenderest parts of my body. The morning found me with swollen face, ankles and wrists, while red splotches on sheet and curtain showed I had slain many enemies, though the blood of the victims was my own.

Hot and inflamed, I sought the bathroom, and found myself in a dark place with a concrete floor, in the middle of which was a large earthenware jar some four feet high which was filled with water. I walked round it wondering how I should climb in, when I saw a tin bucket such as children use on the beach, and noticed it had a handle across the top. I decided to use this as a dipper and soused myself with deliciously cool water; then a good soaping with carbolic, and then another thorough douching with the can.

I never enjoyed a bath more, and when I entered the breakfast room in a clean white cotton suit I was greeted by Hornby who asked me if I had enjoyed my tub and if I had found it difficult to get into the water? When I told him I had

A first attempt at an 'Indian' bath, from W. S. Caine, *A Trip Round the World in 1887–8*, George Routledge and Sons, London, 1888.

not got into the jar but used the bucket, all at the table roared with laughter and said:

'Pay up, Hornby—he has beaten you this time.'

It was explained to me that nearly everyone tries to get into the jar the first time they bathe in the East, and that I had guessed right when I used the bucket. It may be primitive, but it is the pleasantest way to bathe in the tropics.

Hornby was very kind and showed me the ropes. He introduced me to the Colonial Secretary and took me to call at Government House. Later I had an interview with His Excellency Sir Charles Clementi-Smith, with a view of getting a cadetship in the Malay Service, and I hoped that I might have obtained a commission in the Governor's Bodyguard, a very smart body of mounted Sikhs armed with lances. I still had a great longing to serve in a mounted regiment and here seemed my chance.

Mr Dare, an old friend of my father's in Japan, asked me to stay in his beautiful bungalow at Tanglin. Here I met my first cobra in the middle of the drive. I stopped dead and he stood up and spread his hood, and for a minute neither of us seemed inclined to take the initiative. At last I summoned up my courage, gripped my walking-stick firmly and advanced cautiously to the attack. Almost within striking distance I raised my cane. Suddenly, like a flash, he uncoiled five feet of writhing scales. I jumped clear and hit wildly out, while he slithered into the grass in the opposite direction. It was the first time I had faced death at close quarters, so may be forgiven for letting him escape.

The following evening there was a great hullabaloo in the next bungalow: Cries of 'Rimau! rimau!' and Dare rushing out with a rifle.

It appeared that a tiger had jumped through the open window of the kitchen, which in the East is separated from the house, and seized a leg of mutton that was lying on a table, scaring the Chinese cook out of his wits.

We were at first disinclined to believe his story, but there were the pugs outside the window, and Captain Owen of the police, came up the next morning to breakfast and tracked him into a thick swamp in the jungle. Two days afterwards, Owen shot this tiger within a mile of the centre of the town, and we went down and saw him carried into the city by eight coolies, slung on a pole and exhibited to a crowd outside John Little's stores.

R. V. K. Applin, *Across the Seven Seas*, Chapman & Hall Ltd., London, 1937, pp. 50–2.

38
A Visit to the Sultan of Johore

SURGEON-MAJOR JOHN MACGREGOR
1893

The author was a member of the Indian Medical Service, who served between 1885 and 1887 as senior medical officer of the Frontier Brigade at Bhamo, and in various other capacities during the Anglo-Burmese War. In 1893, on leave from India, he visited Borneo, Thailand, and Singapore, where he attended a reception given by the 60-year-old ruler of Johore, Sultan Abu Bakar, then experiencing the social stigma resulting from charges of breach of promise brought against him by his former mistress, Miss Mighell, in the High Court in

London. The case gained wide publicity in the British press, but in November 1893 the High Court ruled that it lacked jurisdiction to try the case as the Sultan was the ruler of an independent state. He was the grandson of Temenggong Abdul Rahman, with whom Raffles had concluded his treaty in 1819, and had succeeded his father as ruler of Johore in 1862 under the successive titles of Temenggong, Maharaja, and, in 1885, Sultan. He was said to have had the tastes and habits of an English gentleman, and he certainly had all the trappings. He kept a stud of horses and carriages, and played billiards and cricket. Because of his hospitality, and early reputation as a sportsman, he was very popular in Singapore. He had, as Macgregor observes, a great love of 'the North', and he visited England first in 1866, when he was granted an audience by Queen Victoria. He travelled widely in Europe, meeting the Kaiser, the Hapsburg Emperor, the King of Italy, and the Sultan of Turkey. In 1887, for her Jubilee, he presented Queen Victoria with a silver model of the Albert Memorial, and she gave him a marble bust of herself. He died, perhaps appropriately, in Mayfair in June 1895, and his remains were brought back to Johore.

SINGAPORE, indeed, is a pretty sight, not so much the town itself, the business part of which is too cramped, but the beautiful broad harbour, with such a lot of ships in it every day in the year. But what particularly distinguishes Singapore is its jinrickshaws. Various cities in the East receive nicknames from certain predominant peculiarities. Thus Calcutta is nicknamed the 'City of Palaces', Bombay, the 'City of Ducks' (that is to say, Bombay Ducks), while Madras is the 'Benighted City'. On the same principle Singapore is the 'City of Rickshaws'. There is probably no other place with the same number of rickshaws, and generally speaking they are very good ones too. Not in Hong Kong, not in Shanghai, and not even in Japan itself, I think, has the institution of rickshaws grown so great. I was riding in one of them some day, and noticed that the number of another one going on in front of me was considerably over 6,000, though the population of Singapore is considerably under 100,000 inhabitants. This surprised me, but I was afterwards told that nearly 8,000 rickshaws run daily on the streets of this tropical city.

Not very long ago an enterprising syndicate who believed in the blessings of steam started extensive steam-cars over the city. But they had to shut up shop shortly after. For the two-footed ponies in the jinrickshaws actually worked the iron horse off his legs. Nay more, jinrickshaws have become quite fashionable. Only the other day, and if you suggested a ride in a jinrickshaw to a woman of quality in Singapore, the woman of quality would turn up her nose at you. But all that is changed now. The governor of Singapore was away at this time, but I was told that his wife had lately taken to riding in a jinrickshaw and keeping a private stud of Chinese two-legged ponies for that purpose, just for fun. Mrs Bumble, the woman of quality, immediately followed suit, and if you now suggest a ride in a jinrickshaw to Mrs Bumble, far from turning up her nose, she makes it look quite archaic (that is to say, with an arch) with the happy pleasure of anticipation. Such are the freaks of fashion.

But to speak in earnest, a good jinrickshaw is really a pretty little carriage, with its elegant wheels and its brass shiny mountings; and there is no reason why any one should turn up his predominant feature at it. As a rule they will cover the ground nearly as fast as four-wheelers, such as the four-wheelers one meets at Singapore. The two-legged ponies are almost invariably Chinamen all over the Far East, with the single exception of Japan, the country from which the jinrickshaws originally sprang. They are generally strong sturdy men, but yet perspire a little too freely in such sultry climates. By constant exercise the calves of their legs get so developed, and their hips so plump, that they move between the shafts with all the ease and elegance of sturdy little Highland ponies....

There was comparatively little for me to see at Singapore this time, as I had been there several times before. There was, however, one notable exception, and that was His Highness the Sultan of Johore. Some years ago I went over to his capital of Johore itself, from which he takes his designation, but he was then in Europe, for he dearly loves the North, like many other people. Johore is at the extreme southern point of the long and narrow Malayan Peninsula, and is practically the furthest south point of the whole vast continent of Asia. It is separated from the small island of Singapore by a sound only a mile or so wide, and the drive across the island from

Sinking under the burden: a rickshaw coolie in Singapore, from Hugo V. Pedersen, *Door den Oost-Indischen Archipel: Eene Kunstreis*, H. D. Tjeenk Willink & Zoon, Haarlem, 1902.

the town of Singapore to Granji Pier opposite Johore is under twenty miles, and is a particularly pleasant one.

I intended to go over this time once again, as the Sultan was at home. But while staying at Singapore there was an announcement that His Highness was going to have an 'At Home' at his town residence, on the outskirts of Singapore itself. This would do away with the necessity of going over to Johore, as I would attend the 'At Home' instead. I wished to see His Highness, partly because he was a very interesting person in himself, and partly because he was very much before the public when I started from India, on account of his very amusing breach of promise case.

The Chinese two-footed ponies in the rickshaws are obtuse enough in their intellect—all ponies are; but the drivers of the four-wheeled 'groaners' are vastly worse. If you told them that you were going to Jericho, they would instantly take upon themselves to drive you there. But they are extremely bad at reaching their destination if you do not know the way yourself, especially if you cannot speak the 'pigeon'. Our driver on the evening of the Sultan's 'At Home' was particularly dull of comprehension; but by patient perseverance we reached the Sultan's palace at last, probably among the very last arrivals.

Mrs Brown-Potter, the once famous American beauty, had already sung her song, for she was then at Singapore with a company of strolling players, and was acting for the time being at the Town Hall, and the function of presentation had also been already over. I was sorry I was so late, as I wished to be presented to His Highness, which, however, I afterwards managed through the English aide-de-camp attached to His Highness's person. The Sultan appeared affable and simple enough, as he moved to and fro among his guests. I did not expect to see any ladies at this function, as I was afraid His Highness would be unpopular with the fair sex, on account of his having so recently jilted an English lady. But not at all: His Highness was very popular in Singapore, and all the beauty, as well as the chivalry of the place, were there in all their bravery.

His Highness was a man considerably over sixty years of age, of a light olive complexion, and so gentle and mild in his manners that no one would expect him to play the part of a wicked Lothario in breaking women's hearts. He would be considered small of stature for a European, but quite the average height of the race to which he belongs, as he is a pure Malay by blood, and very few of this roving race are of anything like tall stature. And they are also far more uniform in height than Europeans, as they seldom differ from one another in this respect for more than two or three inches at the most.

His Highness, who was very popular in Singapore, spoke English thoroughly well, and was quite European in everything except the red fez on the top of his head, as became a true and faithful follower of the Prophet. He gave these 'At Homes' now and again, and they were immensely popular when they came off. But the mere occurrence of this 'At Home' naturally gave rise to gossip about His Highness; and his recent jilting affair would have revived again, even if it had died out, which it had not at this time.

Like many another personage of exalted rank, he delighted occasionally to drop his greatness and his rank, and go about *incognito*, under an assumed name, as if he were mere ordinary flesh and blood like other people. And nothing could show both the humility and fascination of His Highness better than the way in which he stormed the citadel of Miss M—'s heart, for he was then living under the very ordinary name of Mr Albert Baker, an English name that bore a convenient resemblance to his own real Malay name of Abu Bakhur.

The Sultan had a large revenue, but his heart was larger still. And he was, therefore, very expensive in his mode of living, especially when he went among his friends in the North, where he spent a considerable portion of both his time and fortune. The natural consequence followed. His Highness was in debt. Many people regretted the late breach of promise case, more for the sake of the Sultan than for the broken-hearted one, who suffered so grievously by the conduct of her truant lover, Mr Albert Baker, of that ilk. The trial of the case lately in England will still be in the memory of many readers, and it will also be remembered that it elicited one important fact, namely, that though the Johore territory is under British protection, yet that the Sultan thereof is practically an independent prince, over whom the British law-courts have no jurisdiction whatever.

J. Macgregor, *Through the Buffer State: A Record of Recent Travels Through Borneo, Siam, and Cambodia*, F. V. White & Co., London, 1896, pp. 225–30.

39
Coaling a Ship

WALTER DEL MAR
1899

Walter Del Mar left London on his journey round the world in January 1899, aboard the P&O steamer Oceana. *He called briefly at Singapore in February on his way to Java, and returned there between 9 and 15 March, before sailing for Hong Kong and Japan, which was the main country of interest for him. His book,* Around the World Through Japan, *which was published in London in 1902, contains a good deal of specific information for travellers proposing to undertake a similar journey, including the advice to take sufficient linen to last a month as no laundry was available on British ships. He therefore regarded two dozen shirts as essential, and further advised that if letters of introduction to governors or ambassadors were taken, it would be necessary to take a frock-coat and silk hat. It was also essential to take a deck chair, as these were not provided for passengers on ships. He travelled home via San Francisco and New York, and reached London in September 1899.*

WE went to Raffles Hotel where, we were told, we should find the best rooms, although the Hôtel de l'Europe is said to have better cooking; but we found this was a matter of no consequence, as our friends, with characteristic Eastern hospitality, so arranged that we never had to dine at the hotel, and we went to the club for tiffin. The Adelphi Hotel, patronised by German and Dutch visitors, was also well spoken of. Perhaps the first thing you will notice on the way from the wharf is the good surface of the roads, and the painstaking care with which every little inequality is immediately repaired by the coolies who seem to patrol them. The road metal is too soft, however, and while it packs well and makes a good surface, it will not stand heavy traffic, and requires constant care to keep up. The bearded Sikh policemen will attract your attention, as well as the native-born Chinese (*babas*), with the crimson silk plaited into their pigtails. As you approach the bridge crossing the Singapore River, which divides the business quarter from the residential district, the Exchange Building, where the Chamber of Commerce is located on the ground floor, and above it the Singapore Club, will probably be pointed out. The river itself is crammed from bank to bank with junks, tongkangs, sampans, and prahus,—a hopeless jumble of Chinese, Malay, Siamese, and Indian boats and cargoes. After we had our luggage unpacked, our first duty was to don the frock coat and silk hat, which custom, throughout all the Eastern colonies and possessions of Great Britain, requires should be worn in making official visits, and pay our respects to H.E., the Governor. Then back to change into a costume more suitable to the climate before going to the club—the great gathering-place of all the male Europeans for half an hour before, and at, luncheon, and later, before returning to their homes for dinner.

As far as I could discover, in the Singapore Club a man is considered abstemious if, before lunch, he has a 'peg' of, say, whiskey and tonic-water, followed by a *stengah* (the Malay word for half, usually pronounced *stinger*) or split drink, succeeded by a *suku*, or a split divided between two. The same allowance at lunch and a similar quantity before going home is all the liquid refreshment habitually taken, and the members say that this conclusively proves that a man can live comfortably almost on the equator with an extremely small

The call of the East, from *Salubrious Singapore*, Kelly and Walsh Ltd., Singapore, 1920.

allowance of alcohol. The club has a fine billiard room, and there are many good players among the members. The game known as 'snookers' in England is played here under the name of 'Shanghai snookers'. An excellent standing dish at lunch, in place of pudding or other sweets, is *gulu Malacca*,—boiled tapioca, with milk and burnt-sugar syrup.

From Suez to Japan one gets a great variety of fish, but on the restaurant menu no further description is given than is conveyed in the word 'fish', and it is the same at private houses and at the clubs. The American peanut or ground-nut, known as the monkey-nut in England, is very plentiful in Singapore, and goes by the Malay name of *cachong tana* (earth beans). The local Chinese name for them is *fasang*. Singapore housekeepers time their dinner-parties to take place a day or two after the arrival of the boat from Shanghai, which brings down beef from Japan, and game and other delicacies from North China....

There is little twilight in Singapore and if you want to enjoy the best part of the day, you must rise before 6. One morning we started from the hotel at 6.45 for Johor, driving up the Esplanade to the Bochor Road and into the Bukit Timah Road past the Lock Hospital—behind which lie the race course and golf links—the cemeteries for Europeans, the one for Chinese, the Chinese Club, and so into the country. Turning to the right at the fork into the Kranji Road we arrived at 8.30 at Kranji on the Johor Strait fourteen miles from our hotel. It is a charming drive in the early morning air and the road has a splendid surface and is almost level except for an easy hill at the eighth mile-post and another about a mile before Kranji. The road is lined with tress and is well ditched, some of the culverts being dated 1888. The mile-stones are marked with Arabian and Chinese numerals but the quarter-mile-stones in the fractions only. There is running water in the ditch and it serves many purposes. It is the bathing-place of the Chinaman's stray dogs and pigs; the bath-tub for small Malay children; the wash-tub of the Indian *dhoby* who afterward hangs his wash out to dry without clothes-pins or pegs by twisting two small ropes together tightly, stretching them out taut, and pulling them apart sufficiently to introduce the ends of the article, which is thus held fast; the receptacle for house drainage; and lastly the place where the coolie who is bringing your daily supply of vegetable stops to wash the harmless soil from them so that they may look fresh and clean when he delivers them! You go by sampan across the strait to Johor Bahru (or Bharu) to visit the Palace (*Istana*) and the gambling rooms, and to have tiffin at the Rest House opened by the sultan in 1898. This is almost a club-house with two double and four single bedrooms and every possible comfort....

On the way back our sampan coolie took advantage of the breeze and hoisted a large sail made up entirely from flour-bags bearing the names of American millers in great blue designs.

The Singapore sampan is licensed to carry eight passengers. The boatman, standing at the stern of the boat facing forward with right foot firmly planted athwart-ship, grasps the ends of the crossed handles of the oars so that he has his left-hand oar in his right hand and the right-hand oar in his left. He supports himself on the right foot and leans forward, pushing slowly at first and then with a sudden shove at the same time advancing his left foot with a sliding movement, and at times rising on the ball of the right foot. On the recover, the left foot is drawn back again until the heel touches the hollow of the right foot. The oars are made in three pieces, a small handle set at right angles to a shaft and a paddle joined thus. Each oar is attached by a loop of rope to an upright, with two notches, similar to those on the Venetian gondolas. The sails are nearly square and have bamboo booms top and bottom. When required for use, they are unrolled and hoisted to the top of the mast by a rope tied round the middle of one of the bamboos. There are ropes fastened to each end of the other bamboo and the boatman holds these in one hand while he steers with the other.

We stopped halfway between Kranji and Singapore to ascend Bukit Timah (Tin Hill), the highest point on the island. There is a fine view from its top, five or six hundred feet above the sea, and part of the hill is still covered with virgin forest. Returning by Cavanagh Road we drove through the grounds of Government House and back by the Brassa Brassa [Bras Basah] Road. Another morning we drove out Orchard Road to the Botanical Gardens and visited the Museum on our return.

One of the most curious things in Singapore is to watch the coolies coaling a big ship. Two of them carry, suspended to a

Coaling by night at Singapore, *The Graphic*, 4 November 1876. (Antiques of the Orient, Singapore)

short, thick bamboo pole, a large basket containing about a hundred weight of coal, and they go on board by one gang-plank, and back by another, keeping up a continual stream that soon fills the bunkers. And it is claimed that this method of coaling is not only cheaper but more rapid than any other. Coolies get one cent a basket from ship to wharf, or *vice versa*, more if carried any distance, and the merchant who undertook the contract informed me that during the war in the Philippines he had put on board the U.S. transport *Grant* 1200 tons in four hours, and had put 3000 tons on a British man-of-war in eight hours, or 375 tons an hour. But the record was made in 1888 when 1500 tons were put into a ship over two gang-planks in three hours, and it is said that smaller quantities have been put aboard ship at the same rate of 500 tons an hour. An average of 200 tons an hour in loading from alongside by steam cranes is considered to be very fast in England, and 250 tons an hour the outside limit, although 360 tons have been put aboard a German battleship in one hour. While at the wharf we could not help noticing the extreme expertness of the Malays who dive for coins from tiny dug-out canoes which they propel by using the hands for paddles; and the feet are employed in a continual scooping movement to keep the miniature vessel, which is over-whelmed by every wave, free of water and afloat....

There is another feature of Singapore life to be studied, after night-fall in Malay Street, where the native courtesans, as well as contingents of Austrian and Japanese women, have their abodes, and where the dusky beauties are always willing to sacrifice their natural coyness and modesty upon the purely commercial basis of three Mexican dollars in hand paid.

W. Del Mar, *Around the World Through Japan*, Adam and Charles Black, London, 1904, pp. 63–8.

40
John Chinaman, Master and Man

FRED RILEY
1899

Fred Riley, a British journalist and barrister-at-law, sailed from London in February 1899 aboard the P&O mail steamer India *bound for Bombay. After travelling in India and Ceylon, he arrived at Singapore on the P&O steamer* Parramatta *on 23 April, and stayed for a couple of days before sailing to Shanghai. During his journey round the world he contributed articles to local newspapers in Darwen, Rossendale, and Southport, and gathered them together for a book on his return home in 1900. This was printed for private circulation only, as the author did not want it 'to be judged by a critical and cynical public'.*

ON the Sunday morning we were all up betimes to view the magnificent scenery which is passed as you enter the harbour, and by 9.30 we were moored alongside the P. and O. wharf some three miles from the town. And what a scene met your eyes! No other town in the world possesses such a conglomeration of peoples as Singapore. And they all seemed to be gathered on the wharf. Native Malays, in brilliantly coloured cloths twisted round the waist and hanging like a petticoat in front; Chinese in black and heliotrope and white, wearing hats of all kinds, from a fashionable 'Trilby' to an umbrella-shaped 'straw', their pig-tails hanging to the ground almost in some cases, and in others coiled round and hidden in the hat; Parsees in their fly-catchers; Japs, with their slit-eyes; Tamils and Bengalis, with chocolate-coloured skins and dirty loin cloths, mixed with Europeans and Jews, Eurasians and Armenians, swarthy Arabs and African negroes, sleek-looking Cingalese and dapper little men from Siam, Achinese from Sumatra, Filipinos from Manila, Burmese from Rangoon, men from Java, from Anam, from Persia even. It was a veritable gathering of the nations of the East, brought together by the fascinating spell of 'trade', and the East was chiefly represented by the workers. But in Singapore John Chinaman is both master and man: he is capital and labour; and the shops and warehouses are for the most part owned by sons of the Celestial Empire. Indeed, the Chinese in Singapore number some 125,000 people out of a population of 190,000, and strange to say most of these are men, the reason being that the Chinese women do not leave their homes so readily as do the men....

There seem to be three towns: the English town, circling round Commercial-square, where are the chief banks and shops, and from which as a centre eight streets radiate; China town, where every other sign seems to belong to a 'Sing from Shanghai', and where the streets reek with the smell of opium and cooking; and Malay town, where the native Dyaks and Malays carry on their trade in fruits and fish. And in the streets of these districts some interesting street scenes present themselves. Here is the market: the stalls laden with pineapples, retailing at $\frac{1}{2}$d. each, with golden clusters of bananas, with mangoes, cocoa-nuts, green oranges, persimmons from China, and the far-famed mangostern, a delicate pulpy fruit, about the size of a small apple, with a slightly acid flavour. The pulp is found in the centre of a brown husk about half an inch thick, and the contrast between the brownish red of the husk and the ice creamy whiteness of the pulp is a veritable study in colour. Here are shops laden with meat from Siam and India; with fowls from Cochin China; and fish, fresh and dried, shark, cuttle fish, bonita, huge prawns, and crabs, brought alive to the market daily from the craft which stud the creeks and channels flowing between the archipelago surrounding Singapore.

Now you are in the Chinese quarter. In the workshop the 'toff' of the wharf has doffed his gown and works barebreasted. Turners, braziers, and tailors, they are all hard at work; a Chinaman never seems to dawdle,—except when he smokes his pipe of opium. And even then he does the thing thoroughly. Here you have the food shops: reeking with roast pig, with roast duck, with salt and dried fish, for all these things are dear to the Chinese stomach. Here is the 'Chow Chow' Avenue, every shop containing strange looking foods and preparations, which are eaten with relish by the pigtailed workers. That weird beating is the call of the itinerant restaurant keeper, who visits the workers in their dens, and who carries his tempting viands on two trays, each at the end of a bamboo. Yonder, in that dark corner of the shop, you can see a circle of Chinese, all men, partaking of their common meal. The Chinese seem to be always working or eating, smoking or sleeping,—but never playing.

In the shops of the Chinese you can buy anything. Malacca canes are as cheap as twigs, almost; clothes, which are more serviceable than stylish, you can have at prices which will make even a Jew open his eyes; baskets and wicker chairs are sold at a figure which renders even the competition of a co-op. store of no avail. But you must be careful in dealing with the Singapore shopkeeper. His porticoed shop may be clean; his sign may be embellished with brilliant portraits of his gods; but he is still a 'Heathen Chinese', whose object it is to get as much from the 'white devil' as possible, and he will cheat you by giving you bad coin, or by charging you a double price if he gets half a chance.

The public buildings of Singapore are not very imposing. The residence of the Governor is nicely situated on a small hill, but it scarcely compares with some of the residences of the Chinese millionaire merchants; the Post Office, the Town Hall, the Public Library, the Cathedral, the Presbyterian Church, the Gaol and Police Barracks, the Raffles Institution, and the Malay College, are all large and serviceable buildings, whilst the Government Offices are well situated near the harbour. But Nature has glorified Singapore sufficiently to dispense with architectural embellishments, and open spaces, well laid out, abound. The Chinese park is a pleasant garden in the middle of the most densely populated district, whilst on the Esplanade facing the Cathedral is a fine open space, ten acres in extent, with a sward like velvet, and with shadowy trees forming an avenue of great beauty. The Esplanade is a fine drive of about three miles in length facing the harbour and connecting the three towns.

F. Riley, *A Trip Round the World: Being Jottings Made on a Tour from London to Liverpool, via Africa, Asia, Australia, and America*, J. J. Riley, Darwen, Rossendale and Southport, 1900, pp. 116–19.

41
Singapore's Royal Visitors

WILLIAM MAXWELL
1901

The British journalist, William Maxwell, was assigned as special correspondent of the London Standard *to cover the royal tour of the British Empire by the Duke and Duchess of Cornwall and York between March and November 1901. He sailed from Portsmouth on 7 March aboard HMS* St George, *one of the four ships escorting the royal party in HMS* Ophir. *The Duke and Duchess, the future King Edward and Queen Alexandra, arrived at Singapore on 21 April, and stayed two days before sailing for Albany in Western Australia. They were received on landing by the Administrator (Governor from 26 September) of the Straits Settlements, Sir Frank Athelstane Swettenham, and the Malay rulers of Pahang, Perak, and Selangor. A durbar was held the following day at the Town Hall, when Sultan Idris of Perak was invested with the order of the Grand Cross of St Michael and St George. It is interesting to note that Sir John Anderson, who succeeded Swettenham as Governor in April 1904, accompanied the royal couple on their world tour as representative of the Colonial Office.*

SINGAPORE has attractions, but they are of the kind that are seen at their best in blue-books. It is very nice to know that this is one of the greatest ports in the world, that ten thousand ships enter the harbour every year, and that the value of its imports and exports is four hundred and fifty million dollars. These are facts gratifying to our imperial and commercial instincts. But most people who are not salamanders, and have not had the privilege of being brought up in incubators, would rather view them from the cool distance. Only when we escaped this vapour bath did we think of the scenic and social potentialities of Singapore. There are beauties beyond the town—gardens and orchards where the red mangastine grows and the evil-smelling durien for which men cultivate an unnatural taste. I have pleasant memories also of a drive, in the cool of the evening, to the impounding reservoir, and of meeting the Princess of Wales on her way to admire this beautiful English lake that was lately a swamp. But Singapore after all is a business house, and a port of call for the far East. It is supposed to be a British Colony. It looks like a bit of China with a leaven of Dutch and German. You can smell the Chinese as soon as you have left the little land-locked harbour with its border of perspiring green. The Dutch and German you have not long to search after, for their names are written large on the great warehouses and stores that proclaim the prosperity of Singapore. On the road from Borneo wharf, where the *Ophir* and her escort filled their bunkers, your rickshaw runs past acres of coal piled like ramparts, and coolies from China, who swarm like ants in dirty loin cloths and conical hats of straw, with baskets slung on bamboo poles. They are carrying coal to the ships. Despite their multitude and activity, ships have to wait every day to their loss, for wharfage is limited. It is whispered that the Tanjong Pagar, or company that controls the docks, has grown too fat to be enterprising, and that masters of ships in want of coal are beginning to patronise the Dutch establishment, Pulo Way.

But Singapore was not thinking of business. For two days there was holiday in honour of the Royal visitors. They landed on April 21st, under a remorseless sun, and were received by the Governor, Sir Frank Swettenham surrounded by the British community, and some of the principal Chinese. The Sultans of Pahang, Perak, and Selangor were in the company, but the Sultan of Johore had taken a holiday in Europe. The reception was of the conventional kind—a pavilion hung with flags and flowers, three or four banks of ladies in cool, white dresses, and five score perspiring Englishmen in frock coats and silk hats. After a few presentations, the Prince and Princess drove to the house of the Governor among the trees overlooking the bay.

It was Sunday, but the people have no fine scruples. In their quiet, Oriental way, they made the most of the occasion. The streets and buildings—Singapore has some fine shops and offices—were gay with flags. The esplanade, running close to the blue edge of the bay, with its crowded shipping, and bordered by a belt of trees, amid whose rich green shone the scarlet 'flame of the forest', or flamboyant acacia, looked bright and refreshing. Groups of coolies found it a pleasant retreat and a safe place for indulging the national vice of gambling with dice and a small square of cloth divided like a chess board. These games are prohibited, but no one pays attention. The Chinese quarter was especially gay. These inscrutable yellow men in shiny black or blue, with pig tails getting into the way of their heels, have peculiar aptitude for decoration. Their principal street, a long, broad thoroughfare that might have been transported from Pekin, was covered with a canopy of blue, white, red, yellow, and green, from which hung thousands of coloured lanterns. At either end stood an arch, round whose columns fiery-tongued dragons coiled themselves under hideous masks. The Chinese were very proud of this display, and certainly it did credit to their taste as well as to their patriotism. My rickshaw boy, I am convinced, took me a couple of miles out of my way in order that I might admire the dragons and the lanterns, and would have kept me circling all day round a pagoda erected at a cost of two thousand dollars. After I had driven him off he kept his head turned for half a mile, so that he might not lose a glimpse of this coloured paper monstrosity, around which a small Chinese population were squatted with wondering eyes. The Tamils, too, had done their best to show their pleasure, and had built an arch of many-shaded reds and golds. In short, nothing appears to be wanting to impress the Royal visitors with the wealth and loyalty of this strange and interesting community.

At the durbar, in the Town Hall, on Monday, were men of many races—Chinese, Arabs, Malays, Tamils, and all the medley of blood that makes the East. They came with tributes of loyalty, and laid them at the feet of the son of their suzerain—tributes of words, and of gold, and silver, and ivory. In the twelve deputations that added to the pile of precious caskets were men whose history one would have listened to with eager interest. Who was the Chinaman in feminine dress, with the peacock feather stuck in the back of his fool's cap? Why did he appear and reappear as if no presentation and no address could be regular without him? What were the thoughts of the two sober-looking Malays, sons of a deposed Sultan of Johore, when they noted the absence of the occupant of their father's throne, and saw men smile and shrug their shoulders? But the figures that attracted most were the four behind the chairs of the Prince and

Princess. They were picturesque if not imposing men, in shining raiment. Three of them wore jackets and trousers in which gold and silver threads were cunningly blended with heliotrope and green. From the waist to the knees hung the graceful folds of the sarong, or skirt of shimmering silk, in tartan and deep orange shade. The fourth and central figure was dressed more after European fashion, though the blue sarong and the brown irregular features proclaimed him Malay. These were the native rulers of the Federated Malay States—the Sultans of Perak, Pahang, and Selangor, and the Yam Tuan of Negri Sembilan. The deputations filed past with addresses and caskets—British-born subjects, the municipality of Singapore, the general community of Penang, the municipality of Penang, the general community of Malacca, the Singapore Chamber of Commerce, the Malays, the Chinese, and the Straits Chinese British Subjects Association, the Arabs, the Tamils and Chetties, the Chinese representatives of the Federated Malay States, and the Moslem Association—a microcosm of East and West, in silk hat and turban, frock coat and burnous. The heap of scrolls and caskets grew larger and larger until it overflowed the table. Malays brought a fine tusk mounted in gold, the men of Penang a lordly bamboo set in gold, and Chinese of Malaya a fire-screen on which their most famous craftsmen had employed their ornate skill, and had graven the address. When these presentations were at an end the Sultan of Perak—he of the semi-European dress—was invested with the order of a Knight of Michael and George, the Prince putting on his shoulders the blue and red ribbon....

W. Maxwell, *With the 'Ophir' Round the Empire: An Account of the Tour of the Prince and Princess of Wales 1901*, Cassell and Co., Ltd., London, 1902, pp. 57–61.

42
A Perpetual Turkish Bath

MARY MACFARLANE PARK
1901

The Scottish writer, Mary Macfarlane Park, left London in February 1901 aboard the Mary Park, *a tramp steamer chartered by the Government to take cattle and stores to St Helena and South Africa. She sailed in the ship from the Cape to Sydney, Manila, back to Australia, and then to China, Japan, Singapore, Ceylon, India, and Burma. She arrived at Singapore in November 1901, and in her account she relates some of the hazards confronting a visitor in hiring a rickshaw. She also refers to the distinguished Chinese, Dr Lim Boon Keng, who was at the forefront of all social and educational reforms among the Chinese in Singapore during the late nineteenth and early twentieth centuries. He had graduated Bachelor of Medicine from Edinburgh University in 1892, and three years later was appointed the Chinese member of the Straits Legislative Council.*

OUR run to the Straits Settlements was a time for indulging in *dolce far nienti*, the whole passage being pleasant and uneventful, till, on the 16th of November, we entered the fine harbour of the beautiful Island of Singapore, which is the capital. The bay is well sheltered, and the harbour was filled with shipping of every kind. The oldest inhabitant told us he remembered the time when there was hardly a German vessel of any size in the harbour, but he thought Britain was now taking 'a back seat', especially in the passenger traffic to the East. At one time Britain had an absolute monopoly in this important matter, but now magnificent German ships were constantly passing to and fro....

The magnificent harbour is well defended by several batteries, with heavy guns. The population includes a considerable portion of Chinese, regarding whom it has been said that 'They are the bone and sinew of the Malay States—the labourers, miners, shopkeepers, contractors, capitalists, holders of revenue, farms, and the contributors of nearly the whole of the revenue. We never make friends with them because they do not understand being treated as equals. But they are easily governed by the man of determination, and they are intelligent enough to understand that, under a strong, just administration, they can make money, which is their great object in life.'...

Britain's possession of Singapore secures for her 'the maritime superiority of the Eastern Seas'. In commercial phrase it is called one of the best 'corner stands' of the world—a place of call for large ships, in which the seas about it abound. Before landing we were introduced to the Malay boys, who swarmed around the 'Mary Park', in their small hollowed-out canoes, ready to dive for any contribution thrown into the sea. In the good old days silver bits only would be cast over the ship's side, but as soon as the splash of a copper is seen now-a-days the youthful divers will quickly follow after each, and never a piece is allowed to get to the bottom. We thought it an enviable occupation as we stood in the sweltering heat watching them.

This is the spot where the too, too solid flesh appears to melt, as at Singapore most Europeans feel as if in a perpetual Turkish bath. Being almost on the line, the temperature hardly varies, except that the nights are cool; and the island is clothed with richest verdure. Here, truly, 'Nature hangs her mantle green on every blooming tree', the daily equatorial showers giving the luxuriant vegetation a freshness that entitles Singapore to vie with fair Erin as Emerald Isle. As it is too hot for walking, there is the choice of the Japanese jinrickshaw or the Indian gharry, or small brougham, drawn by the sturdy little Delhi ponies. The gharry has a well-covered roof, open at the sides and end, but its Venetian blinds can be drawn up over the openings as a protection from the burning sun, and, while our drivers at home have often to climb laboriously to their seats, the Malay gharryman, gaily dressed in full native costume, lissomly rolls himself into his.

The town has a number of fine public buildings, banks, warehouses, and shops, the latter—especially the Indian and Chinese—being most enticing. The architecture is also enriched by Mohammedan mosques, Hindu temples, and Chinese joss houses. A handsome Episcopal Cathedral, dedicated at St. Andrew, and the oldest cathedral in the East, occupies a good site, and the Presbyterian Church is prettily situated, and well attended by the Scottish residents. Government House is a conspicuous building on Mount Sophia, a special feature of it being its lofty rooms and spacious ballroom. As we drove through the beautiful Botanical Gardens it was easy to imagine ourselves in a terrestrial Eden, for here, in this tropical isle, growing in perfection and profusion in their native heat, were all the plants upon which such care and attention is bestowed in our conservatories at home, and added to this was a forest of trees, many of them aflame with a mass of Hybiscus blossom. Every kind of tropical fruit is to be had in Singapore—the juicy mango, the golden banana, the custard apple, the cocoa-nut, and the much-thought-of mangosteen, as well as more common varieties; though to the Scottish taste probably a good strawberry would surpass them all.

It was a novel experience to form one of a party at an evening promenade in the gardens. Not a few fine carriages moved slowly along the well-kept paths, enabling their occupants to enjoy the excellent music of the band; but great numbers of people promenaded, all wearing evening dress, and regaled themselves with refreshments consisting of fruits, ices, and coffee. As we drove through the surrounding country with our kind host, at whose hospitable home we stayed for some days, we saw many interesting and curious things. One thing which amused us was to see the monkeys sitting as unconcernedly among the branches of the trees quite close to the roadsides, as though they were in the heart of a primeval forest. A feature of the place is the many houses scattered here and there, a few of which are built in bungalow style and stand within spacious compounds.

Like every other visitor, we went to see the garden of the retired Chinese millionaire merchant, Whampoa, which is one of the sights of Singapore. As you traverse its many acres, the variety and richness of its charms are a source of continued and increasing surprise....

To their credit it may be said that the Chinese seem to be both loyal and grateful to Great Britain, apparently realising that they owe a debt of gratitude for the even-handed justice they receive, and for the opportunities given them of earning a comfortable livelihood on British soil. Wealthy Chinese merchants occupy some of the finest houses in Singapore, while it may safely be said that their horses and carriages are among the best to be seen on the Padang. Dr Lim Boon Keng, the leading medical practitioner, was a graduate of Edinburgh University, and sat for several years in the Legislative Council. Needless to say he had shorn his pigtail and donned European dress.

Rejoicings in honour of the birthday of King Edward took place while we were on the island, and there was a considerable amount of festivity, most of the Celestials doing their share by making a brave show of flags and bunting at their residences....

One morning I had rather an exciting adventure. Getting into a 'rickshaw, I thought I had made the coolie understand that he was to run me to the harbour, but soon I found myself in paths unknown. On remonstrating with him he merely shook his head and led me to understand that it was all right. Further and further we got into the country until not a house was to be seen, and still, with short intervals of rest, he went smilingly on. In the circumstances I could do nothing but wait hopefully for something to turn up, and by-and-by we came upon a Chinese lady who had come out of her palanquin on seeing us.

Not much more than a child in appearance, and with a child's unabashed simplicity, she smiled upon us, and with her small black head, on which there was not a hair awry, she looked as though she had just stepped from a picture on an old tea chest. Fortunately for me she knew a little English, and, telling her bearers that I wished to get to the harbour, the coolie, who seemed to have taken possession of me, now turned and went in the right direction. On getting near the ship I was very thankful to see my host, and to be transferred to his trap. His explanation of the conduct of the coolie was that he knew perfectly well where I wanted to go, but hoped to earn more coin by taking me for the long run, a practice which is not altogether unheard of even in the British Isles....

One thing I never could get accustomed to in the East is the hateful mosquito, and Singapore will ever be remembered by us on account of the swarms of them that plagued us there. Everything in the shape of remedies—ammonia, oils, and anything supposed to have virtue—were applied to my smarting flesh, but to no purpose, the abominable little pests refusing to be exorcised.

Mary Macfarlane Park, *Greater Britain and the Far East, or 60,000 Miles on the 'Mary Park'*, The Grant Educational Co., Ltd., London & Glasgow, *c.*1918, pp. 144–51.

43
Exiles on a Cramped Little Island

ETHEL COLQUHOUN
1901

In 1901, the year following her marriage to Archibald Colquhoun, the writer and explorer, Ethel Colquhoun travelled with him to Singapore, Java, Borneo, the Philippines, Japan, Korea and Russia, returning home by the Trans-Siberian railway. She described these journeys, and her impressions of Singapore, in a delightful book entitled Two on their Travels, *illustrated with her own drawings. Her husband died in 1914, and she remarried and went to live in Southern Rhodesia, where she was appointed a member of the Legislative Council. She edited for a time the* Journal *of the Royal Colonial Institute, and she was also a member of the executive committee of the Women's Emigration Association.*

ON Christmas Eve we arrived off Singapore and anchored outside for the night....

The next day we all landed, and Andrew [Colquhoun] and I felt rather forlorn at having no one to meet us or wish us 'Merry Christmas'. I was, however, consoled by the novelty of my first ride in a 'rickshaw'. This was before I had learnt that it is not *comme il faut* for a lady to be seen in a 'rickshaw' in Singapore, but indeed there are so many things which are incorrect in that most particular place that it takes a long while to learn them all. For instance, white duck coats buttoning up to the chin, such as are worn in most parts of the East, are not *comme il faut* for gentlemen, and there is some unspoken law about waistcoat buttons and another about trousers which I am not competent to explain. Once the novelty has departed, however, 'rickshaws' are as little attractive as they are correct, for I could never get accustomed to a bare brown back bobbing about in front of me, and frequently streaming with perspiration!

Singapore is an island. It is flat with the exception of one hill, and that is very steep. Owing to circumstances the only place where people can be conveniently isolated is the top of this young mountain, and therefore honeymooning couples frequent it, and spend a week in a sort of *dak* bungalow or rest-house on the top. As there is nothing particular to do, and one must take one's provisions and servants, the young couple are usually delighted to return to Singapore, and cease to abuse it for a day or two. Singapore is not singular in the fact that, although it is freely maligned by all its inhabitants among themselves, they do not permit criticism on the part of visitors. They won't even admit the vileness of the climate, though pale cheeks and lack-lustre eyes attest it. As a matter of fact Rudyard Kipling said the last word about it when he called it a hot-house. There is a constant, damp, muggy heat. The cooling shower, which I had been told fell every day and cleared the atmosphere, turned out to be a sort of thunderous explosion which left the air as hot as ever and charged with moisture. In such a climate trees and vegetation thrive, and the island is a verdant mass of greenery through which wind the white roads. The town proper lies on the shore, and contains a fine *maidan* (open space) and many handsome buildings. Almost every one lives in what are called the suburbs, pretty shady quarters, where bungalows nestle in little gardens on either side of a grass-edged road. The town is continued towards the suburbs by straggling native streets, and there is a whole quarter in Singapore itself given up to the Chinese. The first thing that strikes one about the East, or the Orient as Americans call it, is that nearly every one of the native inhabitants keeps a shop. The shops are just boxes without lids lying on one side, and are decorated elaborately with red and gold letters. Sometimes there is a counter, sometimes the goods are merely stacked on shelves round the box, but there is always a Chinaman in a scanty blue dress with a long pipe in his mouth somewhere about the premises, and some very nude babies playing in the gutter just outside. If the babies are not nude they are fantastically dressed like little men in all the colours of the rainbow; their faces are thickly powdered and perhaps sprinkled with gold-dust. The native streets of Singapore are full of fascination, for the queerest medley of Oriental races may be seen there. Klings, as all the Hindoos are called here, stride along swathed in diaphanous white garments, looking more like chocolate skeletons than men, and wearing their hair long, and fierce moustaches, while their dark eyes gleam and flash under folded turbans. Their slender women sway along beside them, little olive faces and wondering sombre eyes peeping out from their yellow draperies. There is a peculiar sap green beloved of these Hindoos which rises before my eyes as I write. A touch of it in the veil, while the body is shrouded in reddish ochre—it sounds barbarous, but how marvellously Orientals understand colour! Against a background of golden fruit, oranges and bananas, the slender figure so swathed makes a dark vivid spot in the sunlight and as we watch the brown, yellow and green melt into each other, we feel wonder-stricken that we should ever have cared for the washiness of 'French grey' or 'eau-de-Nil'.

There are, of course, a variety of costumes even among the Klings. Students outrage both taste and propriety by wearing white shirts *outside* their trousers, and black coats or waistcoats with round black caps, while coolies are lightly attired in turbans and loin bands. The Cingalese are unmistakable, and surely theirs is the most absurd of costumes, although undoubtedly comfortable....

Singapore is ... far more Chinese than Malay. Small Malay fishing villages exist on the coast, but the Chinese swarm over the whole island, and are elbowing even the Europeans out of the best residential parts. On the fashionable drive along the sea-front in the afternoon the smartest carriages belong to Chinese merchants, and I have special recollections of a particularly *chic* turn-out, a phaeton and spirited pair, driven by a young fellow in the most correct suit of light tweed, with buckskin gloves, fashionable soft grey hat—and a long black pigtail hanging down behind! John on a bicycle is another Singapore sight, especially when he adheres to his own loose jacket and trousers but crowns his head with a billycock. His tail is neatly tucked into a small pocket to prevent it catching in the wheels.

The English colony at Singapore is, of course, largely made up of males, and the proportion of unmarried girls is even smaller. 'How lovely!' exclaims Miss Wallflower, and pictures to herself the good time she could have in such a favoured spot. Of course, as far as dancing is concerned, it must really be a blessing, for there is no dancing girl or woman living who does not hate to 'sit out'. But I am not sure that I should care for attentions bestowed on me *faute de mieux* and, as far as general society is concerned, it seems a very deplorable state of affairs. After all, one can't talk comfortably to more than one man at once, and when one's attentions have to be impartially distributed among twenty-five the whole affair becomes a bore. As in all small communities, the great drawback is that all the women know each other so extemely well, and all the men know each other (and the women too) even better, so that social intercourse is apt to fall into the familiarity which breeds contempt. The Singapore club is a great institution. Andrew never started out anywhere without ending up at that club, having always, as he assured me, been literally dragged there by some casually-met acquaintance: and the stories he picked up were wonderful; being a new man every one was glad, of course, to secure him as an audience. Singaporeans are not, perhaps, so charitable to each other as they are to their climate, but for hospitality and kindness to the stranger within their gates they are bad to beat. They put us up, dined us and drove us about; they paragraphed us in the local papers, and generally did everything they could to prevent us from feeling home-sick. Poor dears! They live in the baleful atmosphere of a hothouse. They are exiles and prisoners on a cramped little island, from which they cannot even escape for a short holiday at times, only to go 'home'. They naturally get to regard Singapore as the hub of the universe, and to feel as if the whole creation centred round their tiny world of small civil, military, and mercantile duties. They can't exercise charity to their poorer neighbours—for neither Chinese nor Malays are exactly subjects for my Lady Bountiful—so that it is not perhaps wonderful that that much-abused virtue gets rusty in their intercourse with social equals. By the way, who *are* social equals in a place like Singapore? If that point were settled by an Act of Parliament, which would provide the exact order of precedence from the Governor and his lady down to a mercantile skipper and his good woman, much heart-burning would be avoided.

The servant question is not so pressing in the Far East because there are always plenty of 'boys', as Chinese domestics

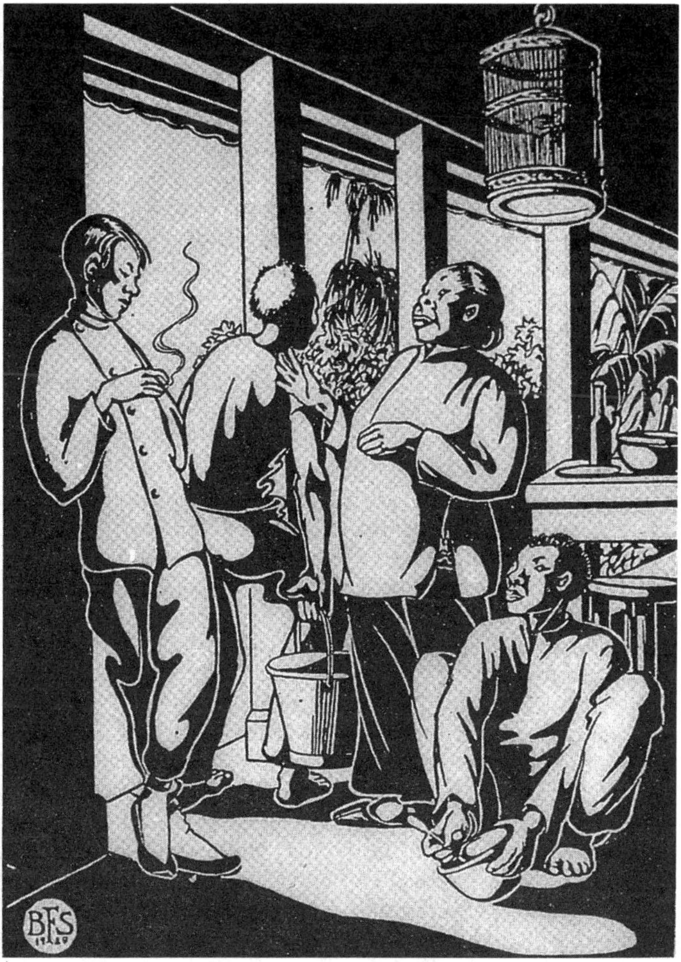

Domestic staff—the 'boy', water carrier (*tukang ayer*), maid (*amah*), and cook—in a well-to-do household, from Ashley Gibson, *The Malay Peninsula and Archipelago*, J. M. Dent & Sons, Ltd., London, 1928.

are called in pidgin-English, the equivalent for a male child in the same lingo being 'smalloboy'. John the cook-boy does all the marketing, and arranges all the meals after a short morning colloquy with his mistress. John the house-boy looks after master's clothes, and keeps them in such perfect order that master himself never gives them a thought; at any moment John can always produce exactly the garment needed. John the parlourmaid (or head boy) will arrange the flowers, look after guests, concoct cooling drinks, and do anything and everything. Every household employs besides a *toucanaya*, often a Malay, who does the dirty work of the house, and is a sort of social pariah. There are, of course, more Malays for the stables and Chinese for the gardens, but these are the usual house-servants. Children have Chinese *amahs*, and the same sleek-headed creatures, with big rings of jade in their ears, loose blue coats and wide trousers, act as ladies' maids.

Ethel Colquhoun, *Two on Their Travels*, William Heinemann, London, 1902, pp. 8–16.

44
Chinese Theatre

GEORGE C. MORANT
1905

George C. Morant was involved in the British insurance business, and in that capacity travelled widely during the late nineteenth and early twentieth centuries. In 1913 he wrote a book entitled Odds and Ends of Foreign Travel *in which he describes some of his experiences, including a visit to a Chinese theatre in Singapore in 1905. In the Preface to the book he reminds his readers that the facilities for modern travel were much changed from what he knew: 'As regards Ocean Steamers the cabins were very different from what they are now; they were lighted by candles in a glass-protected opening in the partition; the bunks were of the old type with wooden laths; the food was sometimes far from appetising, and such things as electric light and electric fans were, of course, unknown.'*

CHINESE constitute the majority of the population of Singapore, and, although they come from various provinces, most of them are Babas or those born in the Straits Settlements. They speak various dialects according to their origin; and, although none of them apparently understand the Cantonese and Pekinese languages, in which theatrical performances are usually given, they are passionately fond of such entertainments, from the humble outdoor 'penny gaff' (if I may so call it) to the more classical representations in the regularly constructed and more imposing 'opera house'.

Many have written about the Chinese theatre, and particularly those who have visited San Francisco, where it used to be considered one of the stock sights; but I do not know if many have entered into details, or if they have, they have not come under my notice; and I am therefore writing this ... from the notes taken by me of a performance at the principal Chinese theatre in Singapore, in order to make good the apparent deficiency.

Europeans were certainly not frequent visitors to the theatre in question, for our little party was at first refused admission point-blank; though this was probably only done with a view to obtaining increased prices, for the Chinaman is an astute man of business wherever met with, and our arrival had evidently put the money taker upon his mettle.

However, after considerable discussion and bargaining, we were ultimately allowed to pass the screen which shut off the view of the interior from the doorway, and found ourselves in a large and crowded hall with a stage at the further end, a gallery on either side, and a third gallery above the entrance. The ground floor and the last-named gallery were reserved for men, and the two side galleries for women and children. Outside the rails of the galleries was a broad ledge, along which vendors of tea, fruit and other 'chow' walked, supplying the requirements of the audience, most of whom were eating, drinking or talking with absolute disregard to the performance which was proceeding—but then the play had been going on for several days, and was likely to go on to the end of the week, so that one or two Acts more or less made little difference to the habitués.

Seats were found for us in the end gallery, at the back of which facing the stage was the usual Joss (or Chinese Altar if it may be so called), though as this is usually connected with personal ancestor worship, its appearance in a theatre was somewhat inexplicable. But Chinese manners and methods are all to a great extent inexplicable even to those foreigners who know most of them.

After the audience, the first thing that naturally attracted my attention was the stage, which was merely a platform approached by doors from the back (left and right) and by two short flights of steps from the body of the auditorium. It was absolutely devoid of scenery and the stage furniture consisted of a table and three chairs, while on the wall at the left was hung for general information the Play Bill, a sheet of red paper about 18 inches broad by some 2 feet 6 inches in length.

Members of the audience walked up one or other of the flights of steps at intervals and sat at the sides or on the edge of the stage with their legs hanging over, while children sat, squatted, or rolled about it at their pleasure, no notice whatever being taken of them by the actors.

In this connection it is interesting to note that it is recorded by Leigh Hunt in 'The Town' that in London until the time of Garrick, 'members of the audience often sat about a stage as at the sides of a room, and the actor had to make his way among them, sometimes with the chance of being insulted'.

At the back of the stage sat the orchestra who wore no dress in particular, the majority of them being clad only in the short, full knickerbockers from waist to above the knee, the usual costume of the coolie class. But what they lacked in clothing they made up for in noise, punctuating the libretto apparently at their own sweet will, and the greater part of the time drowning the voices of the actors altogether by the beating of a gong and the clashing of cymbals, interspersed with occasional taps on an instrument sounding like a xylophone.

In what I presume were the more sentimental passages, the noise ceased and the musical accompaniment was taken up by a fiddle; and, when the play had worked up to a sensational point, a kind of clarinet burst in with bagpipe-like tones, winding up with a long-drawn, ear-piercing shriek. This instrument, however came in very seldom, the brunt of the work falling upon the gong and the cymbals.

But the play, 'the play's the thing!' This particular one, as I

Performance at a *wayang*, or Chinese theatre, *Illustrated London News*, 20 August 1887. (Antiques of the Orient, Singapore)

was informed by a friendly Chinaman who sat behind me, had been going on for three days and would probably not be finished for another three days, so that one had to pick up the threads of the subject as best one could. In any case it would have been impossible to do so from the words, which could only be heard at rare intervals, owing to the noise made by the orchestra; while, as my Chinese friend told me, the language was high-class Cantonese, which only a few of those present (including himself) understood, the majority of the audience being Hokkiens and Babas, to whom it was absolutely unintelligible, and who consequently followed the plot by means of the action only....

I was desirous of seeing the interior of a Chinese private house in Singapore, and Mr Tan Keng Swee, a wealthy contractor, upon the introduction of a mutual friend, courteously gave me the opportunity.

Accompanied by the friend in question I accordingly presented myself at his residence at 8.30 a.m., the hour fixed by him, and as I understood, one of the usual visiting hours in Chinese polite society.

His grounds were surrounded by a high wall entered through large and solid gates embellished with figures and, to me, unknown animals, beetles, birds, and flowers in a highly coloured enamelled ware. Passing through these gates I found myself in a large and beautiful garden kept with a degree of care and neatness which could not be surpassed; flower borders were interspersed with fancy pots and vases containing rose trees in full bloom and various other flowers, yews and box trees cut and trained in a variety of fantastic designs and patterns, the inevitable dragon predominating, and stone ornaments of more or less quaint appearance.

Facing the entrance gates and carried along the whole length of the house was a broad verandah, from the ceiling of which hung numerous ornamental cages containing birds of varied hues, not the least interesting of which was a small bluish-black 'magpie' (so called) which whistled to order on a wave of the hand.

On this verandah I was received by a Chinaman, whom I took to be my host, who gave me the names of the various plants, flowers, and birds, and other interesting information; but as etiquette did not permit of my taking notes at the time, most of the names and much of the information had slipped from my memory before my note book was available.

We did not, however, seem to be getting any nearer to the interior, and I was beginning to fear that my visit would commence and end on the door-step, when an older and more dignified gentleman appeared, and I then learned that I had been talking to his younger brother, Mr Tan Keng Wah, who, on the arrival of his senior, stepped aside with the deference shown by the Chinese to their elders; and although he accompanied us over the house he did not again open his lips until the time came to say farewell!

After introduction and a short conversation in which my friend acted as interpreter, my host, with a stately wave of the hand, invited me to enter the reception room, a lofty chamber, of which the walls were hung with inscriptions and designs on silk materials. Round the walls were arranged stiff high-backed chairs and settees of carved blackwood, upholstered in coloured marble, which did not offer much in the way of comfort; while on either side were doors leading to private apartments (presumably bedrooms), which were not at that early hour open to inspection.

From the reception room we passed through a corridor to a spacious courtyard partly open to the sky, and containing numerous articles of furniture and ornaments which would have delighted the eyes of the curio hunter. Prominence was given to several large specimens of grotto or rock work with miniature houses, bridges, pagodas, and figures dotted about them; and one grand specimen, which my host informed me came from Canton, represented a mountain, on the sides of which innumerable dwarf trees (Cedars, Junipers, Pines and other species) were growing to represent a forest, many of them being of very great age; while here and there houses and figures were introduced, and down the mountain side trickled a miniature waterfall into a lake at the foot.

Other interesting objects were glass tanks standing on ornamental tables and containing shoals of little fishes, less than an inch, and many of them half-an-inch only, in length, of the brightest colours, sapphire, ruby, topaz, and emerald, which rushed to the surface in a crowd when Mr Tan Keng Swee tapped the glass, and followed his finger round the tank in a state of great excitement. I could not gather whence they came or what they were, but the effect produced was most beautiful as they swam round the tank like so many little flashing gems. What struck me on this occasion, as on others, was the love of birds, fish and flowers shown by the educated Chinaman, which is not altogether what one would expect from them, judging by the ordinary descriptions of their characteristics!

But I had almost forgotten one of the great features of the Courtyard, which was a magnificent Joss (I call it a 'joss', but am not sure that this is the correct description) in crimson lacquer, 12 feet high and 8 feet broad. It contained the history of the owner's ancestors, and in front of it were two handsome vases, which, had I not known that the Chinese bury their dead, I should have assumed contained their ashes. The Joss, or Screen, or whatever it should be called, was placed at the bottom of the Court, and when all the intervening doors were thrown open it made a splendid finish to the vista from the verandah.

I spent more than an hour in looking at the various specimens of Chinese art, and in conversation with the Towkay, and came away impressed not only with the courtesy but also with the intelligence and dignity of the educated Chinaman....

A circumstance which frequently came under my notice in Eastern cities was that, as a rule, the European residents took little or no interest in the manners and customs of the native inhabitants, and saw or knew less of what seemed to me the interesting features of native life than the casual visitor who went about with his eyes and his mind wide open, losing no opportunity of investigating local practices and witnessing local scenes.

I do not wish to imply that all casual visitors go about with their eyes open, for I have often met travellers who knew little or nothing of some of the places they had visited beyond the names of the hotels at which they stayed, the club where they may have been asked to tiffin, and one or two of the principal sights usually brought under the notice of the personally conducted tourist.

Nor, on the other hand, do I mean to say that no European residents take any trouble to inform themselves upon such matters; but the majority of them appeared to me to be too much concerned in their business affairs and personal European surroundings and amusements, and it struck me also that in many instances there was a certain amount of affectation, real or assumed, in their ignorance.

G. C. Morant, *Odds and Ends of Foreign Travel*, Charles and Edwin Layton, London, 1913, pp. 68–70, 74–6.

45
Malay Theatre

WILLIAM GEORGE BLACK
1907

After travelling through India and Burma, the Scotsman, William George Black, reached Singapore in March 1907, and shortly afterwards sailed for Hong Kong. During his brief stay he visited the Malay theatre, which was playing Shakespeare's A Merchant of Venice. *He gives an amusing account of the performance in his book,* Winter Days in India and Elsewhere, *which was privately printed at Glasgow in 1908. He later became chairman of the Ophthalmic Institution and of the Ministry of Pensions Board in Glasgow.*

AT Singapore the brilliancy of the green grass at once surprises and delights the eye accustomed to the burnt-up soil of India.... The health of the community is very good; the mosquitoes are intolerable, but they are not malarious; there is no plague or fever. I was speaking to a resident, formerly of Glasgow, who has lived in the island since 1873, and in all that time he has only, he says, been one week away from business from ill-health, and he has only once gone home. Certainly all the white population, ladies and men alike, look surprisingly fresh and vigorous, and this they attribute to the very thing which tries so severely their visitor, viz., the excessive humidity. There are great wide roads most beautifully smooth and well kept, handsome public buildings, and a general air of prosperity....

We went one night to the Malay theatre, where the 'Merchant of Venice' was played in Malay. What Irving missed!

What Beerbohm Tree has to learn! Among the incidental novelties, Shylock, Antonio, and Bassanio sang their parts to each other to modern waltz airs; but at intervals the action of the play stopped altogether, and two weird children came on to sing an American coon song; that finished amid loud applause, Shakespeare was resumed. Under such circumstances little wonder that the performances usually go on till two a.m. Portia was a little difficult to identify at first, but we found her at last in a plump and serious Malay girl with a wealth of heavy black hair hanging down her back and a very short skirt; she had however, magnificent gold anklets, and sat in a sahib's cane arm-chair with the dignity which befitted the lady of Belmont. She also sang several ballads in Malay, which I cannot think were Shakespearean; so, too, each suitor in the casket scene covered his sorrow by a judicious interjection of a pathetic or comic song, and Portia joined frankly and openly in the merriment. I cannot say of Shylock 'this was the Jew that Shakespeare drew', but he was vigorous. The Malay scene-painter's Venice had been developed out of his inner consciousness of what Venice should be, and certainly St. Mark's Piazza might be improved by a large group of tropical plants in the centre. A 'Street in Venice' owed something naturally to Singapore—particularly as regarded a large Union Jack on the top of a small hillock at the extremity of the perspective. But why cavil? It was a street, and would not any street in Venice or otherwise be improved by the Union Jack in full flow? I am glad I saw the 'Merchant of Venice', but I am sorry I did not see 'Hamlet', for there must be great capabilities in it, from a Malay point of view....

I went one morning to the Law Courts of Singapore and heard the Chief-Justice deliver a considered judgment in a very intricate case as to certain rights in a property, the title to which it was admitted by both sides was a forgery. Courts at home are a trifle too warm for comfort; here the air was delightfully cool, for the Courts were great, wide, open halls, well shaded, and with many punkahs unintermittently waving. The Chief-Justice wore a gown but no wig; the members of the Bar wore no wigs, but as regards the upper portion of their persons they were otherwise immaculately correct in white ties, black waistcoats, and gown; but, without exception, they all wore white trousers, for the Law (which loves fiction even in the tropics) supposes lower limbs to be invisible. White, of course, is the universal dress of every European in this land. The newspapers are trenchantly written and interesting, and there can be little wanting to the happiness of those who can stand the climate, where turtle is the cheapest food and pineapples are a drug in the market. The present Governor is Sir John Anderson, an Aberdonian, who was long in the Colonial Office; he lives in a stately palace on a height above the town, and takes a vigorous and discriminating share in the administration of this happy little Colony, where, of course, there are many Scotsmen. Scotsmen, indeed, and men of Devon seem to share between them nearly all the positions of enterprise in the East, whether in the tea gardens of Assam, or the teak forests of Burma, or the tropical islands of the Malay Archipelago.

W. G. Black, *Winter Days in India and Elsewhere*, James Maclehose and Sons, Glasgow, 1908, pp. 52–7.

46
A Picturesque Medley

JAMES CARTER
1907

The Canadian writer, James Carter, began his world tour in Newfoundland in March 1907, when he sailed for New York and travelled across the United States to San Francisco, where he boarded the steamer Korea *for Japan. He transferred to the* Mongolia *for Nagasaki and Shanghai, changed ships again for Hong Kong, and then boarded the P&O steamer* Moravia, *which arrived at Singapore in the early morning of 12 September and sailed for Penang and Ceylon 30 hours later. Despite the brevity of his stay, Carter managed to acquire a good deal of information about Singapore for his book,* In the Wake of the Setting Sun.

SINGAPORE appears to consist of three towns—the business, or English town, Malay and China town. They are all connected by a wide esplanade facing the

The Padang, by A. L. Watson, *c.*1905–10. (National Museum, Singapore)

harbour, between two and three miles long. In the European quarter the streets are wide and macadamized, with handsome shops, having plate-glass windows and all the modern improvements, and well furnished with a high-class stock of goods of all kinds. There are many fine public buildings, the principal of which are the City Hall, post office, police barracks, public library, museum, court house, numerous public offices, Colonial Secretary's office, banks, steamship and insurance offices, clubs, etc.; all handsome stone edifices of considerable pretensions. There are numerous hotels, high class and modern in construction, such as 'Raffles', 'Adelphi' and 'de l'Europe'—splendid large erections, handsomely fitted up, and containing accommodation for 300 guests. Some of them have garden roofs. The ecclesiastical interest is well represented: a very fine, stately English cathedral with a high spire, and Roman Catholics, Presbyterians and Wesleyans have all handsome erections, besides mission-houses, Young Men's and Women's Christian Associations and Nonconformist chapels. In fact, Singapore is a handsome city, of which its citizens may be well proud. It has an extensive esplanade along the waterfront lined with business houses. The harbour is safe and secure, and at the time visited had a large number of steamers of all nationalities, which, with the numerous steam-launches and large and small craft and boats, made quite a busy scene. There is an extensive market, with quite a display of vegetables and fruit. Tramcars run the circuit of the town, and there are vehicles of all descriptions, including the jinrikishas, of which there is quite a number; the European carriages, well equipped with picturesque drivers and well-goomed horses, including what is termed the Indian 'gharry', containing four persons, drawn by active, wiry little ponies about eleven hands high, which bowl you along at the rate of eight or nine miles an hour, with wonderful endurance. Their drivers are Malays in full native costume. The smart dress of the Malays forms a striking feature. It consists of a single piece of silk, woven in as many and varied colours as Joseph's coat, twisted round the waist and hanging down petticoat-fashion to below the knees; a piece of white muslin or cotton cloth thrown picturesquely about the shoulders, and a turban of crimson silk. This finery is only for the street; for a glimpse into house or shop reveals these same dandies squatting about on floor or counter with nothing on but a loin-cloth. Another picturesque feature is the number of carts, some of them covered, each drawn by a pair of bullocks. The animals are of Indian breed, with hump and large, spreading horns. The native cattle have a peculiar long head, but small body. The crowds in the streets contribute a picturesque medley of dresses, the costumes of all nationalities adding to the local charm, which would be hard to match elsewhere even in the East. The residential dwellings and mansions of the influential citizens deserve more than a passing notice, but in my short visit I could observe only a few. I did not visit Government House, but could see that the grounds leading to it were beautifully laid out. The Sultan's palace is a large building, bordering the road to the Botanical Gardens; there were many fine mansions on the same road, situated in handsome grounds, with palms and trees, etc.

J. Carter, *In the Wake of the Setting Sun*, Hurst and Blackett Ltd., London, 1908, pp. 310–11.

47
The Singapore Mutiny

ANON.
1915

The mutiny of part of the 5th Indian Light Infantry Regiment at the Alexandra Barracks south-west of the city, on the afternoon of 15 February 1915, caused consternation and fear in Singapore. The mutiny stemmed from the dissatisfaction among the Rajputs in the regiment with conditions of service, and from the spread of anti-British feeling by Muslim extremists. About half of the regiment mutinied, shortly before it was due to leave for service in Hong Kong. The mutineers killed—within half an hour—one Malay and three British officers, seven British and two Malay non-commissioned officers, and wounded a number of others. Their attempt to enlist the support of German prisoners of war at the camp at Tanglin met with little success, and one German was killed. Other civilians were killed as the mutineers fanned out towards the city. The 5th Indian Light Infantry Regiment was the only regular army unit in Singapore, and apart from local volunteer forces the Government had to rely on the assistance of marines on Japanese, French, and Russian warships to quell the mutiny, while at the same time arranging for the European women to be accommodated on ships in the harbour. Altogether the mutineers killed some 40 people during their rampage, and although the mutiny was essentially contained within a couple of days, it took the authorities some weeks to capture all the mutineers. Some 202 Indian officers, NCOs, and sepoys were put on trial, and all except one were convicted; 47 of them were executed by firing squad, while the others were sentenced to transportation and imprisonment for terms ranging from seven years to life. The mutiny occurred at the height of the First World War, and the alarm it caused among the European population of Singapore is reflected in the account of an Englishwoman which was written and published in the same year.

CHINESE NEW YEAR fell on Sunday, 14th February, and as usual the town had a holiday, all business premises being closed until Wednesday morning....

About four o'clock, as I rested, we heard several loud reports like rifle-shots quite near, but as the Chinese were continually sending off Chinese crackers, and we had been enduring the noise for days, I thought nothing of it....

The German prisoners were interned in a barbed-wire enclosure near the barracks, and had been guarded by Indian soldiers, all the white troops having gone to the front. Volunteer officers were up at Tanglin, and some volunteers were guarding the prisoners, as the Fifth Light Infantry were to leave for Hong-Kong during the next day or two. The Sultan of Johore's Malays had come over to relieve the Fifth, and I believe some of them also were at Tanglin.

L. went into another room where he could hear better.... He went into his dressing-room to dress, but just at that moment a R.A.M.C. soldier, unarmed, white and breathless, and followed by a white-faced woman without a hat, rushed up the servants' stairs at my door. He called to L., 'The Fifth have risen and are firing on the hospital; will you look after Mrs V.?' I heard his voice but not the words. Immediately L.

called out, 'Get up and dress,' in such a voice that I knew something terrible had happened.

I jumped up, looked over the screen door, and saw the woman. I called her in, at the same time getting into the first clothes I could find. Mrs V., wife of a sergeant-major in the R.A.M.C., was the only white woman left in the barracks. All the others had gone Home with the regiment. She told me that she was standing on her verandah looking across to the Military Hospital, expecting her husband to come over to tea, when suddenly she heard firing and saw the Chinese boys and two patients (Germans) come tearing out of the hospital. Down below the German prisoners were playing football. Then a soldier rushed across and called out, 'Come down, Mrs V.; don't wait for anything.' She ran down and they both fled along the back lane at the foot of our garden, passing the M.'s back gate, but as bullets were falling around they came on to us....

I never felt more frightened in my life; my knees seemed to be giving way, and I kept saying to myself, 'Keep your head—keep your head.'...

The Indian Mutiny flashed into my mind; also the fact that we had no white troops. L. was splendid, so cool and collected, but his face was as white as death. I knew he felt pretty desperate. However, we got off and drove straight to town....

We drove straight to Hotel Europe, and Mrs V. and I went up to a friend who lives there, while L. gave the alarm....

The mutineers had entered the guard-room at Tanglin Barracks, passed the Sikh on guard, and killed the three officers who were there....

It is a strange thing that the mutineers seem to have avoided killing women. I heard it said that their religion forbids it, but I can scarcely believe that; they did not hesitate to kill women in the Indian Mutiny.

Can you fancy the feelings of this handful of women sitting waiting to be told what to do, darkness coming on so quickly as it does out here in the East, no one knowing where the trouble was,—it seemed to be everywhere (it really started in three places at once), and no one knew who was in it. In this town of many nationalities and creeds, we are so few Europeans compared to the Chinese and other races. We half feared a rising of all the natives, Chinese too. I met a woman in the hotel corridor that evening who said to me, 'If the Chinese rise the only thing to do is to shoot ourselves—don't you think so?' I said I did not believe I should have the courage, but I suppose I should have done it....

At the Club I found lots of women, nearly everyone I knew, and heard all about their experiences and escapes. We sat about and waited, and then Commander R. and Lieutenant C. came in and said all women were to go on to the *Ipoh*, a Straits Steamship steamer lying in harbour. It was not yet martial law, nor yet the Admiral's orders, so I and some other women refused to go, as it meant leaving our husbands who were not volunteers, and so might be with us for a bit. Most, however, went on board the *Ipoh*, and I returned with L. and a few women and odd men to the Europe....

On Monday night many women and children were taken to Government House.... A guard was set round Government House, as they expected to be attacked.

There were 818 men in the Fifth Light Infantry, and they were almost all out, only a very few remaining faithful, and these did nothing to prevent the others in their dreadful work. They are Punjaubees, and look fine big men. They say this is a Holy War, but we believe it is instigated by Germans and financed by German money. At Government House the staircase was barricaded with mattresses and chairs, and men with rifles put there on guard; the women were told to go on the roof should it be attacked....

We heard later that some hundreds of the mutineers were marching on the town that night, and were stopped by the volunteers and the men of H.M.S. *Cadmus*, which is lying here just now....

Next morning we got up very early and came down to hear more reports of people killed, and not much news of any other kind....

On Tuesday morning the Admiral ordered all women and children to go on to a ship, the transport *Nile*....

We arrived at the *Nile*, a boat built to carry 100 passengers (Canadian Pacific Liner), now made into a transport, and found it packed—not a chance of a berth....

As news was good on Wednesday, I and other women

wrote to our husbands telling how awful it was and asking them to make other arrangements, and at last we were taken off....

We were always hoping to see the *Montcalm*, the French cruiser recalled by wireless, come in. We looked to her for rescue, but as events turned out the worst was over before she returned on Wednesday night, because our own volunteers and the H.M.S. *Cadmus* men had saved us. The French landed on Thursday and assisted in clearing the mutineers off, but I don't think they saw much fighting. Indeed, there was little of that after the first night and day following. The sniping continued, and the hunting down of small bodies of mutineers who were most of them too scared to come in and surrender, but had no more spirit to fight. Report says that at the beginning the mutineers heard that we had got big guns and were going to use them, so they scattered and were leaderless, which proved their undoing and our salvation.

Two Jap gunboats came in, and they also landed men later on to assist, as did the Russians from a volunteer cruiser lying in harbour. The Russians had two men seriously wounded about a week after the mutiny began. We have had a French review, a Jap review, and a Russian review since, when the Governor came down and personally thanked them all for their assistance.

There were wonderfully few casualties in the fighting. Most of the deaths were caused by cold-blooded murder. The Germans were unguarded the first night, as the volunteer guards were shot by the mutineers, and all the other men had to go to protect the residents of Singapore. Some of the Germans escaped, but found life outside so unpleasant under the circumstances that they returned to their prison....

We were not allowed to return to our house until very late, because it was in the unsafe area. The rebels had been all about it, but not in our compound. The 'Kebun' found bullets in our compound, and that firing must have been done during the time we were in the house. Seventy rebels went all over the D.'s compound, and entered the next house, where they drank water, but took nothing and damaged nothing. They also went into Mount Echo, but did no damage; and then searched a Chinaman's house opposite, looking for

Europeans; they would not believe him when he said that the house belonged to him. That was, of course, quite near us. They went to several houses to ask the 'boys' if the 'Tuans' had returned.

One mutineer was found outside Raffles' Hotel disguised as a Chinese coolie, and wearing a large straw hat. A gharry-wallah spotted him, and he was taken to the Drill Hall and recognised at once as one of the Fifth L.I. Two others were caught near the Europe Hotel, sitting on the padang by the sea. Some were found disguised as Malays, but most were caught in the jungle, hungry and miserable.

Later on there was a public execution of two mutineers, and since then many have been shot inside the jail. L., as Special Constable, had to go to the public execution. He with the others was put through a little drill before starting, so as to look more impressive to the natives. After this preliminary they marched to Sepoy Lines, and there on the bank, beside the 6th hole on the Golf Course, were thousands of natives, all creeds and colours, come to see the sight. The Volunteers and Special Constables formed a square, the prison wall making the one side facing the crowd on the Links. The two prisoners were brought out by European warders and tied to stakes in front of the prison wall. A British officer read out their crime—of mutiny and murder, I suppose,—but L. was too far off to hear. Then a Malay interpreter read it out in Malay, and lastly a Chinaman in Chinese, the crowd listening in silence. The firing party of the M.S.V.R. men then stepped forward and fired.

Anon., 'A Lady's Experiences in the Singapore Mutiny', *Blackwood's Magazine*, CXCVIII, No. MCCII (1915), pp. 781–94.

48
Visit of a British Press Baron

LORD NORTHCLIFFE
1921

In July 1921 the journalist and newspaper proprietor, Alfred Charles Harmsworth, Viscount Northcliffe, founder of the London Daily Mail *and* Daily Mirror *and chief proprietor of* The Times, *set out from London on a world tour, traveliing across Canada to Vancouver, and thence by steamship to New Zealand, Australia, Sabah, the Philippines, Hong Kong, Japan, China, and Singapore, which he reached on 30 November aboard the steamer* Nyanza. *During his short visit of two days he stayed with the Governor of the Straits Settlements, Sir Laurence Guillemard, and his wife, at Government House. He returned to London in February 1922, and died shortly afterwards. His observations on his travels were dictated daily to one of his private secretaries, and dispatched home for circulation among members of his family. They were published in book form in the year following his death.*

WE arrived off Singapore last night at about 11.30. Curiously enough, it was a cool night, down to 82, and every one slept like tops.

The Governor at Singapore wired me, saying that I should be met at seven o'clock, the boat being due at the quay at six. It is seven o'clock, and we are still waiting for the quarantine doctor—the beginning of the Singapore slowness we have heard so much about.

We wondered what Singapore would be like. We had read a good deal about it. As we approached the land, it seemed to consist of a long series of low-lying islands. The place is very green, like Fiji or Ireland.

Landed, we are at once in a very busy place; boats of all kinds; and rickshaws running about everywhere.

There was the usual meeting on the landing-stage; aides-de-camp, reporters, cinematograph operator, dark and grinning, and the rest of them. An excellent English motor car drove me off to Government House. We passed through the town, seeing all sorts of people we have never seen before.

The place looks bright and gay, not quite like any other place we have been to. The reason it is green is because there is rain every day, at this time of year, about four o'clock. It is not so hot and steamy to-day as, I believe, it usually is.

Government House stands high over Singapore, and I have a fine view from my window overlooking the green forest. I am busy with cables and letters, which follow us steadily around, with invitations from Ceylon and Bombay which one must deal with.

His Excellency Sir Laurence Guillemard and his Lady are old friends of ours. They are very nice people. There are all sorts of local difficulties here—labour, tin, rubber, and the rest. Everywhere we go the Governor has his difficulties.

This morning I drove with her very nice Ladyship, who is a great admirer of Lady N., to the museum, where I saw many strange birds, beasts, and fishes. I did not realize before what a figure the kingfisher is in this part of the world. I had noticed him in Borneo, and he is very numerous in China. Many kingfishers don't catch fish at all, but are fly catchers. Here I saw also that horribly human proboscis monkey with long human nose....

The Governor has kindly let me have a quiet day to-day.

It takes at least twenty-four hours to find one's bearings here; everything is so different. I am surprised to find the Chinese living in palaces and the English in very modest houses. The best motor cars are occupied by Chinese—notably the only Rolls-Royce. All sorts of things are surprising. The food is surprising. I had a fruit called the mangosteen, certainly the most delicious fruit in the world. His Excellency says that the fruit has never got home; they have tried again and again. I am sending some by Pine. The mangosteen is a little larger than the walnut in its outer covering. You squeeze it, and it opens, and you find little sections, as in an orange, though white.

Just a word as to clothing outfitters who know about the Far East. Be careful about them. My bootmaker has provided me with ridiculous shoes which won't stand the heat. My hatter gave me a hat which weighs a ton.

The European children here seem happy. I saw them playing to-day guarded by their Chinese or Malay amahs, of whom they are very fond. These nurses spoil them, however, and they have to be ordered home when they are seven years of age. On the whole, the children look very well....

It is half-past eight as I write this. A quarter of an hour's walk in the shade would make one wet through, but these folks are hurrying about, riding in motor cars and rickshaws, making their way to work. There is supposed to be business depression in Singapore just now, but I see no signs of it.

This morning I thought it quite cold, but at six o'clock I found that it was 82.

Government House life here is like Government House life elsewhere. Except for the difference in climate, I might be in Melbourne or any other Government House. The Governor and his Lady are very kind. They have left me very much alone. I saw interesting people this morning. Their Excellencies are having a State banquet to-night, so that I may meet more.

I went out in the business section of the town this morning—Malays, Chinese, and Eurasians working in the blazing heat. It is funny to go into offices and see black clerks and typists. The Malays wear little velvet caps. They are well-mannered people.

Singapore is a very big port, they say the fifth in the world. In Singapore no one knows about any other place. We are trying to find out about Saigon (Indo-China) and Batavia (Java). No one knows. It is said that rival steamship companies won't tell about each other.

It is curious to notice all the Christmas goods in the shops; 1922 almanacs and the rest. It is a much more prosperous and much bigger place than we at home know. The cost of living here is said to be the highest in the Far East.

As I have said, it rains here every afternoon, hence the beautiful greenness of everything.

In the early evening I played golf with General Sir J. S. Fowler (commanding troops) and the Chief Justice; the same queer kind of golf I play everywhere, but greens this time, much of the grass being sensitive grass, as in Borneo. The caddies were little Malay boys.

It is very interesting to see John Bull's governing machine at work in these places. I do admire the way the people tackle their jobs in this infernal climate, for such it is. Everything is damp. As I dictate I am eating Huntley and Palmer's biscuits, which are like putty. The men and women are wonderfully vigorous with their golf, lawn tennis, and riding. On talking to them I find most of them long to get home; none would stay here but for the absolute need of earning their living, and the enthusiasm they have for their work.

My secretary tells me that they have jazz dancing here in the afternoon, as everywhere else. St. Andrew's Ball took place last night; people were at it till four o'clock this morning.

I had a gorgeous orchid given to me to-day, six foot three in height! It is a sort of tiger-lily, a very beautiful thing.

On the golf course this afternoon, soldiers were drilling. They are South Staffordshires. They wear khaki shorts, their knees bare, and pith helmets....

Last night's dinner was what used to be called in the days of Champagne Charley, the Coal Hole, Thackeray and Leech, 'a slap-up affair'. It was the first time I have ever dined with Chinese ladies. They were incrusted with diamonds. Out here, the O.B.E. is a high distinction. Chinese ladies and the leaders of the community wore it, and it looked well midst their soup plates of diamonds. Against their dark skins, diamonds look extremely well. Two of them spoke English as well as we do. I was glad to see them in Chinese costume. One arrived in a Rolls-Royce, and a gorgeous one at that.

His Excellency and his Lady do things very well here. I am not fond of pomp and circumstance, but those who are told me that the servants, in their white liveries, red hats, and silver staffs in their hands, wore the costume of the old John Company (East India Company). There was a good deal of ceremony. During the dinner the band of the Staffordshires played toppingly.

Lord Northcliffe, *My Journey Round the World (16 July 1921–26 Feb. 1922)*, ed. C. & St. J. Harmsworth, John Lane, The Bodley Head Ltd., London, 1923, pp. 160–4.

49
The Prince of Wales in Singapore

SIR PERCIVAL PHILLIPS
1922

The author, an American by birth, worked on newspapers in the United States until 1901, when he joined the staff of the London Daily Express *and, after 1922, that of the* Daily Mail. *He had accompanied Edward, Prince of Wales, during his tour of Canada in 1919, and he joined him again for his tour of the Far East during 1921–2. He wrote the official account of the tour, which lasted for eight months and involved a journey of nearly 41,000 miles. After spending four months in India and Ceylon, the Prince of Wales sailed for Japan aboard HMS* Renown. *The royal party called briefly at Singapore, where a crowded two-day programme of events had been arranged to welcome him.*

THE two-day programme at Singapore kept the Prince fully occupied from the moment he landed at Johnston's Pier on Friday morning. The drive through the streets from the water front to Government House gave him a wonderful picture of the composite population of the busy port. Malays, Chinese, Indians, and Japanese were hardly less industrious than his own countrymen in helping dress the route in gay colours, and in adorning it with arches of original design. In a great amphitheatre built for the occasion were assembled 10,000 children of many nationalities, and the Prince made them happy by walking around the tiers of seats and listening to their singing. He unveiled an imposing War Memorial on the Harbour front. In the grounds of Government House he found 400 wild warriors from Borneo—Dyaks, Kayans, and other tribesmen—lightly clad in jackets covered with fishskin, and ornamented with strange necklaces of bones, shells, stones, tiger-cat teeth, and silver coins. As the Prince passed they brandished their spears and gave loud cries of welcome. The women were shy but interested, and one plucked up sufficient courage to show the Prince her arm which was sore and swollen from the effects of vaccination, as a protest against an inexplicable 'punishment'. The Prince saw the warriors again in the afternoon when he opened the Malaya-Borneo exhibition. A replica of a Dyak village had been erected on stilts in the exhibition grounds, and fitted with the rude furniture and household implements of these primitive people. They had even brought clusters of human skulls—the trophies of head hunting expeditions undertaken by their forefathers—and suspended them like chandeliers from the grass thatched roof of the long common room. Nothing pleased the men of Borneo more than for a visitor to examine these gruesome heirlooms and ask questions about their family feuds.

P. Phillips, *The Prince of Wales' Eastern Book: A Pictorial Record of the Voyages of H.M.S. 'Renown' 1921–1922*, Hodder and Stoughton Ltd., London, 1922.

50
Perennially Fascinating Singapore

HERMANN NORDEN
1922

Having had his plans of visiting the Pacific Islands changed by missing his ship at San Francisco, the American writer and traveller, Hermann Norden, went instead to Sarawak, Malaya, and Thailand. He arrived at Singapore from Labuan aboard the steamer Deli, *and booked in at Raffles Hotel. He noted a new feature of the period, the beach combers of Singapore—unemployed British planters thrown out of work due to the post-First World War crash in rubber prices, and the consequent closing down of many plantations: 'Handsome young Englishmen, still dressed in the whites of the tropics, though whites no longer immaculate, who come into the clubs and hotels to borrow small sums from any who will lend. A white man without resource in a yellow man's country is always a tragic sight, and Singapore is now full of these tragic sights. Beach combers there have always been, of course; but this type did not exist on my former visits. It is a product of post-war conditions.'*

THREE days of rest on the steamer, and we were at Singapore, and anchored opposite Johnson's Pier. Grey-haired David, the veteran hotel-runner of the Raffles, and, like James, a Madrasee, appeared, took charge of my belongings, and we crossed to shore in the steamship company's launch. Disdainfully I walked past taxis, motor-buses and horse-drawn gharries, and chose the time-honoured rickshaw for my drive to the hotel. It was still too early for the bank, which was my most necessary port of call.

Perennially fascinating is Singapore, with its hundred tongues; its port alive with steamers, big and small, on their way to every part of the globe; and with its hustling, bustling life ashore. All the races of the world, representatives of every stage of civilisation jostle each other in the streets. I found the aspect of the city somewhat changed in the eight years since my last visit, but the changes are in the way of additions. The old is still there, unmodified, though crowded by the new. For example, automobiles have multiplied, but the gharry and the rickshaw still carry travellers who prefer picturesqueness to speed.

Sunset finds many strollers on the Esplanade, watching the ball and tennis games on the green lawns set aside for sports. I enjoyed, too, walking along the very busy Raffles quay, with its mile of feeding stands for the coolies. Here, in these open-air markets filled with merchandise of every description, the Chinaman reigns supreme. Well he may, for he represents the majority of Singapore's three hundred thousand population. On the quay he is ever busy trying to make trade with customers of his own race, and with Hindus, Malays, Javanese, Tamils, Anamese, Cambodjans, and with many another out of the maelstrom of humanity that whirls in that busy harbour.

A cinema theatre was attracting crowds. I looked in. Charlie Chaplin was the star. Of all the audience the rickshaw coolies seemed the most appreciative; perhaps they were glad to see someone else getting the kicks, for once. The life of a rickshaw coolie is very hard. If he does not run fast enough to please his patron he is apt to get a jab in the ribs. If he goes too fast to please the police he is fined. Just that day, an ambitious coolie had run me into a street car, and had been fined a dollar (fifty cents in our money), which was a day's earnings. The entry in the police blotter read, 'For exceeding reasonable speed, and endangering public safety.'

I peeped, too, into the well-remembered cosy nook on the second floor of John Little's big department store, set aside for the hungry and thirsty and flirtatious of the foreign born of Singapore. It was, as always, crowded. Everybody loves Little.

But Singapore, with all the rest of the world, is changed, by the way. Much of the old-time gaiety is gone; the Europeans are preoccupied and restrained. The planter is lying low, hoping for a better price for his product. The business man is having a bad time with the exchange situation, and the breathless race with competitors for the little business that is being done. The Chinese alone are prospering, and that only as a class. Individually great losses are being suffered. Recently some Tow Kays (Chinese bosses) lost hundreds of thousands of dollars in one deal, and they are 'hitting the pipe' in order to forget. Of course in times like these all luxuries go begging for purchasers. An Indian dealer in High Street told me that he had just sold a bird of paradise for fifty Straits dollars—twenty-five dollars in United States money. In the old days there would have been a scramble for it at five times that price. The lucky buyer was a lady from the China coast.

H. Norden, *From Golden Gate to Golden Sun: A Record of Travel, Sport and Observation in Siam and Malaya*, H. F. & G. Witherby, London, 1923, pp. 61–3.

51
The Great Crossroads of the East

HUBBARD HUTCHINSON
1923

Hubbard Hutchinson was an American traveller who sailed round the world by way of Madeira, Gibraltar, the Mediterranean, Egypt, India, Ceylon, Burma, Singapore, Java, the Far East, Guam, Suva, Apia, and Panama. He stayed only one day in Singapore, but he seems to have spent it fully. He had the usual problem with rickshaws. Having asked to be taken to the Sri Mariamman (Hindu) Temple in South Bridge Road, the rickshaw coolie took him to a railway dump: 'Frantic inquiry of many passers at last elicited English, and presently symphonic Chinese, and eventually we drew up before the desired edifice.'

IN this great crossroads of the East, the Forty-second Street and Fifth Avenue of Oriental trade, we had just one all too brief day, which remains inevitably a rather kaleidoscopic affair. In the morning we wandered freely, in the afternoon we took a long and swift motor drive, and at five we sailed away over glassy and gorgeously opalescent seas to the equator and Java.

As we drew up toward the West Wharf, we had a faint echo of long-gone Madeira—for the water swarmed with small boats containing Malays who in raucous voices howled for coins. Their canoes were slim splinters, guided with incredible skill by clumsy-looking paddles. We threw coins down the naked brown bodies, glistening and muscular, curved gracefully over the side, and picked up their canoes again with the nonchalance of a European picking up his hat. One pantherish glide, and they were inside; a flutter of hollowed foot like a waving fan, and the water was bailed out and they were raising another lusty howl for more nickels.

Motors conveyed us through busy, broad, and very English-looking streets to the famous Raffles Hotel, among a population of fascinating variety. The myriad rickshaws were pulled by Chinese in pointed hats like pagoda roofs, and with legs whose muscular development is only equalled by that of Nijinsky and Isadora Duncan. Moving sedately through scurrying motors and carriages were slow ox-carts upon which sat sooty Tamils from southern India, Aryan of feature but black as ebony. The coppery bodies of Malays gleamed here and there, sometimes light as a tanned Caucasian. It is curious how the mind changes; if one bare-chested man walked up Tremont Street there would be well-bred faintings in all directions; here we looked at nakedness everywhere about us, and the most fastidious were not seen to bat an eye! Modesty seems largely habit and geography.

Once at the hotel, we changed our money into the Straits dollar (worth fifty cents American), and sallied forth in quest of the article for which Singapore is most famous (to the tourist), Malacca canes. These slender reeds, which grow on an adjacent island, are here made up and marketed to all parts of the world—with ultimate prices that would paralyze the simple Chinese maker, as any one who has bought them in New York knows.

We finally found a shop where they were made—a little dark place with evident residence above. The Chinese keeper grinned and promised. We picked out two canes from unbent lengths. Yes, he would have them ready by night. We haggled about prices and finally secured two for just one third the price of one in a New York shop....

After vague and pleasant ramblings through the many-peopled streets, I returned to the Raffles' pleasant terraces for an excellent lunch, and set off at once thereafter on a long drive.

This led past government buildings along Alexandra Road to the Botanical Gardens, a small edition of those at Peredinya, to the Hindu Temple of my morning experience, and back past the hotel to the Chinese section of the city. This is extensive, gay, and prosperous; huge lanterns bedeck little shop doors, and the elaborate carving, later to become so familiar in the shops of Peking, appeared. Through these we swept out into the country along the East Coast road, lined with magnificent palms and following the sea, to the Sea View Hotel, most attractively located on the coast, a little suggestive of Mt. Lavinia, with its swimming beach, and diving board, and broad, comfortable verandahs.

H. Hutchinson, *Far Harbours Around the World*, G. P. Putnam's Sons, New York, and The Knickerbocker Press, London, 1924, pp. 166–71.

52
The Europe and Raffles Hotels

HORACE BLEACKLEY
1925–1926

In October 1925 the 57-year-old British novelist and biographer, Horace William Bleackley, joined the Messageries Maritimes liner André-Lebon *at Marseilles, bound for Colombo, Singapore, and Saigon, where he began a tour of Indo-China, Malaya, Java, Sumatra, and Ceylon. He arrived back at Singapore on the* Paul-Lecat *on the last day of December, in time to observe the New Year festivities at the Raffles and Europe Hotels. The two hotels held a dance on six nights of the week, but apart from these dances Bleackley found few public amusements in Singapore. He noted that behind the façade of the hotels and public buildings lay the mean streets housing the mass of the Chinese population. He died five years after he returned to England from his Asian tour.*

THERE is an air of grandeur about Singapore and everything appears to be on a large scale. The size and populousness, the wealth and importance of the great seaport are manifest at first sight. It has natural surroundings of much beauty; it is a handsome and stately city in itself.

Unlike Saigon, evidence of its riches can be seen before one disembarks. All around the shores of the harbour there are docks and store sheds, workshops and factories, indicating the extent and volume of its commerce. Its numerous wharfs always seem to be occupied by great liners and cargo ships from every country in the world. The Roads within the breakwater are crowded with coasting vessels of all descriptions. When driving from the quay through the business part of the town its opulence is still more conspicuous. The offices and warehouses, the shops and stores suggest that its trade must be equal to that of any port in the Mediterranean.

Not only is it an imposing city, but an exceedingly attractive one also. When passing over the Cavenagh Bridge across the river from the commercial into the residential quarter of Singapore, the first glimpse is seen of its picturesque aspect. The bridge is a suspension bridge, narrow and inadequate, but the river that it spans is full of interest. It was the old harbour, and its left bank, which bends almost in a half-circle, is crowded with ancient Chinese houses. Of various elevations and in different styles of architecture, they appear to be painted in all the colours of the rainbow; and, when the sun is revealing every line and shade of them, the curved frontage of the irregular buildings seems as complex and kaleidoscopic as a street in Venice. The water is covered with craft of every description, laden with merchandise. Canoes and barges, filled with busy lightermen, flit about in all directions up and down the stream. No scene in the East has been painted or photographed more frequently than the view of the Singapore river from the Cavenagh Bridge....

Beyond the Victoria Memorial a wide lawn extends along the sea-front for four or five hundred yards, an expanse of grass-land known as the Padang, which is spacious enough to contain two cricket fields as well as a football ground. At one extremity is the fine club-house of the Singapore cricket club; at the other a large pavilion for the use of Eurasians. In front stretch the Roads, filled with ships of every shape and size, and beyond is the open sea.

This portion of the city is singularly beautiful. Inland, across the avenue that skirts the Padang, is the Anglican Cathedral, a graceful edifice with a tall spire, surrounded by a broad lawn resembling the close of an English cathedral and encircled by trees. It is like a vision of home. Skirting the close a fine street leads away from the sea; and, passing through more pleasant open spaces with public buildings and abundance of foliage, it enters at last into the Orchard Road. This highway ought to be the most splendid in Singapore, for it forms the approach to Government House and to the chief residential quarter in the suburbs. But, alas, its whole length almost is disfigured by squalid Chinese dwellings. It is to be hoped that the municipal authorities will be strong and of good courage and take heroic measures, demolishing without scruple every hovel from end to end of Orchard Road, so that a great boulevard may come into being, worthy of one of the proudest and richest cities in the East.

Likewise, it is possible to make splendid improvements on the sea-front. For about a quarter of a mile on the verge of the Padang a marine drive has been constructed along the

Luggage stickers, *c.*1920. (Raffles Hotel Collection)

shore, a fine promenade indeed, but wholly insufficient. Unquestionably, Singapore is destined to become the first and most important seaport in Asia, if not in the whole world....

Driving away from the gates of Government Park down the Orchard Road, past the open spaces occupied by the Museum, a Tennis Club, and the Raffles Institution, we arrive once more on the sea-front at the eastern extremity of the Padang, where stands the huge Raffles Hotel. It has been celebrated by Kipling, and is the chief resort of the American tourist. Abutting on to the garden and facing the sea is a spacious pavilion—open on three sides, and adjoining the dining-hall—where dances take place in the evening three times a week. The bedrooms in the various annexes communicating with the main building are cool and airy. Excellent though the Raffles Hotel may be in every particular, it must, however, give precedence to the Europe Hotel, which is situated at the western end of the Padang nearer to the business quarter of the city.

The Europe Hotel, too, faces the sea and is divided from the Padang merely by a road. Its reception-rooms have been made adequate after elaborate alteration, and there is a restaurant and a lounge and a large dining-hall, which, unlike that at the Raffles Hotel, has to serve also as a ballroom. But the rest of the building is old-fashioned and ill-suited to the tropics. It is wonderful that a first-class hotel can be conducted under such circumstances.

No one is more anxious than the manager to level the place to the ground and build anew.

This manager is a genius, otherwise he would have been unable to create the best hotel in Asia in such an uncompromising environment. His name is Arthur Odell, but he is no relation to the famous veteran of the Savage Club. All sorts of stories are told of his prowess. Once upon a time, it is said, the whole of the kitchen staff went on strike when the hotel was full, whereupon he cooked the dinner for all his guests, aided by two European chefs, without turning a hair. And none of the mutinous staff were ever allowed to come back again. Beyond all question, Mr Odell is a master of his craft. There are few things beneath his roof—except the architecture of the premises, and for this he is not responsible—at which the most captious person can grumble.

Such a man is a splendid asset to the colony. He has made the name of the Europe Hotel as familiar a household word as that of Singapore itself. The renown of one is inseparable from that of the other; the two cannot be dissociated. A superlative *maître d'hôtel* is sure of a place in history. Ciro and Ritz will be remembered when most contemporary statesmen are forgotten. And thus it is inevitable that Arthur Odell will occupy a niche in the temple of fame beside the three other paramount benefactors of Malaya—Birch and Swettenham and Raffles....

Upon arriving at an Asiatic town it is a good plan to take a rickshaw for an hour at a time, permitting the coolie to trot whither he chooses, and stopping him at any place of interest. In this manner one soon acquires a knowledge of the locality. In Singapore, however, there are two objections to this method. It is probable that a rain-storm will descend during the drive; it is inevitable that the 'boy' will lose himself irretrievably. The *coolie-pousse* of Singapore is the most thick-headed Chinaman that ever breathed, and, if you tell him 'pergi Europe Hotel', he is quite likely to take you to Raffles. Moreover, the hood and the apron of the rickshaw are by no means impervious to a tropical deluge. For a short course a rickshaw is well enough, but for a long journey it is better to take a motor-car....

A fresh part of the pretty island may be seen by following the eastern road through one of the native slums of the city as far as Sea View. Traversing dense mangrove swamps and groves of coco-nut trees, we arrive at a commodious hotel standing upon a wide lawn amongst clusters of palms close to the beach. Not far away is a plantation of casuarina trees. On every Sunday night—the only night of the week when there is no public dance in Singapore—dinner is served on the terrace of the Sea View Hotel, followed by an open-air cinema exhibition.

But the most famous drive of all takes one across the island from south to north—a distance of fourteen miles—to the Johore Causeway. This is the artificial isthmus—a fine engineering feat completed recently—that joins Singapore to the mainland of Malaya. It spans the narrow strait, which is only half a mile in width, over which it conveys both a motor road and the railway. It is possible now to travel by train from Singapore to Bangkok in Siam through the whole length of the Malay Peninsula.

On the eastern side of the straits, several miles from the Causeway, the excavations for the new Naval Base have been commenced. During its construction thousands of coolies will be employed in addition to scores of English engineers. When completed it will be the headquarters of a great fleet, as important an arsenal as Malta. The officers and crews of the ships, together with their inevitable entourage, must increase the European population considerably. The effect of the new development on the trade and prosperity of Malaya will be incalculable....

Upon my second arrival in Singapore, on the last day of 1925, the city was on the eve of its festivities for the New

Year. There were fancy-dress balls at each of the four or five principal hotels, that at the 'Europe', which I attended, being perhaps the most popular. It was a pretty and elaborate spectacle.

The women of Singapore dress well. Indeed, their frocks seem as though they were fresh from London and Paris. All the latest fashions appear here soon after they are in vogue at home, and no one has any difficulty in keeping up to date who can afford to do so. Most of the ladies are good-looking, too, and have boundless energy. Occasionally, one notices a pale cheek when the holiday to Europe has been postponed too long, but almost every woman recovers her bloom after she has been home to England. A visit to the highlands of Brastagi in Sumatra, a journey of a day and a half, seems just as efficacious. Unfortunately, there is no such excellent hill-station in the Malay Peninsula.

The ballroom costume of the men, for the most part, is ordinary evening-dress, the most unsuitable attire for dancing in the tropics that could be imagined. But some are wise enough to wear a drill mess-jacket, and soft shirts are not uncommon. At Government House, however, a tail-coat is compulsory, with white tie and waistcoat in addition, terrific instruments of torture when the temperature is eighty-five degrees in the shade. Its wearer feels just like an ancient Crusader must have felt in his suit of mail armour on a midsummer's day in the Holy Land. Yet, in spite of the heat the men of Singapore are the keenest of dancing men, which is not strange since they have pretty and pleasant dancing partners. There is a dance on six nights of the week either at the Europe Hotel or at the 'Raffles'.

While watching the New Year's ball at the Europe Hotel it occurred to me that there was something unusual in its appearance. And presently I understood what it was. All the dancers were young! No woman in the room appeared older than forty-five; there was not a man of more than fifty. The colony, of course, is peopled for the most part by youth. When folks become elderly they retire home; or, if they stay, they do not cumber the dancing-floor. So, unlike our English ballrooms, where the grey-beards and the dowagers crowd out the poor young folk, those in Singapore are a scene of youth and beauty....

The hospitality of the people of Singapore is embarrassing

in its profusion. Nothing could be more kind than my welcome from every one to whom I had an introduction. It was not long before I discovered why the residents looked so healthy and were so healthy. Their avidity for all forms of exercise is not the main reason. It is because of the excellence of the food. Although cold storage is responsible for the exotic dishes in the restaurants of the hotels, the private houses can command a plentiful supply of fresh meat and poultry and vegetables of as good quality as are obtainable at home. And a Malay curry is the best curry in the world....

The elegant and the sordid are found cheek by jowl in Singapore. Behind the handsome public buildings a labyrinth of mean streets branches in all directions, where the Chinese population—more than three hundred thousand in number—are conglomerated. There is no separate Chinatown as at Saigon and the Celestial has spread himself over the centre of the city. Although no one could be more cleanly when in domestic service, John Chinaman cannot help making his own home into a pig-sty, abominable both as regards odour and dirt. A stroll of little more than fifty yards from the Europe Hotel brings one into the midst of his squalid habitations.

For the most part the houses are of two storeys, the ground floor being usually a shop with dwelling-rooms upstairs, the windows of which are screened by latticed shutters. Every conceivable trade is carried on in these little shops, and a piazza often extends along the pavement in front as a protection from the sun. The streets swarm with rickshaws and bullock-carts, the latter being a replica of the Cambodian bullock-cart of a thousand years ago, drawn by two small oxen with humps on their backs. There are innumerable Ford motor-buses, always full of black and yellow men packed like sardines. The tramway, too, has wide ramifications and is patronized principally by natives.

Both the Tamil and the Chinese women act as beasts of burden, staggering along the road in vest and skirt or a suit of black pyjamas with a bamboo pole across the shoulders, at either end of which a bundle of firewood or a can of water is dangling, balanced like a pair of scales. Food stalls can be seen everywhere as well as numbers of travelling kitchens, where scraps of offal are fried in sausage fashion; and these never lack patrons, for the Chink appears to be always hungry. At the corner of the more important streets a Sikh policeman is stationed to watch the traffic, a black-bearded fellow with gay turban and khaki uniform. Sometimes the policeman wears a long and narrow strip of wickerwork strapped behind his shoulders, which he uses as a road signal....

At present, the city lacks an adequate service of taxicabs. Those in use are insufficient and decrepit, and cannot be summoned from the ranks by telephone. A new rate of charges, registered by taximetre, should be established. The existing system encourages the extortions of private garages, run by the hotels. If you require a car to go out to dinner you have to pay three dollars (seven shillings and sixpence) for a distance of half a mile, or—counting by time—for a drive of five minutes. On the return journey the same rapacity has to be endured, although in London the double fare would not exceed a florin. In comparison, other charges are not exorbitant. The price of a good room, *en pension*, at either of the leading hotels, varies from a pound a day to thirty shillings.

On the whole the cost of living is about the same as in England. Labour is cheaper, but used more extravagantly, and rents are on a higher scale. Still, the absence of custom duties encourages moderate prices, while most of the products of the country, owing to the industrious Chinese, have not become expensive. The tendency, however, is towards inflation; even the Chinaman, instigated by the tin and rubber boom, demanding higher wages. In a recent tailors' strike the employers had to surrender after a stoppage of six weeks.

The shops in Singapore, situated in High Street or in the neighbourhood of Raffles Place, charge little more for their goods than similar shops in London. There are some first-class English chemists; the Kodak Company has a branch here, and there is an enterprising bookseller who supplies all the latest publications. Suits of linen or drill, as well cut as those made in Savile Row, and at a tenth of the price, can be procured from the Chinese tradesman. The great emporiums obtain most of the European custom. Little and Robinson and Whiteway-Laidlaw, all have large establishments on the model of Harrods', and are 'universal providers'. John Little's, which advertises itself as 'the finest Store East of Suez', contains a spacious tearoom and is a popular meeting-place in the afternoon....

Besides the nightly dances at the two principal hotels there are few public amusements in Singapore for English people. A performance at the theatre takes place at rare intervals, and the cinemas are unattractive. The natives, on the other hand, are well catered for. On the outskirts of the city an open-air exhibition—called 'The New World'—is run for their benefit on the lines of Earl's Court, and the man from Cook's insists upon taking his clients to visit the place. It is well worth a visit, for the enlightenment it affords into native life, especially in the evening. The exhibition, which covers a space of several acres, is crowded with stalls where inexpensive commodities are to be purchased. At one of these I observed a display of cheap thermos flasks, a popular article, no doubt, with the Chinese gastronome. Obviously 'The New World' is patronized largely by Chinamen, since there are so many refreshment booths.

But the chief attractions for foreigners as well as natives are the various dramatic entertainments. The visitor comes upon one of these immediately he has passed through the turnstile, a show that is placarded as a Javanese comedy. It took place in an open kiosk with a thatch on top, the replica of an ordinary bandstand, and the spectators assembled around the rails outside to watch it. Within, high up in the roof, a cluster of electric lights cast its radiance upon the actors. The orchestra sat in a circle upon the floor—a couple of drums, a phono-fiddle, a sonorous gong and a xylophone.

The development of the plot was leisurely and wholly incomprehensible to a stranger. Its heroine, a tragic young woman with a high-pitched voice, went through a series of slow contortions as she meandered to and fro with stilted steps, caterwauling at intervals. But her poise and balance were not ungraceful, and she made wonderful play with her arms, while her fingers, which were as flexible as reeds, vibrated like tiny serpents. She was dressed in a black gauze skirt and Turkish trousers, a broad blue sash encircling her waist. On her head she wore a silver turban with a long bead tassel. Another principal character was a comic man with purple cheeks and goggle eyes, produced by a mask of coloured indiarubber.

In a little while our guide hurried us away to a large booth, where one paid to enter, which enabled him no doubt to make a few cents for himself when he purchased our tickets. Inside we found ourselves in a spacious theatre with stage and footlights and scenery, where a Chinese drama was being enacted. The place was crowded, but we secured seats upon a wooden bench in one of the front rows of the stalls.

Most of the parts in the play were taken by children, the two leading ladies being represented by girls, who seemed about fourteen years of age. The faces of both shone with enamel, making them look like wax dolls, and they spoke in thin sing-song voices without modulation. Their dresses were gorgeous, magnificent embroideries worked in gold and silken thread, glittering in all the colours of the rainbow. Only two or three of the characters were adults, one being a comic policeman in command of a troup of boys and girls who marched on and off the stage in single file incessantly. Apparently, the villain of the piece was intended to be Thanatos or the Devil, for he had a skull instead of a face, and persecuted the two little heroines without mercy. At last, one of the damsels retired up stage, and, with the assistance of her friend, seemed to give birth to twins, a couple of extremely wooden dolls being produced suddenly from nowhere in full sight of the audience. After this conjuring trick the mother was led off the stage in a state of exhaustion.

The next performance that we saw was a Malayan opera in a well-equipped theatre with an orchestra of European instruments. Although the music was not untuneful, the voices of the singers were shrill like those of all eastern people. The story of the libretto was complicated, but not altogether incoherent. In the first scene a Malay gentleman dressed like Hamlet, but with a red fez, was having trouble in his harem, being obliged for some reason or other to command his favourite wife to commit suicide with a sword. Taking the weapon from his hands she appeared to acquiesce, and then, during a *tête-à-tête* of some length in which she palyed off all her wiles and coquetry, he was persuaded to forgive her. In the next act Hamlet and his courtiers sang a song in another apartment of the palace in praise of a rich cake, which one of the attendants carried aloft on a platter. The third scene represented a cavern full of black demons, who seemed harmless at first, but upon the appearance of Hamlet and his retinue they became exceedingly enraged and threatened the intruders with death. They were appeased, however, when the magic cake was produced, being tranquillized in a moment; and judging from the laughter of the audience, who were convulsed by their quips and cracks, they must have said a lot of funny things. The fourth scene took place in a street in the suburbs. Two dusky young women in Parisian frocks were brought on to the stage in rickshaws and talked interminably; but, as Hamlet did not appear again, and the story seemed to have run off the lines, we did not wait any longer. Throughout the play the acting had been admirable.

Another of the important sideshows of Singapore is the Chinese restaurant, where every traveller who is interested in the manners and customs of the East ought to take luncheon. Many of these are large establishments of three storeys with several commodious dining-rooms, patronized by opulent tradesmen. For English visitors, however, there is always a cabinet *particulier*, a small chamber with panelled walls carved and painted and gilded in Chinese fashion. An open window mitigates the odours of the eating-house.

The repast commences with green tea, brought in little bowls and then poured into cups, Virginian cigarettes and plates of red beans being handed round at the same time. For the first course at my luncheon party we had chicken Souey, composed of minced chicken, nuts and small pieces of a green vegetable, either melon or cucumber, a hot dish and most appetizing. The second course, which was just as good, was another Souey, no doubt, consisting of a farrago of rice, fish and prawns, accompanied by little plates of curry sauce with chutney, chilis and the usual concomitants. Everything was served in a set of pretty blue china. The chop-sticks were difficult to manipulate, but spoons and forks were provided for our benefit, and the waiter was helpful and deliberate, expatiating upon the virtues of each dish with enthusiasm. Generally, the Chinese boy at hotel or restaurant is a 'plate-snatcher' of the worst kind, which is the reason, perhaps, why so many of the residents in Malaya eat quickly.

The restaurant was in the heart of Chinatown and the window of our room opened into a narrow streeet, which teemed and effervesced with Chinese humanity. Fat Chinamen, stripped to the waist and looking like so many Buddhas, watched from their shop doors with inscrutable expressions in patient expectation of customers. Busy little Chinese women in shiny black cotton pyjamas staggered along under appalling burdens, and crowds of small Chinese girls with long pig-tails danced and prattled and shrieked with laughter. Itinerant vendors passed along in swarms, carrying their stoves or baskets, and sometimes they would halt at a favourite pitch, squatting with their backs against the wall with their stock-in-trade beside them.

During the whole time that we were sitting at luncheon a Chinese orchestra was making a terrific din on the top storey of the restaurant. We went upstairs eventually to inspect and found the musicians in one of the larger rooms, a fine apartment with many open windows that were all framed with trellis work, ornately carved and painted. A couple of vigorous young Chinese women were playing what looked like nigger bones while their two colleagues thumped a big gong and a xylophone of metal bowls. Our waiter escorted us to the kitchens, tiny places scattered in various parts of the building, where Chinese chefs, stripped to the waist, were achieving a maximum turnover with a minimum of material. In one room a youthful cook was painting cochineal on a board to colour the paste for his cakes before putting them into the oven.

H. Bleackley, *A Tour in Southern Asia (Indo-China, Malaya, Java Sumatra, and Ceylon, 1925–1926*, John Lane, The Bodley Head Ltd., London, 1928, pp. 117–24, 127–8, 131–3, 153–9.

53
Singapore's Seething Life

W. ROBERT FORAN
1934

In 1934 the popular British novelist and travel writer, W. Robert Foran, undertook a special journalistic assignment to write about the countries of South-East Asia, and for six months he travelled by rail and road through Malaya, Thailand, Sumatra, Java, and Bali. He sailed on a

Rotterdam-Lloyd steamer from Marseilles for Singapore, which he had visited 20 years earlier. 'My recollections of the earlier visit', he wrote, 'were dim and vague, for twenty odd years impose too great a strain upon the clearness of fleeting impressions of any city. Naturally I knew there was a Raffles Hotel. One associates the port and hotel as a matter of course, just as one connects Shanghai with the proud distinction of owning the longest bar in the world. Beyond Raffles Hotel my memory refused to function. The city was, to all intents and purposes, virgin soil to be studied and explored.'

THE entrance to the harbour from the westward is infinitely more attractive than that from eastwards. I have seen many lovely harbours in the course of over thirty years of world-travel—Sydney in Australia, Dar es Salaam in Tanganyika Territory, Kilindini and Mombasa in Kenya Colony, and Pago Pago in Samoa instantly recur to mind. The western passage into Singapore compares favourably with them.

Shipping from the west enters the harbour proper and the docks at Tanjong Pagar through a narrow strait. It is hedged in by green islands and red rocks, while attractive bungalows, perfectly in tune with their setting, nestle cosily among the tropical vegetation. I registered an impression of scenic splendour immediately we came within measurable distance of the port. There was an air of serenity about the general outlook which was delightfully restful and the harbinger of still better things to come.

The deep-water anchorage beyond this narrow strait has been renamed Keppel Harbour, in memory of Admiral Sir Harry Keppel, who was the first to discover its potentialities; but early in the last century it was known as New Harbour. The Portuguese adventurers of an earlier period were, perhaps, more apt in their christening, for they labelled this the Straits of Singapore. Now Blakang Mati Island stood on our starboard bow and Fort Pasir Panjang was immediately abreast on the port side.

I stood entranced. The wondrous beauty of the panorama steadily unfolding itself ahead was a sedative for ocean-weary eyes. The waters of Keppel Harbour were jade-green, and I gazed over them upon a veritable fairyland. This was indeed a perfect reintroduction to Singapore. A deep sigh at my left elbow caused me to look in that direction. A Singaporean, who had come aboard at Belawan-Deli, stood beside me at the rails, eyes glued on the ever-changing scene, and face all wreathed in smiles....

Singapore's streets are always seething with life. The noise is indescribable. London, New York, Paris and other great cities are bad enough; but they are a haven of peace in comparison with Singapore. The Malay drivers of motor-vehicles have a failing which is highly objectionable. The horns or buttons of the mechanical hooters on cars and lorries prove quite irresistible to their childish minds. Their itching fingers are never off them for more than a few seconds at a time. They behave exactly like infants provided with a drum or cornet to amuse themselves, and make full use of this golden opportunity to render life hideous for others. It does not matter in the least to these native drivers that there is no real occasion to give warning of their approach. They argue that the hooter was provided for use, and are not niggardly in sounding it. They are an infernal nuisance in the city's streets, for they create Bedlam by day and night.

Frequently I saw a long row of taxis on a stand, and each driver was entertaining the neighbourhood with his share in a motor-horn symphony. Some sat upright, putting heart and soul into their contribution to the cacophony of sound; others smoked cigarettes and lolled back in their seats, while keeping *their feet* pressed heavily on bulb or button. The noise produced by this amateur jazz-band can best be imagined than described. It must have been a nerve-racking experience for the occupants of adjacent offices, even as it was for those who passed through the street. The constant sounding of a dozen different varieties of motor-horns and buzzers cannot be recommended as a musical entertainment.

Sleep at night in the hotels, until you grow accustomed to this infliction (if you ever do), is practically an impossibility. Until two or three o'clock in the morning this hellish nightmare never ceases. Two hours later, the obliging church-bells of the city begin to toll forth their summons to prayer, while the impromptu symphony of the motor-driver's orchestra is resumed with renewed vigour. Three to four hours of sleep at night was about as much as I managed to get during the first few days in Singapore. In such a climate, this can lead only to the grave, murder or a lunatic asylum.

Tourists in Singapore, from the *Straits Times Annual*, 1938.

Nobody seems to concern himself with any serious attempt to abate this perpetual nuisance, though all are ready enough to condemn it in strong terms. Apathy, that curse of the East—*tid' apa* (never mind)—is mainly responsible for nothing being done to curb this infernal racket by day and night.

The vehicular traffic in Singapore is no less astonishing for its quantity and variety than that of the masses of craft in the roadstead or on the congested river. Everyone appears to own a car in Singapore—be they European, Eurasian, Chinese, Indian, Malay or Javanese. The tally of the Malay and Chinese operated taxis and buses must run into four figures or more. Motor-lorries, private and public cars and buses, horse or bullock-drawn carts, man-hauled trucks, electric trams, the thousands of Chinese hauled jinrickshas, and a vast multitude of bicycles flood the streets. Almost every day, the busiest sections of the city resemble the congestion of the London streets during the General Strike, when any kind of conveyance was brought into use.

In Raffles Square, during working hours, a solid mass of cars is parked; and in the vicinity of the hotels and clubs, or other popular resorts, there are long lines of other parked motors. Singapore has acute traffic problems, too; but is solving them satisfactorily. The greatest problem of all is to drive about the city without running down a wandering Chinese pedestrian, ricksha or cyclist. Road rules convey nothing to them. They wander about from side to side, or in the centre of the road, with a blissful indifference to their own danger or that of others. Gradually, however, they are being instilled with a modicum of 'road-sense....'

Singapore has a habit of growing upon you. I found it no easy matter to place a finger upon its specific appeal to my affections; but the more you get to know it, the more you like the place. Both the city and its environment possess marked individuality....

There are many odd and curious corners in Singapore which well repay exploration. It is there you can find things that the hardened residents frequently do not know even exist at their doorsteps. Tourist agencies have only a stereotyped programme to offer their clientele, and a little leaven of originality would not come amiss. Too often their clients are beguiled into pursuing the shadows and avoiding the substance. The resulting loss is considerable from the traveller's point of view, for they see only the surface and nothing beneath it....

Hill Street, nestling under the shadow of Fort Canning, is a beehive of Chinese commercial activity. In Singapore it represents the equivalent to London's Oxford Street. Both in Hill Street, and in those cutting across it at right angles, can be found and purchased most of the typical silks, laces, linens and curios of the Orient. There is infinite variety of choice from which to make your selections; and the goods offered for sale had their origin in many different lands.

During my brief sojourn in Singapore, Hill Street drew me constantly like a magnet. I always found it fascinating to wander up and down this crowded thoroughfare; to poke my inquisitive nose into dirty little shops, each crammed with a weird assortment of goods; and to haggle for things wanted or unwanted. I know of few more intriguing ways of filling in a dull hour or so.

Despite the Government's efforts to revive and encourage Malay gold and silver work, laziness and a newly-acquired passion for European cheap wares have doomed this Malay craft to fade into oblivion. It is a thousand pities that this should happen.

A few Chinese have factories in Singapore, where imitation Malay ware is produced by Chinese artisans; but their output is poor stuff in comparison with the genuine work of the Malay people. The latter is not easily discovered to-day, and always in the nature of a rare find. There is, however, an abundance of Malay silverware to be seen on sale, but nearly all of it is fabricated by the energetic Chinese craftsmen and retailed to the unsuspecting as the work of Malays. The Chinese carry out this deception in a most open and shameless manner; and, for this reason, it is always advisable to consult an expert before concluding any bargain.

I spent a number of amusing and interesting hours in browsing through these quaint shops. In the ordinary Chinese general merchant's shop you can buy chinaware unprocurable outside of the Orient, for the simple reason it is so cheap that export trade could not be made profitable. For a few cents only I bought in Singapore the little blue and white spoons, made like an egg-shaped ladle, with which the coolies eat their rice; and for a Straits dollar became the owner of an armful of queer but beautifully coloured bowls and plates. All were absolutely given away at such a low cost....

Rummaging in the Chinese pawnshops for rarities is still another delightful, and often profitable, pastime. I picked up some rare curios at bargain prices in some of these *Pajak Lelap* (drowsy pawnshops) where the pledged articles sleep out the course of their tickets or until such time as redeemed. It is when the former occurs, and the articles are exposed for sale, that a real bargain-day is at hand. The variety of choice is wide and catholic enough to suit even the most exacting bargain-hunter or curio collector.

If luck favours you, it is quite possible to buy cheaply the most gorgeously-hued *sarongs* of silk; genuine jade bracelets; silver, gold and silver-gilt Malay or Chinese ware; all kinds of bizarre jewellery; quaintly patterned *kris* (Malay daggers); brasswork from every land in the Orient; opium-pipes, which have been pawned in a sudden access of virtue or to pay a pressing gambling debt; rare chinaware lodged as security by a wealthy Chinaman, who has been squeezed hardly in some business venture; and a motley collection of other articles, some valuable and others frankly mere rubbish. It is a fascinating game to turn over these heaps of pawned goods in search of some rare treasure. Who knows what may be unearthed?

At first, it is true, you may be greeted by the pawnbroker with a chilling indifference; but with patience, civility and persistence, you will succeed finally in breaking down this attitude and be shown all kinds of queer things. In due course a bargain is struck to the mutual satisfaction of vendor and customer. After my experience in combing the pawnshops in Singapore, I never missed an opportunity to visit them in the towns and villages visited in my wanderings. Often my time was wasted; at others, my finds were disappointing; and, on still other occasions, I became the owner of a valuable work of native art at small price. You can never be sure if luck will smile on you or not.

The Chinese box-wallah (pedlar) is an institution everywhere throughout the East. He is an entirely different stamp of man to the pawnbroker, possessing a keen sense of humour and a greater degree of the milk of human kindness. The box-wallah is generally a bland and cheerful scoundrel, who speaks a number of Eastern languages fluently and passably good English. He is a first-class salesman always—courteous, patient, seldom accepts a rebuff seriously, and can blarney with the best.

The box-wallahs haunt the hotels and ships, or else plod round the residential section of a town with their bales and baskets of merchandise. At their heels staggers a semi-naked, expressionless Chinese coolie, weighted down with even heavier loads. These are types familiar to all who live in the East—from China to India. They are, in fact, the 'Wandering Jews' of the Orient: part and parcel of the daily routine of existence. Without their constant presence in our midst, surely the world must be at an end!

Sunday morning is the box-wallah's favourite time for making a personal call at your residence, for then the *Tuan* does not go to his office and is holiday-making. Any other day in the week will serve for the hotels or to visit the *Mem-Tuans* at their bungalows. He is the most persistent of all traders. Nothing is too much effort, and no time too long, if there is the least likelihood of completing a sale ultimately. Credit he will give readily, if so desired. He knows to a cent your financial worth, and is certain that a *Tuan* will keep his word and pay what and when agreed. Rarely indeed is his trust in the European misplaced.

On a Sunday morning, soon after my arrival in Singapore, a fat and cheerful Chinese box-wallah visited my host's bungalow in Tanglin. We were taking it easy on the veranda after a late breakfast. We assured him, both individually and collectively, that we had no wish to buy anything; that we were just off to play a round of golf; and that, incidentally, we had no cash on us or in the bungalow. It was futile protesting. He ignored our obvious subterfuges, deliberately opened up his packages, spread out their contents alluringly, and held up first one and then another article for us to admire.

He never took his eyes off our faces, except for a fleeting instant while finding some other bait, but watched carefully for the first hint of our interest being aroused. His smile was infectious. I became conscious that my resolve to buy nothing from him was weakening. Good humour, civility and an unlimited store of patience are his chief aids to success in business. A prospective customer is as weak and defenceless as a babe in his expert hands. The Chinese box-wallah is in a class by himself among salesmen. They could sell you anything, given time....

One night my host took me to a Malayan theatre. I would not have missed that treat for worlds. The play of the evening was the Malay version of 'Ali Baba and the Forty Thieves'. I gathered that it is a prime favourite among Malay audiences. It certainly does permit of more scope for the clownish element than the more serious dramas of Shakespeare, in which they also delight.

The performance was excruciatingly funny, and I laughed until my ribs ached and eyes watered. Though not understanding the dialogue, or the ripe jests and often unprintable quips, the pantomime of the players made it fairly simple to follow. The Malays are clever mimics, and the clown of this troupe portrayed a Chinese coolie to the very life. The quaint accent and gestures of the average coolie, together with their hazy knowledge of the Malay language, were so faithfully depicted that I was deceived into thinking the clown was actually a Chinaman. My host disabused me, however. I enjoyed that amusing night in Malay theatreland so much that I never willingly missed any other chance to witness Malay, Tamil or Chinese plays.

We were the only Europeans in that very cosmopolitan audience. The theatre was filled with Eurasians, Chinese, Malays, Indians and Javanese. Most of them either smoked, or munched monkey-nuts, industriously throughout the performance; but were a rapt and appreciative crowd. None laughed more heartily at the life-like caricature of the coolie than did the Chinese members of the large audience.

Those who have never had an opportunity to witness a Malay version of *Hamlet*, *East Lynne*, or *Cinderella*, have missed a rare and unforgettable experience. I spent one hilarious night in the front seats of a Malay theatre, and watched *Hamlet* staged and produced according to Malay ideas and tastes. The occasion will long linger pleasantly in my recollections.

The Chinese players often erect their stage high above a street in Chinatown, and the audience gathers round in much the same manner as children before a 'Punch and Judy' show. No one seems to object to this blatant obstruction of the public thoroughfare, and the stage may remain in position for the best part of a week without protest. Like most things

Chinese, the productions staged are much as they were played hundreds of years ago. As a race, the Chinese have not much liking for changes in their age-old arts. They are strictly conservative in their outlook, which tends to provide a rare degree of charm to their theatrical performances. Their theatre will always repay a visit.

The Malayan opera, or *Wayang Malayu*, represents a most important part in the life of the people of the Peninsula. I can honestly commend the efforts of the local producers, for the *Wayang Malayu* is anything but a dull entertainment. The range of their repertoire is wide, but largely consists of the European pantomime type; but William Shakespeare, and their own plays based on ancient Malayan mythology, are constant favourites....

Beach Road, a purely Chinese and Malay quarter of the city, is interesting if only for its rabbit-warren of hovels, Chinese artisans' shops and factories, movable open-air restaurants, licensed opium-shops, pawnbrokers, second-hand clothes and junk dealers, and the hordes of strange people who throng this evil-smelling artery of Singapore, both by day and night. Here are to be found some of the best examples of local brasswork.

In Rochore Road, which is one of the many streets connecting Beach and North Bridge roads, are located most of the bird and animal shops. Rochore Road is famous throughout the East for its animal dealers, and the Mecca for all collectors of wild birds, reptiles and other creatures for zoological gardens in the West. In that thoroughfare you can buy almost anything from a Java sparrow to a full-grown Malayan tiger. Almost every shop displays many cages of doves, whose value is estimated according to the volume of their cooing notes and the number of rings on their legs. Others have cages filled with a variety of wild beasts for sale; and in one shop I saw a baby Sumatran rhinoceros. Birds, snakes and pythons, monkeys, and all kinds of jungle beasts are brought to Rochore Road for sale to the collectors from Europe. Rare birds and animals vie with monstrosities for pride of place.

If you are blessed with a nose impervious to horrible smells, then a walk up Rochore Road is vastly interesting.

One of the amenities of Singapore is the popular seaside resort at Sea View, where there is excellent sea-bathing and a comfortable hotel. Its local name is Tanjong Katong, but all Europeans know it as Sea View. Near this resort are the European and Chinese Swimming Clubs, where exceptional good bathing is obtainable. Not so long ago, however, you bathed at risk of life and limb from a vagrant shark. Such fatalities were not common, but did occasionally happen....

The road out to Sea View does much to spoil the delights of this popular resort. You must proceed via Beach Road, and through a barrage of smells of infinite variety and nauseating qualities. There is only one other route available—a drive by a circuitous road, which takes you half-way round the island. Notwithstanding, many Europeans and wealthy Chinese dwell at Tanjong Katong, and drive twice or more each day through a series of smells such as rival even the Singapore River at its worst. They are either long-suffering or foolish! If you could escape the pestiferous evil of that drive to and fro, then Tanjong Katong (or Sea View, call it what you like) might be written down as a delightful asset to Singapore. As it is, the approach entirely kills its many charms.

W. R. Foran, *Malayan Symphony: Being the impressions gathered during a six months' journey through the Straits Settlements, Federated Malay States, Siam, Sumatra, Java and Bali*, Hutchinson & Co., London, 1935, pp. 25, 32–8, 40–4.

54
Singapore versus Kuala Lumpur

MARGARET C. WILSON
1934–1935

Margaret Wilson's daughter married a young British engineer in Kuala Lumpur, and she accompanied her when she rejoined her husband after leave in England. She travelled to Malaya aboard the P&O steamer Ranchi, *disembarking at Penang. After staying some time in Kuala Lumpur, she moved to Singapore with her daughter and son-in-law, but she did not like the change, and she did not much like Singapore, at least in comparison with Kuala Lumpur. In the Introduction to her little book,* Malaya: The Land of Enchantment, *one of the rarest of Malayan travel books, she writes: 'For the seasoned traveller, or to those fortunate persons whose circumstances permit of their travelling how and when they please, this book will, probably, have little appeal. There are no high spots; no thrilling adventures, as generally understood, although the whole undertaking constituted an adventure that to me was epoch-making. It is just the simple chronicle and happenings of one whose journeyings have hitherto been limited to holidays spent in various resorts in England and Scotland, with a few trips—at long intervals—to Paris, and other parts of France.'*

AFTER the beauty of Kuala Lumpur, Singapore struck me as being decidedly unprepossessing, but of course, that remark may be applied to the majority of large towns, when viewed, for the first time, from the railway station.

The happiest method of approach to the Island is, undoubtedly, from the sea.

The harbour is magnificent, and full of interest. Stately liners from all parts of the world; coastal steamers, plying between the adjacent Islands, and cargo boats carrying merchandise to all the 'Corners of the Earth', are all mixed up with sampans and quaint, local craft of every variety.

One is also enabled to perceive properly the fine line of the very handsome buildings, that occupy such a commanding position, all along the front.

We found that furnished bungalows were expensive, and difficult to obtain. This scarcity, which is becoming a serious matter, is chiefly owing to the influx of the Army and Navy—not forgetting the Air Force—that are being drafted into the Colony in such large numbers.

Eventually, we secured a small bungalow, situated about five miles from the City, past the Keppel Harbour.

Pasir Panjang Hill, is a delightful little district, overlooking the sea.

Our new domicile was one of a cluster of bungalows originally built, I should imagine, for the accommodation of week end visitors. Certainly, it offered a grateful respite from the heat and noise of the City.

But, after the spaciousness of our late home, we found it terribly small, and restricted as to space. It was promptly christened the 'Rabbit Hutch'.

Also, from the point of view as a permanent residence, it left much to be desired.

In our estimation it lacked everything in the way of conveniences, and, the worst part of all, there was no modern sanitation. After our lovely bathrooms in Kuala Lumpur, those provided for us here, struck us as deplorable. Of course we, and especially I, had been spoilt in this respect. Had I arrived at this bungalow straight out from Home, I should have taken the drawbacks as a matter of course. When we made the obvious comparisons, Norman used to smile, and murmur things about 'Empire Builders' and 'Blazing Trails'. Thereupon, I remarked that so far as I could judge, the Empire was very adequately built, and, anyhow, I had blazed my own trail for so long, that I had no desire to start another one—especially in the Tropics! Incidentally I may mention, he disliked the drawbacks of the 'Rabbit Hutch' as much as we did, and immediately set about having the bathrooms improved, and altogether making the place more habitable, according to our ideas.

Naturally, we also set ourselves to the task of making the best of things, and getting the bungalow to look as home-like as possible.

We gradually found ourselves quite liking the little hill, with its funny little houses perched so high up, that they looked as though a puff of wind would blow them away—and we experienced more than puffs, I assure you.

The climate was somewhat more trying than that of Kuala Lumpur. In fact, it was almost too hot for me—and I can stand a lot—a sticky heat, in which one was always damp....

As we became more acquainted with our new surroundings, we discovered that Singapore, although it could never rival the beauty of the up country districts, possessed a charm of its own....

The town itself is most attractive. A drive along the Esplanade in the cool of the evening, is an experience not to be forgotten.

Three miles from the shore, near the Tanglin Barracks, are the Botanic Gardens, a real beauty spot. Here the flora of the country is to be seen to perfection.

Gravelled walks lead to lovely flower beds; the artificial lake bears many varieties of water lillies on its placid bosom;

the wide spreading trees provide a natural back ground for the well kept lawns, and rare shrubs that are planted around so effectively....

The Chinese quarters are some of the most interesting sights of the City. Endless rows of open shops, line the streets on either side, with the family wash stretched on bamboo poles, suspended from the upper windows.

Every other shop appears to be a restaurant. The Chinese, like the French people—take most of their meals outside their homes. Innumerable children play around, and on the pavements, pariah dogs prowl about, looking for scraps; placid mothers sit outside, nursing their quaint babies, and groups of young men may be seen watching, with keen interest, games of cards in progress. They are great gamblers.

Barbers shops also abound, and their clients, swathed in a sheet, are to be seen undergoing the severe clipping of their black hair, in which they delight. Is this a revolt from the 'pig tail' I wonder?

The names are odd to our ears. The immortal 'Widow Twanky' is constantly brought to our remembrance, by such signs as 'Le Fung', or 'Ah Sing', washerman, suspended over the doors.

I must mention one fact about these streets, that is too potent to be ignored. They are distinctly smelly!

One of the worst offenders in this respect, is actually called Lavender Street. It is the greatest piece of sarcasm one can imagine, and shows a rich sense of humour on the part of whoever was responsible for the naming of this malodorous thoroughfare.

In this district, it is a common sight to see chickens being hatched out in the open, by the heat of the sun.

Chinese coolies swarm everywhere, and they have a most irritating habit of straggling across the road, with a sublime indifference to any traffic that may be coming along. After escaping death by a few inches, and through no merit of their own, but rather the excellence of the driver, and his brakes, they will turn round and give the apoplectic syce a disarming smile, and proceed to repeat the process quite happily, with the next vehicle that comes along....

There is no lack of amusements. Singapore boasts several good cinemas. For lovers of serious, or high brow music, there is the Victoria Institute. The handsome race course is available for those addicted to the 'Sport of Kings', and various golf and tennis clubs provide plenty of scope for the enjoyment of these games. The cricket club is faced by a large *padang*, on which all the important events, and fixtures of the year take place.

But the greatest delight of all, to us, as to many others, was the swimming club. This is a glorious institution, and deservedly flourishes. Membership is reasonable, and confined to Europeans only.

Here, if so inclined, you can spend the whole day, in and out of the water, rest in the afternoon, and have any meal you please to order.

Little tables are dotted about, shaded by large umbrellas. This is a favourite spot for *mems* to meet in the mornings for tea and chat—not forgetting the swim, whilst the *amahs* take the children to bathe in the children's *pagar*. It is a real joy to watch the little toddlers paddling about, and making sand castles, in the manner of children all the world over. Their bonny faces, and sturdy limbs speak eloquently of the benefits derived from the days spent in this health giving spot.

The air is delicious, coming straight from off the sea, and bearing the real salt twang of the sea side.

The adults have their *pagar*, too—a large area of the sea enclosed by a fence, which renders it safe from any marauding shark.

There is, also, a large swimming pool, with diving platforms of varying heights. We witnessed some very fine displays from time to time.

Once a month, the regimental band gives a selection of music, which is much appreciated, and makes for a very enjoyable evening.

Altogether, this Singapore 'Lido' ranks high among the amenities of the City.

Then there are the restaurants and hotels. Of the latter, Raffles holds pride of place for gaiety. Dances, and cabaret shows are always well patronised by a smartly dressed crowd. A dinner and dance at Raffles, is a very usual form of entertainment given by the inhabitants, to any visitors who may be tarrying awhile with them.

Sea View, delightfully situated on the shore, offers a quieter form of entertainment, but none the less enjoyable. To dine in the open, and watch the moon rise over the water is an experience that transforms the repast into ambrosia and nectar—food and drink for the Gods indeed.

An amusing evening may be spent at the New World. This is a permanent place of entertainment, somewhat like our old 'Earl's Court', and is very popular with the native races. You see them here, Chinese and Malays, and Indians, all enjoying the various forms of amusements presented to them.

There are plays in Chinese, and dramas acted by Malays. The stage fittings are of the plainest, and the acting is primitive in the extreme, but no trifles like these detract from the enjoyment of the audience, who stand or sit around (these latter are the opulent ones) and applaud vigorously, as each situation reaches its culminating point.

Stalls selling trinkets and silks, mingle with those exhibiting the most—to our notions—unsavoury looking food; and highly coloured sweets are sucked by all the children with the same relish alike—whether brown, black or yellow.

As may be imagined, the dance halls are fully patronised by the young men and maidens—the latter much bedecked in jewellery and flowers for the occasion.

It is interesting to observe the manner in which the Chinese and natives have adopted our outdoor games. Cricket and football are very popular, whilst tennis and badminton are indulged in by those fortunate ones, whose gardens boast a court.

The boys in the streets too, have their beloved football. It is quite a common sight to see bare brown feet kicking a ball about, on any vacant piece of ground. What they lack in knowledge of the game, is made up by the zeal with which they enter into a scrum in true Western fashion.

And now we come to the wonderful week of the Jubilee—In no other country could it have been celebrated with more zeal and loyalty. We were only a small colony, tucked away in a corner of the Empire; but we did our stuff nobly.

The town itself was beautifully decorated, and illuminated. The ships in the harbour, dressed with flags in the daytime, and blazing with lights at night, added greatly to the gaiety and beauty of the scene. H.M.S. Terror was a particularly fine effort, being entirely outlined with brilliant lights.

The Esplanade, that magnificent thoroughfare in which the Cenotaph stands, sported high pylons decorated in red, white, and blue, and at night was effectively illuminated in the same colours.

One of the most conspicuous of decorative erections, was the large double archway, crowned by two huge cupolas of some silvery substance, which spanned the entrance to Beach Road. This was the tribute of the Arab community. But is was truly wonderful to see the manner in which each section of the mixed population availed themselves of this opportunity to show their loyalty, and to tender their homage to the sovereign whom they had never seen, but of whom they had heard so much, and under whose rule they enjoyed such a measure of peace and prosperity.

But what appealed to me the most, was the efforts made by the little shops in the poorer parts of the town, to produce their best in the way of celebrating this happy occasion. Even the stalls and street barrows in the outlying districts, sported their little coloured lights, and strings of flags.

It all made me feel very proud of my British nationality. If nature had not already done it for me, I should have puffed out my chest, every time I stood up to the strains of our National Anthem.

At 6.45 a.m. on the Monday, we wended our way to the Cricket Club, from whence we watched the Grand parade, and march past of the troops. H.E. the Governor, accompanied by the Sultan of Johore, stood and took the salute.

Afterwards, the Air Force gave a display. The manner in which those huge planes dived and rose in their own particular form of salute, won universal admiration.

The next evening from the same point of vantage, we watched that most wonderful spectacle, The Chinese Lantern Parade.

It was three miles long, and took three hours to pass a given point.

Between beautifully illuminated and decorated cars, hundreds of men walked in single file, each holding aloft the most marvellous lanterns one can imagine.

Ferocious tigers, all kinds of weird birds, and queer, monstrous fishes were there; now and again, dragons, about thirty feet long, and belching forth the most realistic flames, made a break in the procession.

It was a truly wonderful sight, and one never to be forgotten. I wished all the children at home whom I knew, could have seen it. They would have gone mad with excitement.

Towards the end, the Ceylonese contributed their part towards the show, and brought their own decorated vehicles. At one point, a beautiful chariot, bearing a huge lotus flower on the roof, stood stationary, for a few moments. Slowly the petals opened, revealing the lovely form of a young girl, who sang to the assembled throng.

The Sikh and Chettier community had their own celebration. They held thanksgiving services in Silas and Tank Roads. These services were extremely picturesque. Afterwards, their great silver car, drawn by the sacred white bulls, draped in gorgeous trappings, paraded the streets.

These were preceded by grotesque carnival figures, and on reaching the Raffles reclamation ground, the whole show terminated by a great display of fireworks. But the Malays were not behind in their demonstration. The pageant they gave will long be remembered for its beauty and colour. There were nearly forty gaily and wonderfully decorated lorries, depicting various scenes of native life. The procession was accompanied by the Royal Naval Volunteer Reserve, and the Malay Volunteer Corps, looking very smart in their uniforms. Arrived at the Padang, they gave an exhibition of games, dancing and musical scenes, that were warmly appreciated by the spectators. They were afterwards reviewed by the Colonial Secretary, Sir Andrew Caldicott [Caldecott] at the Municipal Buildings. A grand ball on H.M.S. Terror on Friday, brought to a close a week that will live long in the memory of all, but especially those of us whose hearts, at this time, were stretching across the seas—to London—the centre of the Empire, from which rose all this peon of praise and thanksgiving, to spread far and wide throughout the world.

Margaret C. Wilson, *Malaya: The Land of Enchantment*, The Mascot Press, Amersham, *c.*1935, pp. 101–23.

55
The Most Colourful Town in the World

H. D. HARBEN
1935–1936

The Englishman, H. D. Harben, left Genoa in August 1935 aboard the cargo steamer Java *of the Danish East Asiatic Line, on his way to Japan. He chose the Danish line because it offered the cheapest passage and better food than on the more expensive lines. He passed through Singapore at the end of September, and returned there in December aboard the* Java*'s sister ship* Malaya, *on a passage from Shanghai via Manila. He put up at Raffles Hotel, but found it far from comfortable, being kept awake at night by the sound of band music from the ballroom and the outside traffic. After travelling to Kuala Lumpur, Penang, Bangkok, and Cambodia, he returned to Singapore in January 1936, being undecided whether to go to Raffles Hotel or the Adelphi, which did not have running hot water. In the event, both hotels were fully booked, and he had to settle for the Sea View, which, in advertisements at the time, emphasized the fact that it had both 'running hot and cold water'.*

WE left the *Malaya* for good on Saturday last when she arrived at Singapore, where we settled down for five days at Raffles Hotel. There was a month's correspondence waiting for me, and I had also the arrangements to make for the next month's journeys; and there was also washing and dry-cleaning and repacking to be done. The first night we ran up against Stanley, who dined with us with another flying man, G. H., who had lost an eye in an aeroplane smash some time ago. Stanley was leaving on Sunday, but G. H. offered to show us round Singapore. We had no time to do justice to his offer, but one evening we dined with him and he took us in his car to a large place of amusement called the New World, where there were Chinese and Malay theatres and cinemas, many cafés and eating-houses, and a large cabaret and dance-hall. The dance partners were of many nationalities, and two or three of the Eurasians were extremely good dancers, as were also some of the Chinese. But we had only two hours in the whole place and little time for dancing. It was here, however, that I discovered the secret of the dignity and stately carriage of the Chinese girls. They are considerably longer in the leg than Europeans in proportion to their height. I danced with a girl about two inches shorter than myself, but I noticed that her legs were at least three or four inches longer than mine. Then watching the others I found that it was quite common to see the men's legs a little shorter than their partners', even though they were half a head taller. But this was only the case with Chinese girls, not with other nationalities.

Singapore is the most colourful town in the world. In no place does one see so many nationalities at once, and most of them in costumes of the most brilliant colours. Chinese, Japanese, Siamese, Filipinos, Malays, Singhalese, Indians of several races, both Mohammedan and Hindu, all vie with each other in many shades of orange and pink and red and blue and green, magenta and cherry colours predominating. Many of them are half naked, and their brown skins throw the colours of their robes into stronger relief. They tend to live in different quarters, and in order to study them one should visit many distant parts of the town. But they all throng the principal streets as well; and the shortest walk or rickshaw ride is a joy to the eye and abounds in interest.

Unfortunately, Raffles Hotel is far from a pleasant place to stay in. It is in the first place at a very noisy corner of the town, and it is not possible to avoid the sound of traffic. Then they dance nearly every night till quite late, and when the people mount to their rooms they wake up the whole hotel, as there are no carpets and no windows, so the sound of feet on the stone comes through the trellis shutters. The same thing occurs when the staff move about, as they are apt to do nearly all night. By six in the morning sleep is impossible, and it is out of the question after lunch. Five days of this hotel reduced us to a pulp, and we should have moved elsewhere were it not that we had unpacked all our fifteen packages directly we arrived. The hotel is extremely expensive and full of a rather bourgeois crowd of English, who evidently think themselves the best people and whose women dress as if they came from the North of England or Birmingham or the Regent Palace Hotel. After hearing their English in the lounge it is a relief to talk one's mother tongue with the Indian servants, who have pleasing voices and a pure pronunciation....

When we arrived in Singapore on Tuesday last week we were undecided whether to stay at Raffles, where at least there is hot water, or to try the only other hotel, the Adelphi, where there is none, but which might be more comfortable in other respects and at least could not be worse. The matter was decided for us by the fact that there was no accommodation left in either place. So we were forced to come out here, some five miles from the town. The hotel is situated among palm-trees on the very edge of the sea, and the water laps the lawns a few yards from the rooms at high tide. We found it so quiet and beautiful that I again altered my plans, and decided to start for Borneo next Saturday, January 18, instead of on the 11th as arranged, so as to have a good rest after the fatigues of the journeys in Siam. Also there is a good pile of correspondence to be attended to, and the yearly accounts to get straight.

We have been here a week now, during which time we have lazed thoroughly and only been into Singapore four times. One or two friends have been out to lunch or dine, and last night we dined at the 'mess' of the junior staff of the East Asiatic Company, a cheery lot of young bachelors—four Danes and one Scotchman—who have a roomy villa with a cool verandah, a Chinese cook, and a piano. For the first time since last April I played, and we sang all the old tunes in chorus—war songs, film tunes, and the favourite musical comedies for thirty years back. To my surprise it was after midnight when we calmed down, and one o'clock before we got home to bed.

I am awfully well in the climate of Singapore; the heat—just over eighty in the shade day and night—does not incommode me, and provided one changes one's clothes two or three times a day and sponges down, one keeps pretty fresh. I find myself for the first time in my life completely without surplus energy. Exercise, even in the cool of the evening, is an effort; and thinking generally involves collar work. One cannot recall even the most familiar names or numbers, and trying to do so is conscious effort. I was alarmed at first, and thought I was getting old, but they tell me it is the universal experience out here.

I suffer a good deal from the powerful electric fans which whiz immediately above one's head in every room. The old-fashioned punkah worked by hand used to cause a light and pleasant breeze. But the 'rushing mighty wind' of these modern aeroplane propellers cut my bald head like a knife, and as one is always more or less damp with the heat it causes a rapid condensation that I consider as dangerous as it is unpleasant. On one or two occasions I have had to eat my meal in a beret, and the other day in the cinema I took off my jacket and wrapped it over my head and shoulders like an Arab at sunset.

Many other discomforts there are, peculiar not to the climate but to the English way of living. The food is really abominable in the hotels. In this heat it is natural that the meat should be frozen, but the use of cold storage has made it customary to ignore the produce of the district and to serve food from Europe several months old at every meal. You hardly ever get the fish fresh from the sea here, only soles and salmon from England. The vegetables are all canned, so is the stewed fruit, and there is no dairy produce at all—only tinned milk and frozen butter. The inhabitants (British, I mean) attribute their exhaustion to the climate, but it is really lack of vitamins, and they stave it off by constant whiskies. If we lose the East, it will be largely due to our unhealthy habits. I still look back on the three days at the French hotel at Angkor as an oasis in the desert.

Another abomination is the architecture of the hotels. To satisfy their mania for draught, and to combat the heat, all the hotel rooms are open at both ends. There are, of course, two side walls to separate one room from another, but the upper half of the back wall is an open grating, and the front wall is non-existent. You just walk through a low wooden partition into the verandah outside. In an hotel this verandah is the public corridor. The Chinese boys can stand on tip-toe and peer over the swing door into your room, and they do this quite frequently. There is no means of securing any privacy at all, and no means of shutting out either light or sound. At daybreak the light streams on to your bed, and at all hours you can hear everything that goes on in the next room, which is open to yours just round the corner. You know when they clean their teeth, and you hear them when they quarrel or become affectionate. And if, as often happens, anyone in your wing has a gramophone, it is exactly as if it was in your own room.

This all might be worth while if it achieved the object of securing coolness. But the mere fact of letting in all the outside air lets in all the heat as well. In Italy or the Near East everyone keeps their rooms shut up and darkened all day, so that every house is noticeably cooler than the air outside. Here the internal and external temperatures are bound always to be the same. And the broad verandah keeps out all your access to the sun. In the Near East you can sweeten your clothes by hanging them over a chair in the window for ten minutes occasionally. Here that is impossible, as your verandah is the public corridor. So you either have to send everything to the laundry every day, or else put it on wringing wet. For in this damp nothing dries unless it is actually in the sun.

I enlarge on these discomforts not in a spirit of complaint, but because I am amazed at the stupidity of them, and at the long suffering of the British inhabitants. As I said before, they appear to have achieved at great expense the maximum of luxury with the minimum of comfort.

I am much impressed with the immediate possibilities of Singapore. The construction of the new naval and air bases, and the consequent increase of the personnel of the war services, has made a shortage of house accommodation which is already apparent and is bound to become serious quite soon. There is room for two or three good new hotels and hundreds of houses and flats, but I see no signs of supplying the need. Someone with money who formed a syndicate for that purpose would certainly find it a good investment.

The government of the city leaves much to be desired. The smells in many parts of Singapore and the surrounding country are extremely displeasing. The drainage system should be modernised, and the swamps close to the town should be abolished. There has been an alarming increase in malaria lately, so perhaps the matter will soon be taken in hand. It is a pity that a place so pleasant to live in, with so much natural beauty, should be spoiled by these remediable defects. Still, I like Singapore.

H. D. Harben, *Japan and Back*, B. N. Langdon-Davies, Welwyn Garden City, 1936, pp. 173–5, 212–16.

56
Tidy Little Chinese Girls

THORNTON CLARKE
1936

Thornton Clarke was a Fellow of the Royal Geographical Society. He and his wife began their tour of the world by sailing first from London to New York, and then through the Mediterranean to Ceylon, Sumatra, Java, and Singapore. They stayed only 24 hours, arriving early on 4 February 1936 and departing on the following day for Bangkok, Manila, and Hong Kong.

WE docked early at Singapore; too early to see this long island lying among a group of much more beautiful islands, but we saw its fine harbour.

When we got on deck we found ourselves right in the very front of the town, almost moored to its chief thoroughfare.

Soon after breakfast we started off in motors to explore the place.

The houses are higher than are generally seen in the East, and many of them have prison bars on the windows of the ground floors. Nearly all the streets are arcaded; brown and yellow men sit on string beds under the narrow arcades and watch life go by. Rickshaws, and carts with bullocks whose great horns nearly meet, impede the busy traffic.

We noticed a succession of clean-looking Chinese restaurants and joss-houses, all well patronized, as they naturally would be in a place where the majority of the population is Chinese; the rest are a queer hotch-potch of mixed races.

What might be called fourth-class taxis, mostly patronized by the natives, are a feature of the place. And the smells, of course. The farther we penetrated the more penetrating they became. Our noses sniffed various scents, and even the incense of the joss-sticks didn't camouflage the outrageous odours near the house-boats and dwellings by the water.

A policeman, too, was rather a curiosity. With a wicker bar straight across his back, he stopped our procession at the main crossing, and when we were allowed to go on again the bar went up to attention.

By an excellent road we left the town. As we turned slightly inland nice houses, gardens and even blocks of flats came into view; then comfortable little cottages, and a stretch farther on, airy, primitive dwellings of thatch and laths and mats sprinkled about the sandiest of sandy soil amongst bananas and palms.

Many of the Malay villages are built on stilts in the water.

Fishing drives that seemed to be right out at sea were in quite shallow water in which mere specks of men walking out to the nets were only knee deep.

Almost before the town was left behind, rubber plantations started and the soil became red. We saw so much rubber, so many coco-nuts, and such an array of growing pineapples I shall think of Singapore whenever I see any of these products.

As usual during our present visit to the tropics, we noticed the lack of noxious insects—we were warned we should find the most and worst here—and thanked our stars for having come in the off season. Nor was it so hot or moist as we had expected.

Red paper slips with black lettering were plastered on most of the doors and gates of the Chinese shops and houses. These may be New Year blessings and greetings, the extended Chinese New Year still being with us.

Horrible curved black pigs ran about the gutters and in and out of the houses. I think these obscene creatures added to the vile odours that filled each village and settlement; a stench of fifth and decay and blocked-up drains, or more likely, the lack of drains. Fortunately for the inhabitants smells are only danger signals and not harmful in themselves—at least so modern science tells us.

To get some idea of the place we made a long, roundabout drive. After Java and Ceylon the country didn't strike us as being specially beautiful. It often offended the eyes as well as the nostrils.

We forgot the unpleasant villages when masses of gay flowers and bright plants greeted us in Chinese nursery gardens, whose owners' names were just queer little noises.

Very soon we came to a residential quarter. Large houses

were built on rising ground in park-like gardens, tree-shaded and English looking. Generally the architecture was a trifle too ornate, and the climate had made it a shabby ornateness. It struck me that the rich Chinese live in much finer houses than the Europeans.

When we turned homewards the landscape became more varied and undulating, and almost beautiful as we neared the sea again.

What impressed me most on the morning's run round was the sight of so many tidy little Chinese girls, and men of all ages, marketing, carrying back undiagnosable scraps of meat, bits of vegetables and strange tiny fishes hanging from strings. Such a pitiful assortment of oddments each had accumulated gave one the idea the shoppers were both small eaters and not very particular what they ate. Perhaps it was the ogre poverty that restrained their appetites and inclinations.

In the afternoon we set out again, passing the harbour, a busy place full of ships, especially of the smaller craft, sampans and prahus, and 'boats of a peculiar ancestry'.

After leaving the town by a long shore of shops and docks, we drove through the beautifully kept Botanical Gardens. I'm sorry to say we hadn't time to get out of our car. Friendly monkeys were skipping round much after the manner of the wicked little grey squirrels in the London parks. The wide, well-made road into which we turned was as full of traffic as any similar one in England, and heavily loaded motor-lorries and vans were rushing along at a great speed.

I noticed it's the thing to have stucco animals on one's gate-posts. So fierce and scowling some of these are, it's hardly necessary to put up 'Beware of the dog'.

A finely situated, tree-embowered reservoir looked most inviting; we wanted to get out and rest our tired eyes on it for a while, but were hurried on through a pretty stretch of country, slightly undulating and well wooded.

Thornton Clarke, *Round the World Without Worries*, Heath Cranton Ltd., London, 1937, pp. 109–11.

57
The Japanese Journalist

TATSUKI FUJII
1938

In April 1939 the Japanese journalist, Tatsuki Fujii, arrived at Singapore to work on the Japanese-owned Singapore Herald. *He was interned in Changi Gaol with other Japanese civilians on the outbreak of war with Japan, and then transported to an internment camp in India. Eight months later he was included in the first Anglo-Japanese exchange of prisoners, and from Lourenço Marques in Portuguese East Africa he returned to Singapore, where he renewed his journalistic activities. His remarkable book,* Singapore Assignment, *which describes these events and also Singapore during the Japanese Occupation, was published in Tokyo during the war. It is vitiated by feelings of hatred for the British, which sometimes lead its author into farcical conclusions. It must also be said that 'Johnny' Fujii was viewed with great suspicion by American and British newspaper correspondents working with him in Singapore before the outbreak of war. Cecil Brown of the Columbia Broadcasting System consistently refers to him in his book,* Suez to Singapore *(New York, 1942), as 'the Japanese spy'.*

SINGAPORE lay basking in the tropical sun when our ship sailed into the harbor on April 20, 1939. For hours that morning, I had stood on the deck waiting for the first glimpse of Singapore as the ship sailed serenely through blue waters between numerous green islands.

Finally, I caught a glimpse of the white buildings glinting in the sun. Singapore lay quietly asleep. How characteristic this was of Britain's fortress, I thought to myself.

Even before I disembarked. I was startled when the British Immigration Officer greeted me by name. It seemed that the police and even the newspaper reporters had been informed of my impending arrival.

Immediately upon landing, I was taken to the Police Station where I was questioned for more than an hour by Major Morgan, Chief of the Special Detective Branch. He asked me to give details of my trip from the United States, how long I had stayed in Japan and what I was going to do in Singapore.

Much to his disappointment, he learned very little from my replies. I told him that I had come to Singapore to work on the Singapore Herald. That was all I had to say....

Singapore, on my arrival, was not a British city. It was predominantly Chinese with a good proportion of Indians, Malais and Arabs. The Japanese numbered only about 4,000. And yet the British ruled the destinies of the Asiatic population of 700,000 with selfish tyranny.

As in New Delhi, Hongkong and Shanghai, the British in Singapore had built imposing buildings in order to impress the masses. They had stationed troops in Malaya, not to fight, but to remind the Asiatics that the British ruled by virtue of force.

Bridges and roads were built not for public service, but solely for defense purposes. Schools were established in order that British history and language could be imposed upon the children. Hospitals and prisons were constructed because they were needed, not because of any humanitarian motive.

Wasn't it sufficient testimony of British oppression that the Supreme Court and the Changi Prison were the finest buildings in all of Malaya?...

In the early days of British colonial domination, some good men had been sent out in the Malayan Civil Service....

But as years went on, London grew lax and the social and economic misfits of the British Isles began to drift out to Malaya. There was nothing so obnoxious as a British colonial official....

The poverty of the people increased the longer the British remained in Malaya. The slums of Singapore were world famous and in the midst of all this poverty and filth, the British lived in oblivious splendor.

Life in Singapore for the British was leisurely and comfortable. Most of them lived in the suburbs—Tanglin, Bukit Timah or along the East Coast—where it was cool. They built magnificent residences staffed with a retinue of Chinese and Malai servants.

Yes, Singapore was easy and comfortable for the middle-class English officials and businessmen. Many of the wives sprang from the petty bourgeoisie of England and Scotland. Many a police inspector had formerly walked the streets of London as a 'bobbie' while more than one railway official had served his apprenticeship in an English dispatcher's office.

Scrubwomen, farmers' daughters and manicurists—all became Singapore 'ladies'. Many told amazing stories of aristocratic backgrounds which were refuted by the Cockney in their speech.

When Noel Coward, the celebrated English playwright and author, came out to Singapore, he was amazed at the smug, pretentious and bad manners of Singapore society.

After a visit to the Tanglin Club, one would-be lady asked him how he liked the Club.

'You know the Tanglin Club is one of our best clubs,' the 'lady' beamed.

Noel Coward turned to her and said, 'After meeting your best people, now I know why there is such a shortage of servants in London.'

Indeed, the British built up a life of superficial leisure in Singapore. While they drew handsome salaries and did no work, the efficient Chinese and Eurasian clerks slaved. It was only necessary for the British manager to make an appearance every day, sign the checks and dictate replies to letters that came from the head office in London.

The British rolled through town in limousines, lived in sumptuous villas and revelled at exclusive clubs while the rest of the Asiatic population starved, toiled, and died.

Even the young assistants lived well—usually in an apartment or a bachelors' mess which resembled a private club. All of the British managers and most of the younger assistants owned motor-cars driven by Malai chauffeurs. Their domestic needs were taken care of by a Malai or Chinese houseboy, Chinese cook, Malai gardener and a Chinese amah to do the laundry. . . .

For the younger bachelors, life in Singapore was very convenient. They usually started drinking at the Cricket Club, proceeded on to one of the three cabarets where they danced with a pretty Chinese or Eurasian partner and ended up at the cafes which lined Jalan Besar Road and Lavender Street. If the favors of certain dancers at the cabarets were unobtainable, they went along to one of the numerous brothels which served just as well.

Tatsuki Fujii, *Singapore Assignment*, The Nippon Times, Tokyo, *c.*1943, pp. 3–8.

58
Raffles Hotel

CARVETH WELLS
1939

Carveth Wells worked as a civil engineer on the survey of the Malayan East Coast railway line between 1913 and 1918. His health was affected, and although British by birth he sailed to America, where by accident he became a public lecturer and travel writer. In 1925 his popular book, Six Years in the Malay Jungle, *was published, and he later led expeditions to Lapland for the American Museum of Natural History, and to Uganda for the Geographical Society of Chicago. In 1939, after an absence of 23 years, he returned with his wife, Zetta, to Malaya and Singapore, and in his book,* North of Singapore, *he contrasts Singapore with the city he remembered after the First World War.*

RAFFLES HOTEL, named after Sir Stamford Raffles, who founded the city of Singapore in 1819, has always been a famous rendezvous for world travellers. It is an immense rambling structure, with huge courtyards full of coconut palms and lovely tropical flowers. Surrounding these courtyards are tiers of wide verandahs on to which open lofty bedrooms, twice the height of any ordinary hotel room. At the back of each room is a spacious bathroom, but not the tiled affair with glittering fixtures so common in America. These bathrooms are designed for the old-fashioned Malay bath. Instead of filling a tub with water and lying in it, you stand on a wooden grating, dip water from a large earthenware jar and fling it over your head. The last time I had taken such a bath in Raffles Hotel was in the autumn of 1918. The earthenware jar, four feet high and two feet in diameter, used to be filled every morning by hand and covered with a wooden lid to prevent mosquitoes from breeding in it. I remembered that the moment I had thrown water over my head, several large toads emerged from behind the jar, hopped towards me and sat near my feet so that they also might get the benefit of the shower bath.

Times had changed. The friendly toads had disappeared. The artistic earthenware jar had been replaced by an ugly galvanized iron tub underneath a brass tap. Mosquitoes were not given a chance to breed in the bathroom. Fresh water was drawn for each bath and the tub was turned upside down afterwards. Running water was new to me in Singapore, and when I learned that the water in those taps was as pure as any drinking water in the world, I realized that the city had changed indeed. There used to be a time when the name Singapore conjured up visions of people dying of cholera, plague and smallpox. This reputation was quite undeserved, compared with other places, but Singapore was no more a health resort than the Panama Canal Zone was in the days of De Lesseps. Even twenty years ago it wasn't safe to drink the water or eat a salad. Practically everyone took quinine daily; it used to be given away at post offices. Huge pictures of anopheles mosquitoes were placed in public buildings so that everyone might recognize the dangerous little lady. Nowadays, with first-class drinking water brought from a mountain in the Johore jungle forty miles away, and every kind of modern sanitation, Singapore is so healthy that even rats average only three fleas a piece, an important item when the spread of plague is considered.

I had been warning Zetta all the way from America to beware of drinking the water in Singapore. Yet now I drank several glasses of ice water and ordered a delicious mixed salad, which, according to the menu, was prepared from fresh vegetables, grown according to European standards at Cameron Highlands, a health resort high up in the jungle-covered mountains of Pahang and Perak. I suffered no ill effects.

Outside our bedroom there was a Sikh watchman who must have tipped off a local Chinese tailor that some Americans had arrived and would probably need tropical

Raffles Hotel, *c.*1939. (Raffles Hotel Collection)

clothing. It would be unfortunate for our department stores if every traveller to the Orient knew how cheap and good the local tailors are. For twenty-seven dollars American money I had four linen suits, three pairs of khaki shorts and a doeskin tuxedo made to measure and delivered within twenty-four hours. This included labour and material. Zetta had two linen dresses and one silk dress made to measure and delivered overnight, for sixteen dollars. The secret of getting good clothes made in Singapore is to give the tailor a well-cut Western suit or dress to copy and make sure that the cloth he uses has been thoroughly pre-shrunk.

When we entered the enormous cocktail lounge of the hotel I observed many changes, both in drinks and the dress of the people. Although it was eleven o'clock in the morning, I did not see a single gin sling. Those delicious pink, long drinks had apparently gone out of fashion. Gimlettes had become more popular. A gimlette is a short drink made of a mixture of gin and lime juice. For old time's sake, I ordered a gin sling, and when it finally arrived it cost a dollar. But the old pernicious habit of signing chits for one's drinks was evidently still in favour. Money rarely seemed to pass.

Twenty years ago the usual dress of a Singapore business man was a white duck suit with a tunic and high military collar. Nowadays men wear shorts, shirts, stockings, and brown leather shoes. I looked in vain for anyone I might have known and I was about to give up hope when I caught sight of a tall fellow dressed exactly as I myself used to dress. Recognition was mutual. We had come out on the same boat together nearly thirty years before. He was a successful broker and had become one of the city fathers of Singapore. Pointing to the men wearing shorts, he remarked: 'They don't go into the jungle any more, Wells, as you used to. In fact, they won't. We have the devil of a job to get young men even to live on a rubber estate unless they can get into town for lunch!'...

Gradually, as luncheon time approached, the lounge filled up with men in many different kinds of uniforms; it was interesting to note that naval officers, artillerymen and aviators were in the majority. At night, when the tables were cleared away for dancing, the scene was indeed thrilling. In Singapore, before the war, there had been about eleven men to every woman. But with the influx of soldiers and sailors, the proportion of men was even higher; every woman who could walk without the aid of crutches was in great demand. Dozens of male wallflowers stood around the dance floor, patiently waiting for a chance to cut in. With few exceptions, the men were in uniform and, as many of them were veterans of the first World War, their breasts glittered with medals.

Conspicuous among the brilliant company were the officers of the Royal Engineers, whose short mess jackets exposed their tight-fitting trousers with a broad red stripe running down the sides. Tall handsome men of the Royal Australian Air Force showed that far-off Australia had lost no time in despatching reinforcements to the great fortress upon which the safety of their homes depended....

From our hotel we could see a large boys' school. By seven o'clock in the morning the students were pouring through the gates, some on foot, but a great many on bicycles. No crowd of youth could have looked smarter than these Malays, Chinese and Indians, but, even more important than their good appearance was the fact that almost without exception they had gone to school voluntarily.

There are now many fine schools in the Straits Settlements and Malaya and the rising generation is very different from that of twenty years ago. Thousands of young natives speak English well, and the prospect of good jobs for all of them is excellent.

I could not help noticing how Malays, Chinese, Indians and Eurasians had taken the places of English men and women. For instance, in most of the large stores, where I used to be waited upon by Englishmen, I found that only the manager of a department was white, and many, even among the managers, were native. Most of the stationmasters in big cities used to be white men. To-day they are usually Indians or Chinese. I well remember that the engine-drivers of most of the express trains were British, but to-day their jobs are done by the natives they trained. Judges and magistrates used invariably to be Englishmen, but nowadays many of them are well-educated Malays. As for stenographers and clerks, I did not on this trip see a single white man doing such work.

It pays to advertise in Singapore just as elsewhere. The truth of this was discovered by a Chinese, who decided to capitalize on the popularity of the tiger. For centuries the tiger has been regarded as having supernatural powers. The whiskers of the animal are supposed to have magical properties and, though I never heard of a Malay who actually succeeded in milking a tiger, I have been frequently shown a white substance in the jungle which, I was informed, was tiger's milk and very good *obat* (medicine). Probably the substance was a kind of fungus, but the belief that it was tiger's milk no doubt improved its healing qualities.

Some years ago the signboards of Singapore and Malaya announced the discovery of a powerful new medicine called 'Tiger Balm'. Wherever there was a vacant wall or side of a tall building, a brilliantly coloured picture of a tiger was painted. Overnight tiger balm became even more potent than ginseng; and it had the great advantage of being easily identified by the picture of the tiger. Guaranteed to cure every sickness from a pain in the toe to the heartache of a disappointed lover, it brought an enormous fortune to its inventor.

Hearing that he had built a mansion that was worth seeing, we set out to find it. We were well repaid for our trouble. Surrounded by a magnificent iron fence with gateways, crowned with brightly coloured life-sized tigers, was a huge white house. The Chinese millionaire was not at home, but his caretaker invited us in. Large paintings and exquisitely embroidered tigers adorned the walls. There were tiger coverlets on the beds. Even his automobile was painted vivid yellow with black stripes, while the hood and radiator were made to represent an enormous tiger's head with mouth wide open to show rows of large white teeth.

Surrounding the house was the strangest garden I have ever seen. It appears that the owner disliked caterpillars and insects that lived on foliage. He wanted his garden always to look fresh and blooming. Therefore every tree and shrub in it was cleverly made of metal and painted; metal leaves moved in the breeze. Crawling over the rock garden were huge porcelain dragons of vivid colours, while another section of the garden was given over entirely to a menagerie of metal animals and birds. The most prominent place in the garden was devoted to a large replica of Ferdinand the Bull. The gardener had the softest job in Singapore. He had nothing to do but show visitors this fantastic aggregation and occasionally dust off the flowers.

An interesting development that I noticed in Singapore was the commercial cultivation of orchids. I saw many nurseries devoted entirely to raising them for table decoration. Large bunches could be bought for a few cents, but the flowers were all alike....

I think that the greatest change in Singapore, if you do not include the less respectful attitude of the Asiatics to white men, is in the night life of the city. '*Pergi Malay Street!*' (Go to Malay Street) used to be the usual order to the ricksha puller after dinner in Singapore. This street used to be the heart of the segregated area of the city, where street after street was devoted entirely to brothels of different nationalities. Malays, Indians, Africans, Arabs, Chinese, Japanese and Europeans were all on view in all their war paint. European girls in full evening dress used to sit on the sidewalk, while their companions sang songs around a piano in a room one side of which was completely open to the street. Hundreds of Japanese houses were there, with girls on view behind iron bars, like caged animals. Sometimes there were two girls, sometimes six, all dressed in gorgeous kimonos of the kind worn only by prostitutes. Funnily enough, these are often the kind purchased by tourists on cruise ships. It is just as well to know what you are buying, especially when you buy anything with Chinese or Japanese lettering upon it. The wife of a prominent diplomat once bought a very elaborate ricksha, in which she insisted upon riding when doing her downtown shopping. Her husband begged her not to use it, but she insisted until he translated the Chinese lettering which was written prominently but decoratively on the sides and back of the ricksha: 'I am a first-class prostitute. My price is five yen.'

Malay Street and the whole of Singapore's segregated area has been cleaned up and is now a respectable part of the city.

One evening while I was sitting in the lounge of Raffles Hotel I met Joe Fisher, the Sam Goldwyn of Singapore and biggest movie magnate in Malaya. Before Joe Fisher Americanized the motion-picture business in Singapore, a visit to the movies usually meant sitting in a glorified barn crowded with every conceivable race of mankind, including a bunch of brightly-dressed, but veiled, Malay women, and listening to the worst piano player on earth attempting to interpret the most violent and blood-thirsty silent movie ever produced by

Hollywood. Pictures in which white men fought one another were among the best money-makers. Every time the hero slugged the villain in the eye, the crowd yelled with delight. The acme of success was attained when someone was flung violently through a plate-glass window or thrown over a precipice. Slap-stick comedy was even more popular than tragedy, and, even now, Joe Fisher will tell you that Charlie Chaplin tops them all.

To-day Singapore has several fine theatres, but the kind of pictures popular in America are not necessarily successful in Malaya. Marlene Dietrich, Greta Garbo and Joe E. Brown make no appeal to Asiatics, but Norma Shearer, Janet Gaynor and Ronald Colman never fail to fill the house. Mickey Mouse and the Tarzan pictures are as popular with Malays as they are in America.

Carveth Wells, *North of Singapore*, Jarrolds Publishers Ltd., London, 1940, pp. 119–32.

59
The Singapore Military Base

MONA GARDNER
1939

After working on Californian newspapers, Mona Gardner went to Japan, where she lived for 12 years. She visited China as a newspaper correspondent during the 1930s, and witnessed at first hand Japanese aggression against that country. She travelled in South and South-East Asia during 1939, when she wrote an assessment of the British defences at Singapore based on interviews with British military commanders. On the basis of her long experience and knowledge of the Japanese, she warned in the Introduction to her book, Menacing Sun, *that the countries she had visited—Thailand, Indo-China, Malaya, the Dutch East Indies, and India—'all lie on the path of empire expansion which has been mapped out for Japan'.*

SINGAPORE evokes such varied pictures. To the tourist lady it is the place to buy a Malay kriss (they make such interesting paper knives, my dear) and another tube of toothpaste. To her husband it means going to the verandah of the Raffles Hotel to have a red and frosted Singapore gin-sling, and wonder—with the second one—if the town was named after the drink. To junk captains, whose philosophy would never look pretty on the printed page, it is a place to unload their dubiously gotten cargo and get out of before questions become insistent. To the young clerk out from home it means joining the master caste and letting his complexion take him to places his salary never could. A tour of duty there spells malaria to army officers, to the bride it means orchids after marriage, and to Japanese imperialists it is the place where 18-inch guns are waiting to say 'Keep Off The Grass'.

Anything can happen in Singapore, and it usually does—according to story writers. Certainly all the human elements of drama are on the streets for anyone to guess at—with Arabs, Portuguese, Chinese, Dutch, Tamils, Afghans, and a lot of people who look as though they spoke Esperanto, living together. And while you are shuddering and waiting for the scream, some well-informed Public Servant tells you that there is less major crime in Singapore in proportion to the population than there is in New York City.

You can mull over that for days or weeks, according to your temperament; and you may decide that it is because Malayans make better policemen than Irishmen. Or, if you read the names of New York criminals in the daily newspapers there, you might even come to the conclusion that Singapore has less crime because Italians didn't emigrate there and because there is little scope for Jewish shysters.

Perhaps the most curious thing about Singapore is that all these human odds and end who do live there—these Afghans, Turks, Chinese, and others—depend for their well-being upon the American motoring public. The absolute barometer of prosperity in this faraway corner of the British Empire is set by whether the Joneses, the Smiths, and the Johnsons in the United States are actively wearing out automobile tyres. When they do, people in Malaya buy tinned salmon, scented soap, and radios. But let a depression hit the American pocket-book, and almost immediately these same people in Malaya begin to twist last year's *sarong* one screw tighter, concentrate on New York stock-market reports, and read wistful articles in the local newspapers about how business in the United States is bound 'to take an up-turn in the spring'.

If you can't talk rubber—and by that I mean quotas, surplus stocks, market prices, cover crops, the doings of 'the rubber pool', and 'the Colonial Secretary had better be careful, by gad, sticking his finger in the crew-hiring question'—then take along a book to read when you go to dinner parties, because conversation in Singapore begins, runs eight-course circles, and ends with rubber. There is always the possibility that you'll be lucky and draw a dinner partner, as I did one evening, who will keep his conversation to the rubber-level that he thinks you will understand. And in this way you will hear about the mysterious visitation of latex-drinking snails that has recently swept over plantations. You may be alarmed over snails taking to a new diet with such abandon that 5,000 of them on each acre drink so many potential automobile tyres that planters are wondering now if they can't sell the snails instead. But personally, after listening to the talk of rubber, rubber, rubber, I am afraid I felt a little grateful to nature for this biblical-sounding revenge.

Singapore is the great pivot about which trade between Asia and Europe revolves. It has become the extraordinary commercial centre that it is because nature placed it where it dominates this important marine highway. But Singapore was chosen as Britain's base in Asia for two other more important reasons. These are: the mild Malayans offer no political menace in the way of nationalistic longings such as the Indians do, and Singapore, unlike the outmoded strength of Gibraltar, has a good chance of remaining invulnerable to attack by an invading force.

In the first place this force would have to come a very long way; and secondly, nature has done her best to put up serious barricades. The sea routes leading to Singapore are devious. The coral reefs in them would make submarine attacks futile and silly. All the dozens of innocent-looking tropical islands bordering these channels are excellent protection for the big 15-inch guns which, with their shooting radius of twenty to twenty-five miles, are all that is necessary to keep enemy warships at a distance.

Any land force attacking Singapore island (which is joined to the tip of Malaya by a causeway over the narrow blue Straits of Johore) would have first to effect an infantry landing in Siam or Malaya, and complete the operation by a long and arduous overland trek. Aside from Siam's disinclination to be used as an enemy base, there is the insurmountable barrier of hundreds of miles of mountainous jungle without a single road, stretching across the northern province of Malaya. A landing in southern Malaya is not at all impossible, but it would be a slow unwieldy manoeuvre, for the roads by which the infantry could march are narrow chasms in the jungle and therefore a perfect target for plane attack. Three new military aerodromes which the British have just established in various districts of southern Malaya were evidently put there to take care of this contingency.

When it comes to air attack, Singapore's vulnerability is another matter. Citizens' committees are pressing the Government for more bomb-proof shelters, for gas-masks and decontamination chambers. Drills and lectures for all classes of citizens on poison-gas protection are conducted regularly on the island. People don't just talk about drills, they make a point of attending them. And there are a lot of children that you would expect to be busy playing with their dolls who can tell you right off the proper defence against mustard gas, and what to do about the kind that stays on the street and burns the shoes off your feet if you walk on it.

But, although an invading air force could create havoc amongst civilians in Singapore, that is still far from making any dent on the military fortifications which are manned now by more than 6,000 troops. The number will be increased when new barracks are completed.

No outsider knows the actual extent of Singapore's military fortifications, or just how many units there are of the big land batteries with their 18-inch guns. All of this is kept very secret—as it should be. Until the formal opening of the base a year ago it was not even known that 18-inch naval guns had been dismounted from a warship and set up there as land batteries. To-day officers will neither confirm nor deny their existence, but the certainty that these colossi are there is pretty well established.

Some say they are antiquated models—leftovers from the World War—but that doesn't change the fact that they are several times more powerful than anything that can come up to Singapore, and that they can fire projectiles weighing more than 3,000 pounds. There seems to be no question but that these secret batteries, together with hidden garrisons of artillery and engineers on the small islands guarding the straits, constitute a formidable fortress.

The naval base covers some twenty square miles, and is spread out in open view for anyone to look at. Building it was a tremendous engineering feat, which involved moving a river, transporting 14,000,000 cubic feet of earth in the process of excavating hills and filling in mangrove swamps. It has two mammoth docks—the famous floating one towed out from England to the astonishment of mariners and landsmen as well—and another stationary one of vast proportions. Both are capable of holding any battleship that has been built, as well as those still in blue-prints. They are there to provide quick repairs for Britain's Asiatic Squadron if it ever goes into action in the Pacific.

The air base is less impressive to the eye, probably because it consists of three aerodromes on different parts of the island. The chief military field, though, has been built to accommodate the forty odd flying-boats permanently stationed there now. In addition there is a splendid new civil field right in the town of Singapore, which handles both sea and land planes. Considerable attention has been given to the development of flying-boats here because of their potential effectiveness in the long stretches of smooth water in the Singapore channels. Flyers say there is more than forty-five miles of ideal 'flying-water'. There are more of the flying-boat squadrons in India, just as there are troops and bombing planes, all of whom can be called upon to augment Singapore's defences any time.

These grimly expensive units are not gestures. They all mean business. They very definitely and explicitly say that Great Britain is not retiring from Asia. And there seems to be no question in anyone's mind but that this message is intended for Japan. It means that something like (if officer's and men's salaries are included) £50,000,000 have been spent to make the message forceful: to prove that Britain is ready to back up Hongkong or Australia, and probably—though this is not openly declared—lend a hand to Holland if there is any threat of Japanese occupation of the East Indies.

Now, however, the tension in Singapore (which has been prevalent for several years amongst military authorities, businessmen, and rubber planters) has noticeably relaxed because of the fervent hope that Japan will exhaust herself financially in trying to subdue Chinese who won't stop fighting. I was interested in all the scheme of Singapore's defences because I had the horrible feeling that all the people I had been with, the Annamese, the Cambodians, the Siamese, and the Malayans may have their future decided for them by these very cannon, flying-boats, and drydocks.

The astounding thing about Singapore's proud base—that gives a fillip to the whole vast scheme, but may be an unpleasant jolt for the ladies back home in Surrey—is that nearly one-sixth of the funds used to build the base were contributed by some 34,000 Chinese opium addicts. It wasn't a voluntary contribution either. It was—s-sh, s-sh—a part of the Government's whacking good revenue from traffic in the poppy.

Mona Gardner, *Menacing Sun*, The Travel Book Club, London, 1940, pp. 171–6.

60
The Japanese Conquest

COLONEL MASANOBU TSUJI
1942

It cannot be said that Colonel Masanobu Tsuji, Chief of Operations and Planning Staff of the 25th Japanese Army in Malaya, was a traveller to Singapore in the traditional sense. His informed account of the Japanese conquest of the island in February 1942 is included here because the event essentially marked the end of British colonial rule, and also the end of the 'golden age' of travel.

DURING the day on the 5th Division front the battle had raged as violently as in the Keppel Barracks area. Our front line had only been able to advance to the southern end of the reservoir. The troops had never before been under such heavy shellfire, from which the front-line trenches afforded very little shelter. The division had attacked from the main-road sector supported by the full strength of the 'Tiger's Cub' Tank Brigade, but the troops were finally brought to a standstill at half-past three in the afternoon. Then suddenly, ahead of the front line which was renewing its assault along the central highway, there appeared a large white flag.

Major Wylde [C. Wild], an English staff officer, came bearing the flag of truce.

Like lightning this was reported to Bukit Timah headquarters. Immediately on receiving the news Staff Officer Sugita, in charge of intelligence, who was in a plaster cast because of a broken collar-bone, was taken by car to the front line, where he personally delivered to the bearer of the flag of truce documents which had been prepared in anticipation at our Army Headquarters. The British staff officer at once returned to Singapore with them to enable the British commander of the fortress to consider our proposals, which were as follows:

1. At eighteen hours on 15th February, both Army Commanders to meet at Bukit Timah.

2. The British Army to promptly suspend resistance all along the line and disarm.

3. Normal administration of the economic structure to continue to maintain every existing business, obeying our demands in succession, then handing over to the Japanese Army.

4. Ships, aircraft, vehicles, weapons, ammunition, provisions, fuel reserves and so forth, the whole of the buildings and land belonging to or used by the Army, communication facilities, harbour equipment, aerodrome equipment, maps and documents—all are to be handed over to the Japanese Army without damage, demolition, or destruction. There must be absolutely no conduct whatever that will cause injury to the Japanese Army.

5. Those involved in termination of conflict with the Japanese Army must make assurance doubly sure and suppress at once any local conflicts which may arise.

6. All prominent persons on the side of America, the Dutch East Indies, and Chungking are to be immediately held as

prisoners of war and placed under protection of the Japanese Army.

7. All Japanese men held as prisoners of war are to be handed over forthwith to the Japanese Army.

8. Committees are to be appointed for Army, Navy, Air, Finance, Administration, Sanitation, Prisoners of War, etc., the presidents of which are to be responsible for meeting the requirements indicated by the Japanese authorities.

The streamlined motor car with the Union Jack and the white flag crossing each other stopped in front of the Ford Car factory north of the three-pronged Bukit Timah road. The British Commander, Lieutenant-General [A. E.] Percival, accompanied by Brigadier Torrens, Brigadier [T. K.] Newbigging (Deputy Adjutant-General) and Major Wylde, were led to the place of interview by Staff Officer [I.] Sugita. General [T.] Yamashita, who was roughly five minutes behind time, entered followed by his staff officers, exchanged handshakes, and took his seat. How did the English general feel surrendering to his enemy after defeat? The faces of the four English officers were pale and their eyes bloodshot. General Yamashita indicated to General Percival a document written in English, saying, 'I wish you to answer these questions very briefly.'

The questions and answers were:

'Does the British Army surrender unconditionally?'—'Yes.'

'Are there any Japanese prisoners of war?'—'Not even one man.'

'Are there any Japanese men held prisoner?'—'All Japanese civilian prisoners have been sent to India. The guarantee of their position is being entrusted to the Government of that country.'

'Do you agree to this document unconditionally?'—'Please wait until tomorrow morning for the answer.'

'Then, in that case, up till tomorrow morning we will continue the attack. Is that all right, or do you consent immediately to unconditional surrender?'—'Yes.'

'Well, then, there will be a cessation of hostilities from 10 p.m. Japanese time. The British Army, using a thousand men as a police force, will please maintain order. In case of any violation of these terms a full-scale attack on Singapore will immediately commence.'

General Percival then said, 'I wish to receive a guarantee of the safety of the lives of the English and Australians who remain in the city.'

'You may be sure of that. Please rest assured. I shall positively guarantee it.'

In this way the curtain dropped on the campaign for the occupation of Singapore. Even more dramatic was the arrival at that time of the Emperor's military aide-de-camp at Bukit Timah. In 1819, one hundred and twenty-three years earlier, Stamford Raffles had landed on this island. Everything that Great Britain had since built up here in the Far East had now been beaten to a standstill.

Masanobu Tsuji, *Singapore: The Japanese Version*, trans. Margaret E. Lake, ed. H. V. Howe, Ure Smith, Sydney, 1960, pp. 266–9.

Bibliography

Anon., *Singapore Retrospect Through Postcards: 1900–1930*, Archives and Oral History Department, Singapore, 1982.

Anon., *Souvenir of Singapore: A Descriptive and Illustrated Guide Book of Singapore*, Straits Times Press, Singapore, 1905.

Augustin, A., *The Raffles Treasury: Secrets of a Grand Lady*, Singapore, 1987.

Beamish, Jane and Ferguson, Jane, *A History of Singapore Architecture: The Making of a City*, Graham Brash, Singapore, 1985.

Braddell, R., *The Lights of Singapore*, Methuen, London, 1934; reprinted Oxford University Press, Singapore, 1982.

Brendon, P., *Thomas Cook: 150 Years of Popular Tourism*, Secker & Warburg, London, 1991.

Buckley, C. B., *An Anecdotal History of Old Times in Singapore*, Fraser and Neave, Singapore, 1902; reprinted Oxford University Press, Singapore, 1984.

Butcher, J. G., *The British in Malaya 1880–1941: The Social History of a European Community in Colonial South-East Asia*, Oxford University Press, Kuala Lumpur, 1979.

Chew, E. C. T. and Lee, E. (eds.), *A History of Singapore*, Oxford University Press, Singapore, 1991.

Cook, J. A. Bethune, *Sunny Singapore: An Account of the Place and its People, with a Sketch of the Results of Missionary Work*, Elliot Stock, London, 1907.

Cunyngham-Brown, S., *The Traders: A Story of Britain's South-East Asian Commercial Adventure*, Newman Neame, London, 1971.

Edwards, N., *The Singapore House and Residential Life 1819–1939*, Oxford University Press, Singapore, 1990.

Falconer, J., *A Vision of the Past: A History of Early Photography in Singapore and Malaya: The Photographs of G. R. Lambert & Co., 1880–1910*, Times Editions, Singapore, 1987.

Flower, R., *Raffles: The Story of Singapore*, Croom Helm, Kent, 1984.

Gregory, A., *The Golden Age of Travel 1880–1939*, Cassell, London, 1990.

Hall-Jones, J., *The Thomson Paintings: Mid-Nineteenth Century*

Paintings of the Straits Settlements and Malaya, Oxford University Press, Singapore, 1983.

Hancock, T. H. H., *Coleman's Singapore*, MBRAS Monograph No. 15, Kuala Lumpur, 1986.

Hindley, G., *Tourists, Travellers and Pilgrims*, Hutchinson, London, 1983.

Howarth, D. and Howarth, S., *The Story of P&O, The Peninsular and Oriental Steam Navigation Company*, Wiedenfeld and Nicolson, London, 1986.

Jayapal, Maya, *Old Singapore*, Oxford University Press, Singapore, 1992.

Lee, E., *Historic Buildings of Singapore*, Preservation of Monuments Board, Singapore, 1990.

Lee Kip Lin, *The Singapore House 1819–1942*, Times Editions, Singapore, 1988.

Liu, Gretchen, *Raffles Hotel*, Landmark Books, Singapore, 1992.

Makepeace, W. E., Brooke, G. E., and Braddell, R. St. J. (eds.), *One Hundred Years of Singapore*, John Murray, London, 1921; reprinted Oxford University Press, Singapore, 1991.

Moore, D. and Moore, Joanna, *The First 150 Years of Singapore*, Donald Moore, Singapore, 1969.

Pregarz, R., *Memories of Raffles: 22 Years with a Grand Hotel*, Treasury Publishing, Singapore, 1990.

Ramachandra, S., *Singapore Landmarks Past and Present*, Eastern Universities Press, Singapore, 1961.

Reith, G. M., *Handbook to Singapore*, Fraser and Neave, Singapore, 1907; reprinted Oxford University Press, Singapore, 1985.

Seddon, Sue, *Travel*, Alan Sutton, Stroud and Thomas Cook, Peterborough, 1991.

Sharp, Ilsa, *There is only One Raffles: The Story of a Grand Hotel*, Souvenir Press, London, 1981.

Sheppard, M. (ed.), *Singapore 150 Years*, Times Books International for MBRAS, Singapore, 1973.

Song Ong Siang, *One Hundred Years' History of the Chinese in Singapore*, John Murray, London, 1923; reprinted Oxford University Press, Singapore, 1984.

Swinglehurst, E., *Cook's Tours: The Story of Popular Travel*, Blandford Press, Poole, 1982.

Turnbull, C. M., *A History of Singapore 1819–1975*, Oxford University Press, Kuala Lumpur, 1977; 2nd edn., 1988.

Tyers, R., *Singapore Then & Now*, Landmark Books, Singapore, 1993.

Warren, J. F., *Rickshaw Coolie: A People's History of Singapore (1880–1940)*, Oxford University Press, Singapore, 1986.

______, Ah Ku *and* Karayuki-san*: Prostitution in Singapore 1870–1940*, Oxford University Press, Singapore, 1993.

Willis's Singapore Guide, Singapore, 1934.

Wright, A. and Cartwright, H. A., *Twentieth Century Impressions of British Malaya: Its History, People, Commerce, Industries, and Resources*, Lloyds G. B. Publishing Co., London, 1908.

Yen Ching-hwang, *A Social History of the Chinese in Singapore and Malaya 1800–1911*, Oxford University Press, Singapore, 1986.

Other Oxford Paperbacks for readers interested in South-East Asia, past and present

Borneo

Among Primitive Peoples in Borneo
IVOR H. N. EVANS

The Best of Borneo Travel
VICTOR T. KING

Borneo Jungles
TOM HARRISSON

The Field-Book of a Jungle-Wallah
CHARLES HOSE

Fifty Years of Romance and Research
CHARLES HOSE

The Gardens of the Sun
F. W. BURBIDGE

The Head-Hunters of Borneo
CARL BOCK

In Borneo Jungles
WILLIAM O. KROHN

My Life in Sarawak
MARGARET BROOKE, THE RANEE OF SARAWAK

Natural Man
CHARLES HOSE

Nine Dayak Nights
W. R. GEDDES

Orang-Utan
BARBARA HARRISSON

Queen of the Head-Hunters
SYLVIA, LADY BROOKE, THE RANEE OF SARAWAK

Through Central Borneo
CARL LUMHOLTZ

Wanderings in the Great Forests of Borneo
ODOARDO BECCARI

The White Rajahs of Sarawak
ROBERT PAYNE

World Within: A Borneo Story
TOM HARRISSON

Cambodia

Angkor: An Introduction
GEORGE COEDÈS

Angkor and the Khmers
MALCOLM MacDONALD

Indonesia

An Artist in Java and Other Islands of Indonesia
JAN POORTENAAR

Bali and Angkor
GEOFFREY GORER

Coolie
MADELON H. LULOFS

Flowering Lotus: A View of Java in the 1950s
HAROLD FORSTER

Forgotten Kingdoms in Sumatra
F. M. SCHNITGER

The Hidden Force*
LOUIS COUPERUS

A House in Bali
COLIN McPHEE

Indonesia: Land under the Rainbow
MOCHTAR LUBIS

Island of Bali*
MIGUEL COVARRUBIAS

Islands of Indonesia
VIOLET CLIFTON

Java: Facts and Fancies
AUGUSTA DE WIT

Java: The Garden of the East
E. R. SCIDMORE

Java Pageant
H. W. PONDER

Javanese Panorama
H. W. PONDER

The Last Paradise
HICKMAN POWELL

Let It Be
PAULA GOMES

Makassar Sailing
G. E. P. COLLINS

The Malay Archipelago
ALFRED RUSSEL WALLACE

The Outlaw and Other Stories
MOCHTAR LUBIS

The Poison Tree*
E. M. BEEKMAN

Rambles in Java and the Straits in 1852
'BENGAL CIVILIAN'
(CHARLES WALTER KINLOCH)

Rubber
MADELON H. LULOFS

Soul of the Tiger*
JEFFREY A. McNEELY and PAUL SPENCER WACHTEL

Sumatra: Its History and People
EDWIN M. LOEB

A Tale from Bali*
VICKI BAUM

The Temples of Java
JACQUES DUMARÇAY

Tropic Fever
LADISLAO SZÉKELY

Twilight in Djakarta
MOCHTAR LUBIS

Twin Flower: A Story of Bali
G. E. P. COLLINS

Unbeaten Tracks in Islands of the Far East
ANNA FORBES

Yogyakarta: Cultural Heart of Indonesia
MICHAEL SMITHIES

Malaysia

Ah King and Other Stories*
W. SOMERSET MAUGHAM

An Analysis of Malay Magic
K. M. ENDICOTT

At the Court of Pelesu and Other Malayan Stories
HUGH CLIFFORD

The Chersonese with the Gilding Off
EMILY INNES

The Experiences of a Hunter and Naturalist in the Malay Peninsula and Borneo
WILLIAM T. HORNADAY

Glimpses into Life in Malayan Lands
JOHN TURNBULL THOMSON

The Golden Chersonese
ISABELLA BIRD

Illustrated Guide to the Federated Malay States (1923)
C. W. HARRISSON

The Malay Magician
RICHARD WINSTEDT

Malay Poisons and Charm Cures
JOHN D. GIMLETTE

A Nocturne and Other Malayan Stories and Sketches
FRANK SWETTENHAM

The Pirate Wind
OWEN RUTTER

Saleh: A Prince of Malaya
SIR HUGH CLIFFORD

Six Years in the Malay Jungle
CARVETH WELLS

The Soul of Malaya
HENRI FAUCONNIER

They Came to Malaya: A Travellers' Anthology
J. M. GULLICK

Philippines

Little Brown Brother
LEON WOLFF

Singapore

Main Fleet to Singapore
RUSSELL GRENFELL

The Manners and Customs of the Chinese
J. D. VAUGHAN

Raffles of the Eastern Isles
C. E. WURTZBURG

Singapore 1941–1942
MASANOBU TSUJI

Thailand

Behind the Painting and Other Stories
SIBURAPHA

The English Governess at the Siamese Court
ANNA LEONOWENS

A Physician at the Court of Siam
MALCOLM SMITH

The Politician and Other Stories
KHAMSING SRINAWK

Temples and Elephants
CARL BOCK

To Siam and Malaya in the Duke of Sutherland's Yacht *Sans Peur*
FLORENCE CADDY

Travels in Siam, Cambodia and Laos 1858–1860
HENRI MOUHOT

Vietnam

The General Retires and Other Stories
NGUYEN HUY THIEP

**Titles marked with an asterisk have restricted rights.*